W9-DCD-533

THE BLUE GUIDES

Countries **Austria**
Belgium and Luxembourg
Channel Islands
China
Corsica
Crete
Cyprus
Czechoslovakia
Denmark
Egypt
England
France
France: Burgundy
Western Germany
Greece
Holland
Hungary
Ireland
Northern Italy
Southern Italy
Malta and Gozo
Morocco
Portugal
Scotland
Sicily
Spain
Switzerland
Turkey: the Aegean and Mediterranean Coasts
Wales
Yugoslavia

Cities **Athens and Environs**
Barcelona
Boston and Cambridge
Florence
Istanbul
Jerusalem
London
Moscow and Leningrad
New York
Oxford and Cambridge
Paris and Versailles
Rome and Environs
Venice

Themes **Churches and Chapels of Northern England**
Churches and Chapels of Southern England
Gardens of England
Literary Britain and Ireland
Museums and Galleries of London
Victorian Architecture in Britain

Getting water near the desert town of Merzouga

BLUE GUIDE

Morocco

Jane Holliday

A & C Black
London

WW Norton
New York

Second edition 1992

Published by A & C Black (Publishers) Limited
35 Bedford Row, London WC1R 4JH

A CIP catalogue record of this book
is available from the British Library.

ISBN   0–7136–3592–4

Published in the United States of America by
WW Norton and Company, Inc
500 Fifth Avenue, New York, NY 10110

Published simultaneously in Canada by
Penguin Books Canada Limited
2801 John Street, Markham, Ontario L3R 1B4

ISBN   0–393–30966–5   USA

The author and the publishers have done their best to ensure the accuracy of all the information in Blue Guide Morocco; however, they can accept no responsibility for any loss, injury or inconvenience sustained by any traveller as a result of information or advice contained in the guide.

Jane Holliday is a graduate in English Literature (London) and a *diplomée* in *Civilisation Française* (Sorbonne). When married to a senior diplomat, she lived and worked in Sweden, Bolivia and, latterly, Morocco where she spent over four years becoming familiar not only with the major cities but also with the most remote corners of the country. Still a regular visitor to Morocco, she now lives near Oxford and works for a leading British charity.

Maps and plans drawn by András Bereznay, revised by Terence Crump for this edition.

Photographs by Susan Benn.

Printed and bound in Great Britain by
Butler & Tanner Ltd, Frome and London

PREFACE

Morocco, only 14km from Europe and bounded by both the Atlantic and the Mediterranean, is the ideal gateway to the African continent and to the Arab world. Tourism in this richly diverse country has multiplied eight times in the last twenty-five years: not only is it easily accessible from both Europe and the United States but it offers something to suit all tastes—rugged mountains, desert oases, cedar forests, uncluttered sandy beaches, and an inexhaustible supply of atmospheric old towns and kasbahs.

The main attraction for the discerning visitor is, without doubt, the quartet of 'Imperial' cities—Fez, Marrakesh, Meknes and Rabat—so-called because each at some time has been capital of the empire (which stretched northwards into much of Spain and southwards beyond Timbucktoo). Each of these cities has its own unique and irresistible atmosphere and nowhere more so than Fez, the oldest of all (founded in 808) and now preserved as a national treasure with the aid of UNESCO; Marrakesh, equally rich in historic monuments and with a near perfect climate, is rapidly becoming one of the world's most desirable tourist destinations; Meknes, Morocco's very own Versailles, and Rabat, living proof that modern and traditional architecture can exist harmoniously side by side, complete the picture. These cities, above all others, bear witness to over a thousand years of unbroken royal succession and strong Islamic tradition. Unlike its neighbours, Algeria and Tunisia, Morocco was never invaded by the Turks, and successive dynasties, whether Berber or Arab, have always sprung up from within the country itself. Even the forty-four years of French and Spanish occupation earlier this century left the culture largely unchanged (whilst hugely benefiting the infrastructure and educational system). So it is that Morocco retains to this day a remarkably homogeneous artistic and cultural heritage, and a wealth of Islamic architecture which reflects the extraordinary energy of its sultans and frequently a touch of extra refinement from Moorish Spain (el Andalus).

All of Morocco is fascinating and most of it is easily accessible, with good road and rail networks and a well-distributed hotel infrastructure. It is the purpose of this Guide to help readers to feel at home in the great medinas of Fez and Marrakesh and also to encourage them to look beyond the obvious places—to enjoy the supreme majesty of the Atlas, the hot colours of the pre-Sahara, the huge enveloping silence of the forests and the excitement of the country souks. It is based on the personal experience and observations of the author who has spent over four years in the country, visiting and re-visiting all the great cities and travelling extensively in the rural areas. She has been helped and encouraged by a wide variety of people, ranging from the poorest desert nomads to the wisest academicians in the land—all happy to satisfy her curiosity and proud to talk of the origins of their country, its problems and its promise.

The author would like to express her gratitude to all her friends in Morocco who have so willingly given of their time and experience to make the writing of this book possible. Special thanks are also due to Mr John Macrae, the British Ambassador in Rabat, and to Mr Hassane Esserghini, Director of the Moroccan National Tourist Office in London; also to Peter Holliday, Tania Sellwood, Tim Brierly and many others whose help and constructive criticism have been invaluable.

A NOTE ON BLUE GUIDES

The Blue Guide series began in 1915 when Muirhead Guide-Books Limited published 'Blue Guide London and its Environs'. Finlay and James Muirhead already had extensive experience of guidebook publishing: before the First World War they had been the editors of the English editions of the German Baedekers, and by 1915 they had acquired the copyright of most of the famous 'Red' Handbooks from John Murray.

An agreement made with the French publishing house Hachette et Cie in 1917 led to the translation of Muirhead's London guide, which became the first 'Guide Bleu'—Hachette had previously published the blue-covered 'Guides Joannes'. Subsequently, Hachette's 'Guide Bleu Paris et ses Environs' was adapted and published in London by Muirhead. The collaboration between the two publishing houses continued until 1933.

In 1933 Ernest Benn Limited took over the Blue Guides, appointing Russell Muirhead, Finlay Muirhead's son, editor in 1934. The Muirhead's connection with the Blue Guides ended in 1963 when Stuart Rossiter, who had been working on the Guides since 1954, became house editor, revising and compiling several of the books himself.

The Blue Guides are now published by A & C Black, who acquired Ernest Benn in 1984, so continuing the tradition of guidebook publishing which began in 1826 with 'Black's Economical Tourist of Scotland'. The Blue Guide series continues to grow: there are now 50 titles in print with revised editions appearing regularly and many new Blue Guides in preparation.

'Blue Guides' is a registered trade mark.

CONTENTS

8

Maps and Plans

HISTORICAL SUMMARY

The Berbers. Since the beginning of history there have been Berbers in North Africa and they were already well established when the Phoenicians made their first incursions in 1200 BC. Their origins are uncertain but thought to be Euro-Asiatic, and their high cheekbones and light skin colour would seem to point that way. The generic name *Berber* was imposed on them by the Arabs meaning (in a derogatory sense) those who were not Arab, probably following the Greek word 'barbaros', which was used to mean those who were not Greek. In reality they have never been one homogeneous racial group but three: Sanhaja, Masmouda, and Zenata, and their loyalties have always been to their tribal origins and not to one amorphous mass known as Berber.

The Sanhaja, from which sprang the Almoravide dynasty (the founders of Marrakesh), were nomads who in the 11C conquered the desert and much of the region to the south of it for Islam; the Masmouda were quiet farming people who lived in the north and west and in the High and Anti Atlas mountains, and it was they who gave rise (from out of Tin Mal, south of Marrakesh) to the Almohade dynasty which displaced the Almoravides; the Zenata, a sub-group of which—the Beni Marin—swept in from the empty region between the Tafilalet and Algeria to become the great Merinide dynasty, were tough, horse-riding nomads of the cold high plateaux of the interior.

Joined to the Arabs only by Islam, the Berbers have always held themselves proudly separate in all other matters, especially in the rural and mountain areas where there are still families who would not dream of intermarriage with Arabs. There is no standard form of Berber language since each tribal group has always used its own version, and there is no recognised Berber script or literature. Their strongest form of self-expression is music and dancing, which is rhythmic but with little harmony, compelling, loud and often quite intoxicating.

The proudest boast of many Berbers is that they have never been conquered. And this is no idle boast. The Phoenicians and Carthaginians did not try. The Romans finally left, not only because they had pressing matters elsewhere but also because Berber uprisings in the Rif and Middle Atlas were proving too troublesome and too expensive to put down. Berbers lived alongside the Arabs, after being initially quelled, and Islam was not so much imposed as welcomed, insofar as it represented a clearly defined way of life that they could immediately relate to (albeit with some admixture of their own brand of animism) in place of Christianity, which they had toyed with and discarded.

The ruthless, driving expansionism of the first Arab arrivals in the late 7C and early 8C appealed to the spirited Berbers who gladly joined in the early invasions of Spain (though they were somewhat chastened when the Arabs allotted to them the poorer regions such as Extremadura). Subsequent expansion into Spain was Berber led (Almoravide and Almohade) and the conquest, frequently (and mistakenly) referred to as Arab, is more correctly termed either Moorish or Muslim.

From the mid 11C until the arrival of the Saadians in 1554 Morocco was ruled by Berber dynasties, and even during the Arab years Berbers still retained their strongholds in the mountains, particularly in the High Atlas and the Rif, where they were wisely left alone. Nor did the French or Spanish 'Protectors' succeed totally in quelling their ardour, and the greatest Berber leader of all, Abd el Krim (1882–1963), was finally put down by the combined Spanish and French forces only because he over-reached himself by venturing out of his mountain fortress to try to take the traditional capital of Fez.

The Phoenicians and Carthaginians. The first invaders are believed to have been the Phoenicians, coming from the land known then as Canaan in the Eastern Mediterranean in the 12C BC. Gradually they established trading posts along the north coast of Africa and traces of their occupation have been found at Lixus (Liks), which was probably the earliest, Tangier (Tingis), Melilla (Russadir), Chellah (part of Rabat), and Tamuda (near Tetouan). These traces are usually in the form of fish-salting factories and are often heavily overlaid by Roman remains. The Phoenicians were essentially a maritime people, not interested in conquering or colonising, and paying scant attention to the primitive Berber tribes and poor agricultural land of the interior; therefore, their colonies were little more than enclaves along the coast, separated by great open spaces of wasteland which they did not need. Their main centre of influence was Carthage (Tunisia) and later, when Carthage became an independent state, the more civilised Carthaginians arrived and turned the north coast settlements into prosperous towns; they are known to have developed the fish-salting and preserving into quite a major industry and their anchovy paste, called 'garum', was widely exported. They also grew wheat and probably introduced the grape.

The Carthaginians exercised a considerable cultural influence on the Berbers—even outside their small enclaves and certainly in the prosperous region around Volubilis—and this continued long after the Sack of Carthage in 146 BC; indeed it probably increased at that moment as hundreds of Cathaginians fled westwards and took refuge from the Romans in the friendly enclaves along the coast. By this time there were two Berber kingdoms: Mauritania (to the W) and Numidia (roughly where Algeria is now), with the Moulouya river forming a boundary between the two.

The Romans. After they had taken Carthage the Romans moved westwards into the Berber kingdoms of Mauritania and Numidia which became part of the Roman Empire. In 33 BC the Emperor Octavius granted the kingdom of Mauritania to the young Berber prince, Juba, son of Juba I of Numidia who had committed suicide 13 years earlier after defeat by the Romans at the Battle of Thapsus. In 25 BC they added the whole of Numidia to his realm. Educated in Rome and married to the daughter of Mark Antony and Cleopatra, known as Cleopatra Silene, his pedigree was impeccable and he ruled wisely, probably living in Volubilis. This had already become a Berber town of some standing before the Romans arrived, due, in part, to the natural fertility of the region surrounding it and in part to the teaching of the Carthaginians enabling the Berbers to get the best out of the land.

Juba reigned for 48 years and was succeeded by his son, Ptolemy, whose life ended abruptly when the Emperor Caligula, half mad and obsessively jealous of Ptolemy's success with the populace, had him quietly executed. This infamous act marked the end of the Mauritanian kingdom. Caligula himself was murdered the following year and his successor, Claudius, transformed the kingdom into two provinces of Rome, for easier administration and greater control: Mauritania Caesariensis stretched from Eastern Morocco across Algeria; Mauritania Tingitana (named after Tingis) extended as far west as the Atlantic coast. This gave rise to furious and bloody uprisings on the part of the Berbers, led by Aedemon, the late King

Ptolemy's minister, which took 20,000 Romans three years to put down. Thereafter peace and prosperity reigned for a time. Tingis was the capital but Volubilis was the seat of the Provincial Governor. Roman rule stretched as far W as Sala Colonia (Chellah) and not much further south than Volubilis where the Middle Atlas formed a natural barrier. The Berbers of the high mountains and the south were little affected and led their lives as before, only occasionally riding northwards to claim new pastures. It was about this time that the desert Berbers discovered the use of the camel which made them far more mobile and ready for aggression. The Romans built aqueducts and reservoirs and brought water into regions which had hitherto been drought-ridden. But they had little desire to move into the wild south. Pliny in one of his letters describes the region south of Sala Colonia as being 'deserted and the home of elephants'.

After some 300 years of good works and fairly half-hearted city building, though very little of a cultural nature (Volubilis was the main contribution), the Romans began to lose interest in Mauritania Tingitana, which, after all, produced little more than elephants and an almost inexhaustible supply of citrus wood, which was used by wealthy Patrician families for making decorative tables. Uprisings of Berbers (who had been ignored rather than subdued) continued and increased, ranging from minor irritations to deeply damaging and costly battles, and the Romans compromised by moving the seat of their administration northwards to Tingis (Tangier) c AD 250. Shortly afterwards they abandoned Sala Colonia and Volubilis and maintained only a small presence in an area bounded by Tingis, Lixus and Tamuda, which looked to Roman Spain for its administration and was probably deemed necessary only for the purpose of guarding the Straits.

The next 400 years formed Morocco's Dark Ages and very little is known about this period. The Vandals and Goths who were sweeping through Spain may have touched the northern tip of Morocco on their way eastwards to Carthage but there are no traces of their having stayed. The Berbers in the mountains and the desert continued life much as before. The Romanised, part Christian, Berber-Mauritanians of the cities of Volubilis, Sala Colonia, Tingis and others, held on to their mixed cultural heritage and maintained a degree of civilisation, as evidenced by one or two Latin inscriptions, found in several places, dating from as late as the mid 7C. But the weak and divided nature of the country was to prove no match at all for the next wave of invaders.

Islam

The Idrissides. By the 7C AD the Arabs were in full expansion. They were inspired primarily by their fierce desire to spread their own religion of Islam throughout the world. But they were doubtless particularly attracted to North Africa by the endless stretches of desert sand which were to them like home. It was in 670 that the first Arab invasions of the North African coastal plain took place under Oqba ben Nafi, a commander of the Ummayed dynasty in Damascus. He is best known for having founded the city of Kairwan (south of Tunis) and for having built the first ever mosque in North Africa. He swept with his army into what is now Morocco in the year 683, and history records that he was so triumphant at finally reaching the Atlantic overland that he spurred his horse on into the water shouting that only the ocean prevented him from carrying his conquest even further, 'preaching the unity of Thy holy name and putting to the sword the rebellious nations who worship any other gods but Thee'. He called this territory *el Maghreb*, meaning 'the West', and that part which is now Morocco he called *el Maghreb el Aqsa*, or 'farthest West'.

The main part of Morocco had still to be conquered. There followed a period of great violence, and Oqba ben Nafi himself was quickly despatched by the warlike Berbers. But the absolute and dynamic religion of the Arabs eventually appealed to the Berbers, the majority of whom had been little moved by the Romans' Christianity. When a second Ummayed leader, Musa Ibn Nasir, arrived in 703, they were not unwilling to participate in the Islamic expansion into southern Spain and into the more southerly areas of Morocco. However, the progress of Islam remained patchy and small enclaves of Christians still existed in the interior (though many fled to Spain). This lack of national unity persisted until the arrival of Idriss bin Abdallah, a descendant of the prophet Mohammed, in 788. There are very few original Arab sources available for reference about this early period but that which is most frequently cited by historians is the 'Raoud el Kartas', a chronicle by the 13C writer from Fez, Ibn-Abi-Zar-el-Fasi. From this we learn that Idriss bin Abdallah fled into Egypt from the Abbasides, who had earlier displaced the Ummayed dynasty in Damascus and against whom his own father had led an unsuccessful uprising. Idriss was accompanied by his faithful companion Rachid (about whom almost nothing is known) and the two arrived, by way of Kairwan, first in Tangier and then in the former Roman city of Volubilis where they were received by Berbers already fully converted to Islam by the earlier Arab arrivals. The Berber chief Abd el Majid proclaimed Idriss king and pledged the support of his own and neighbouring tribes. It seems that he welcomed the arrival of an assured leader who would guide the country out of the spiritual uncertainties which had increased since the death of Oqba ben Nafi. Moulay Idriss' power increased daily, and more and more tribesmen bowed to the inevitable and allied themselves to this new and formidable group of believers. So powerful did he become that the infamous and jealous Abbaside caliph, Haroun er Rachid of Baghdad, sent a representative to poison him in 791. His body was taken to Moulay Idriss, a town he had founded alongside Volubilis, and it lies there still in what has since become one of the great shrines of Islam.

Fortunately for posterity, Idriss had married and made pregnant a Berber servant girl called Kenza. Idriss bin Idriss (soon to be Moulay Idriss II) was born after his father's death and was educated and prepared for his awesome task by Rachid, his father's faithful friend who acted as regent until Idriss was proclaimed King at the age of 12, in 804. By all accounts he was a remarkable child, able to read at four years old and recite the entire Koran at eight. He was wise and well-loved throughout his reign of 21 years and his faith in Allah as the one and only true God and in the teachings of his prophet Mohammed through the Koran was exemplary.

Idriss was an ambitious and energetic leader and he needed a capital city; Volubilis (now called by the Arabs *Oualili*) was too small, and anyway it was essentially Roman in character. So he founded Fez (or, he may have built on to what his father had already founded). Historians disagree as to who actually laid the first stone of this historic city but it is generally agreed today that Fez began to prosper only from the time of Idriss II. (It was ideally sited in the centre of a fertile, well-watered region and at the crossroads of the natural east–west and north–south routes through the mountains.) In

818, as if to confirm the significance of Fez, 8000 Arab families arrived after being expelled by the Christians from the Emirate of Cordoba in Spain. Seven years later 2000 families came from Kairwan, the city which Oqba ben Nafi had founded and which was by now the most advanced centre of Arab culture in the eastern Maghreb. These 'refugees' were welcomed and installed, respectively, on the right and left banks of the river that divides the town. It was very largely as a result of the coming of these people, with their refinements and skills, that Fez became a great spiritual and intellectual centre whose influence very soon reached to the far north of the country, and later beyond. Moulay Idriss II, a charismatic and unequivocal leader, united warring tribes in a general allegiance to Islam, and to himself as a direct descendant of the Prophet. Thus he created the first Arab kingdom of Morocco. But the oases in the south, and probably much of the great mountain ranges of Atlas and Rif, remained outside his grasp, still uncharted and breeding future dynasties which would wrest his kingdom away.

When Idriss II died in 828 the kingdom was divided between his eight sons and confusion followed. Berber tribes, sensing a lack of firm direction and unity, grew rebellious once more and tried to displace their royal masters; amongst them were the unruly Meknassas who surged in from the east and founded Taza and Meknes. The newly-established Fatimid dynasty entered the country from Tunisia and the Ummayeds arrived from Cordoba to rid the country of the Fatimid threat. In the event neither stayed long: the Fatimids succeeded in conquering Egypt in 969, moved their capital from Kairwan to Cairo and lost interest in the far west. The now weak caliphate of Cordoba collapsed and Spain became a collection of small autonomous units known as 'taifas', which made for ineffectual government; it became necessary for the wandering Ummayeds to return to Spain to strengthen the cause of Islam. Into this vacuum came the next dynasty, from the south.

The Almoravides. The Almoravides were camel-riding Berber nomads of the Sanhaja group of tribes, to whom cultivation of the soil was unknown and who lived off the meat and milk of the camel. They have always been referred to as 'the veiled ones' since they wound a length of cloth around their faces as protection against the sand (as their descendants still do today). For a century or more they had been conquering and converting to Islam the black countries to the south of the Sahara, inspired by their search for the source of large quantities of gold which were flowing into Morocco from somewhere in the region of the Niger river. The emir of one of these tribes went to Mecca and came back convinced of the need to reform his fellow men and particularly his warlike and greedy kinsmen. Other repentants joined him and this large band of pious and fanatic Berbers roamed the south forcing into repentance and submission the Souss valley (an extensive sugar-growing area on the west coast) and the oases, particularly Sijilmassa, the rich market on the cross-roads of the camel caravans, which received most of the gold.

The story of the gold trade is a fascinating one. The Arabs had been aware of the existence of gold in the general region of the Niger since they first arrived in North Africa. Certainly at the time of the foundation of Fez, the exchange of gold for salt was well under way. Arab historians and travellers have agreed throughout the ages that the 'silent trade' was enacted as follows: the people of the Niger region, it seems, suffered from a permanently unsatisfied craving for salt, and just south of Sijilmassa were salt mines. Arab merchants therefore set off across the desert, their camels laden with vast loads of salt, and when they reached a certain river on the far side they arranged their salt in heaps on the ground and then retired out of sight and waited. A crowd of black men would then arrive in boats, deposit a quantity of gold beside each salt heap and retire, leaving both salt and gold. If the merchants were satisfied with the amount of gold, they would take it and journey back across the Sahara to Sijilmassa; if not, they would go away again and wait for the men to add a little more. Both sides were usually well pleased but never met. Lurid tales are told by travellers about the silent black men: that they lived in holes in the ground and were completely naked, etc., etc. But no one actually discovered the source of the gold, neither Berber nor Arab, despite expensive and perilous expeditions throughout the centuries. For a colourful account of this period read 'The Golden Trade of the Moors', by E.W. Bovill.

The campaigns fought by the Almoravides were violent and successful and they soon controlled the whole of the south, under their leader Youssef ben Tachfine, one of Morocco's really great leaders and the founder of Marrakesh. As nomads, the Almoravides had never been used to settling in one place, much less building a city, but as their power increased so did the need for a central store of weapons and food and, it goes without saying, in view of their new-found religious fervour, a mosque. So, after their exhausting crossing of the High Atlas, what more natural than that they should want to stop a while on the vast empty plain immediately to the north, where the mountains offered both protection from sandstorms and an ample supply of spring water. Thus in 1062 the building of Marrakesh began and the mosque was erected on the spot where the Koutoubia stands today. Having established their base the Almoravides went further north to conquer Fez and force submission on the remains of the Idrisside dynasty. This they did without much difficulty (and hugely enriched the city thereafter). From here they flowed over the rest of the country and turned everybody, at least superficially, towards their particular version of strict orthodox Islam; this done they began to venture further afield, and by 1080 Youssef ben Tachfine's Almoravide empire stretched as far east as Algiers. His reputation as a formidable fighter had reached the much beleaguered Muslim leaders in Spain who invited him, now a very old man, to lend a hand against the advancing Christians who had just taken Toledo. In 1086 he took his armies across the straits, regained lost ground and took the important city of Valencia; much of Spain became part of the Almoravide empire. A period of peace and prosperity followed, enriched by the refined culture of the Andalucian courts to which had been added a healthy dose of Berber virility and discipline.

Youssef ben Tachfine, a legend in his own lifetime, died in 1107 at well over 100 years old. He was succeeded by his son Ali whose mother had been a Christian slave from Andalucia. Ali's reign of 37 years was not remarkable though he is credited with having been responsible for much of the embellishment of Marrakesh, some of this during the absences of his father in Spain. But he did not continue the policy of expansion abroad and pacification at home. Born and brought up in the luxurious atmosphere of the Andalucian court and never having known the hard life of the desert, he was too irresolute and too spoilt to command the necessary respect and allegiance of the tough Berber leaders. He chose advisers of the same origins as himself and latterly, as he became increasingly religious, he turned more readily to spiritual advisers than he did to the well-tried and trusted counsellors who had surrounded his father. Unrest began to spread throughout the country. He died in 1144 and was succeeded by three rulers who were even more ineffectual. By this time general dissatisfaction was making itself felt amongst the tribes, whilst in the cities the strict orthodox religious code of the first Almoravides had become almost unrecognisable.

The Almohades. A new power was emerging. The Almohades were Masmouda Berbers from the High and Anti Atlas mountains who had long looked down on the once nomadic Sanhaja Almoravides. They had endured 85 years of Almoravide rule, but now that the vigorous leadership had become effete and aimless they saw their chance to come out of their mountain strongholds and take over.

The first Almohade leader, Mohammed Ibn Tumart, claimed not only Arab descent but descent from Ali, the Prophet's son-in-law. He was a man of extraordinary power and his supporters proclaimed him 'the promised one' of Islam and called him *Mahdi* (meaning messiah). He spoke both Arabic and Berber, and was even more determined in his desire to stamp out weakness and corruption than the early Almoravides had been. The foundation of his doctrine was absolute unity with God, from which stemmed the name Muwahhadin, meaning Unitarian, which was applied to the followers of this doctrine; the term Almohade is a European version of this. In the year 1107 Ibn Tumart went to Mecca where he spent ten years deepening his knowledge of divine matters, and it was on his return that he began gathering up large numbers of disciples, including Abd el Mumene who would eventually succeed him. Son of a simple potter living in Eastern Algeria, Abd el Mumene is said to have attracted the attention of the Mahdi by his intelligence, piety, and good looks, and was persuaded to leave his family with promises that he was the 'Chosen One', and would take over and guide the Muwahhadin to victory through faith. The two men, with a huge band of supporters, re-entered Morocco from the east, leaving behind them a path of undying love, or vehement hatred, as the case might be: for Ibn Tumart would unhesitatingly attack any deviation from the strict creed of the Koran and himself abhorred music and even the company of women which, he maintained, could only divert the soul from its true religious path towards God.

So in 1118, Ibn Tumart began to preach openly and to appeal to dispirited Arabs and Berbers alike, who were more than ready for another strong leader to replace the disinterested Almoravide, Ali. Tribe after tribe of Berbers were impressed by the depth of his understanding of holy matters, his singleness of purpose and his superb skills as an orator. Still, many a bloody battle had to be fought with the Almoravides themselves and in 1130 he attacked their great citadel of Marrakesh, unsuccessfully in the first instance as defences were too strong.

At this moment the Mahdi suddenly died and Abd el Mumene (1133–63) took over quietly, lest news of the sudden death of 'the One exempt from sin' should cause panic and despair. It was to take him another 17 years to put down remaining resistance by the Almoravides and the final blow was a decisive victory in Tlemcen in 1144, followed within the next three years by the total surrender of Fez and Marrakesh.

Morocco was once more pacified and attention was turning again to Spain. Abd el Mumene, now called Emir el Mumenin (Commander of the Faithful), reigned for 30 years and during this time the Moorish (now Almohade) empire reached its furthest limits: deep into Spain and eastwards as far as Kairwan. He was succeeded at his death by his son Youssef, who took greatest pleasure in philosophical discussion and for a time removed to Seville so as to be part of the more developed intellectual life there. It is arguable that much of his father's hard-won territories abroad would have begun to fall away had he not died young (killed in northern Spain in a battle against Alfonso IX of Leon in 1184). His son Yacoub, whose mother was a negro slave woman, was to become as great an empire-builder and as wise a ruler as his grandfather. He was soon to be honoured with the proud title of *el Mansour* (meaning 'the Conqueror') but he is chiefly remembered as a builder of mosques. As he pushed further and further into Spain it was his custom not to execute his captives but to bring them back as slave labour for his mighty building projects, the greatest of which was to have been the Mosque el Hassan ('the Beautiful') in Rabat. The town of Rabat was founded at this time as a convenient *ribat* (camp), used by Yacoub and his army as a launching point for southern Spain. Later it was called Ribat el Fath (Camp of Victory) and the great mosque building project began. Yacoub died before the Mosque el Hassan was ever finished and all that remains today of this unfulfilled dream are the stumps of pillars which would have supported the roof, and an incomplete minaret known today as 'le tour Hassan'. He also completed the Koutoubia mosque in Marrakesh and the Giralda in Seville (both begun by his father).

Yacoub el Mansour was above all a great statesman, deeply concerned with adherence to Islam but not a fanatic, a brave warrior but with an understanding of the arts and sciences, a just and tolerant man, probably one of the most balanced rulers Morocco has ever had. The whole country prospered at the time: spiritually, intellectually, economically and architecturally. Marrakesh (still the capital) and Fez flowered as never before (or since) and the end of the 12C is generally regarded as an apogée in Morocco's history. He died in 1199 and was succeeded by his son, Mohammed al Nasir, who, like so many sons of great men, turned out to be a weakling (in fairness, he was only 17). Enemies of Morocco were quick to exploit this and the empire began to break up, especially in Spain where kings and princes lost no time in regaining much of their land. In desperation Mohammed collected himself and announced he was going to make a supreme effort to 'overwhelm all Christendom'. It is interesting to note that King John of England who was engaged in trying to regain Normandy from the French at the time was much alarmed by this threat and quickly sent envoys to Morocco to plead for co-operation between the two countries against the French. History might have been very different had he not been refused but this nevertheless makes a fascinating moment of contact between two dissolute monarchs with pressing problems abroad and the threat of civil war at home. In the event, the Almohade army got no further N than Las Navas de Tolosa, a town on the borders of Castile and Andalucia, where they suffered a gruelling and decisive defeat at the hands of the Christians in 1212 which proved to be the turning point in the Muslim occupation of Spain. In shame al Nasir crept back to Marrakesh where he died the following year, having already abdicated in favour of his 16-year-old son, Youssef al Mostansir. This pleasure-loving youth had little chance of regaining control of the resentful and increasingly ungovernable tribes in Morocco. He reigned for 10 years and was followed by a string of equally unsuitable monarchs.

After such a major reversal in Spain and a succession of weak rulers at home, chaos inevitably broke out once more. Throughout the early years of Morocco's history, the multifarious and high-spirited tribes were held in check by one or both of two things: religious fervour and merciless control by the sword. When both these elements were missing, high spirits would

The incomplete Hassan tower, Rabat, begun by Yacoub el Mansour in 1174

naturally erupt and disorder turn quickly to anarchy, until the arrival of the next recognisably strong ruler. None was forthcoming at this time from the Almohade camp and a new and threatening force was gathering in the east.

The Merinides. The Beni Merin, or Merinides, were a tribe of nomadic Zenata Berbers who came from the empty area between Taza and Algeria. They had been edging their way westwards for some time as they sought better pasture for their flocks. Their driving force was not fanatical desire for religious reform (unlike all their predecessors) but greed for land and, latterly, as success whetted their appetite, for conquest and power. They had no particular creed to preach and were content to go along with the orthodox Islamic faith which had returned to the country after the excesses of the early Almoravides and Almohades. Their leader, Abd el Hakk, was a wise and pious man whose father had fought in the war against Spain. He was quick to sense the absolute disarray of the Almohades, and in 1213 (one year after their demoralising defeat at Las Navas de Tolosa) he slipped quietly into Fez and was enthroned there with very little ado, and with hardly any effect on the rest of the country, which continued in a state of dissension and inter-tribal violence for some years to come. He died soon after his enthronement and his successor, Abou Yahya, a man of little sensitivity, aroused such fury in that proud city that he did not finally take it until 1248, after nine months of siege.

Abou Yahya was succeeded by his brother Youssef, who occupied, without too much difficulty, the Almohade capital of Marrakesh and put an end to the last Almohade ruler, Abu Dabbus, in 1269. By this time virtually all of Morocco had been won over and tribes were ready, as before, to fall in with a new and forceful leadership which had by this time gained favour by winning back some territories in Spain. Youssef was a wise and forward-looking monarch who set out to calm the bitter resentment in Fez by firmly making it his capital and then founding a new city (Fez Jdid) alongside the old one in 1276, for the old one already filled its ramparts and could expand no further. Fez Jdid was essentially a royal city consisting almost exclusively of palaces and military buildings set in vast open spaces. It also became an administrative centre and the Merinides go down in history as having been the first Moroccans to introduce a simple form of civil service. Moreover they saw to it that the posts of caids and regional authorities were filli d by leading local figures who had proved their worth rather than by members of the royal family, and many influential positions were allocated to Moors returned from Andalucia.

It is often said that the Merinides lacked the panache and passion of either of the preceding Berber dynasties, and that their conquests abroad were not remarkable. But their policy at home was enlightened. One example of their imaginative domestic policy was the introduction of the mellah or Jewish quarter in all the major towns, Marrakesh and Fez in particular, so that Jews could live secure and unmolested. Hitherto Jews had been scattered throughout the old cities in isolated groups, officially tolerated by Muslims but not welcomed, often abused and frequently made scapegoats. Nevertheless, it is recorded that many Jews converted to Islam at this time rather than be forced to leave their homes and move to the mellah and today some of Morocco's most distinguished families have Jewish origins.

Youssef's successor, Yacoub, was a philanthropic man, one of the first Berber sultans to seek to improve the lot of the disadvantaged: the blind, the sick, and, above all, the impoverished students who often walked vast distances to their university or place of learning. The medersa—an elaborately ornamented students' lodging hall with one or two lecture rooms—probably originated in Baghdad in the 11C and later found its way into Egypt. The Merinides were certainly the first to introduce the concept to Morocco, and Fez in particular is liberally scattered with fine examples within easy walking distance of the Karaouyine. No expense was spared; Sultan Abou Inan (1351–58) who built the Bou Inania medersa in Fez, the most famous medersa of all, is reported to have said upon being told how much it cost: 'what is beautiful is not expensive however great the price', which sums up the Merinide belief that gold was of no value unless converted into beauty. Every town was enriched. Certainly the later Merinide sultans much preferred the ornamentation of their environment to the waging of endless and costly holy wars against the Christians in Spain. Despite the ostentatious splendour of the medersas, it has to be said that the students themselves lived a frugal and often unhealthy life (as the size of the cell-like rooms signifies). Sometimes two or more would share a room which was dark, often damp, and certainly ill-ventilated; and there they would sleep, cook, eat and study. But their lodging was free, and they also received drinking water and bread daily from the town. Anything else, such as books, meat or vegetables, they had to finance themselves: some lectured in the mosque, some acted as temporary servants in rich houses, and others were forced to beg for charity (which was not too difficult since Muslims must anyway give away a proportion of their income to the poor and there were enough rich Fassis around who were happy to support the cause of knowledge).

Within their extravagant setting Merinide sultans surrounded themselves with scholars who could talk not only about the Koran but about science and law, poetry and geography. The well-known traveller Ibn Batuta (1304–78) was an honoured member of the court of Abou Inan, who gave him a secretary to write down stories of his travels as far afield as the Black Sea and Timbucktoo. Ibn Khaldoun, the 14C historian and Spanish Muslim brought up in Seville, spent many years as an adviser and close associate of Merinide sultans. The cultural prestige of the court in Fez was further enhanced by the arrival, in 1268, of some 13 mule-loads of ancient Arab manuscripts, Korans, etc. which Spanish Muslims had lost to the Christians over the years and which were now being returned as part of a former peace treaty with the King of Castile. Moreover, the Merinides were the first to introduce a code of conduct into what had hitherto been a fairly rough and mannerless mode of life depending solely on the laws imposed by the Koran. To these laws were added rules of courtesy and hospitality which are still today an integral part of the Moroccan character and which strike a charming—if slightly anachronistic—note upon the Western ear: upon meeting a friend or aquaintance, (after the traditional greeting of *Salaam Aleikum*, meaning 'may peace be with you') a ritual of questions and answers as to the health of each member of the family and the state of the harvest or business of each will be enacted before any objective conversation can begin; and the visitor should be aware that even today admiration expressed for one of your host's possessions puts him under an obligation to present it to you as his guest.

The great and beneficial ruler Abou Inan was murdered in 1358, seven years after he had come to the throne, by which time he was reputed to have well over a hundred sons. He was succeeded by a series of less worthy rulers and pretenders, including some from Moorish Spain, who fought amongst themselves for power. Almost exactly one hundred years after its arrival from the east, the Merinide dynasty began to lose its grip, its leaders obsessed by personal advancement and by the pleasures of the court and the harem within it. By now only the kingdom of Granada remained as a Moorish enclave within Christian Spain and even that was to go in 1492. At the height of their power the Merinides had raised the spiritual and cultural levels of Moroccan society to new and dazzling heights; their eye for architectural beauty was astounding (it is a sad fact that virtually all of their graceful palaces were destroyed by succeeding jealous rulers and only the medersas remain as a legacy). Their military achievements, however, were negligible and towards the end of their time actually in a state of reversal. At the turn of the 14C the dynasty was feeble and its sultans gorged with too much luxurious living. The empire had all but slipped away and Spain and Portugal were now beginning to turn envious eyes on Morocco, encouraged by their recent successes. Moreover hordes of Christian merchants were spreading throughout Morocco, bringing with them outrageously liberated views which must have horrified any remaining orthodox Muslims.

Upon hearing of the death of one of the last sultans, Abd Allah, in 1398, another ruler, El Wattas, who was of the same tribe but not of the same family, left his home town of Asilah (on the north coast) and came to Fez to avenge his kinsman—unwisely as it turned out, for the Portuguese, who quickly sensed a weakness in their hitherto indomitable enemies, invaded Asilah and caried off 5000 of its inhabitants as slaves, including the son of El Wattas and other members of his family. Understandably enraged, El Wattas was forced to make a treaty with Portugal ceding not only Asilah but also Tangier and Ceuta. Afterwards he turned once more to Fez, besieged it for a year, ousted the killers of Abd Allah and proclaimed himself king. The minor dynasty of El Wattas is remembered now for the easy way in which it gave up large portions of Morocco to Portugal. (Portuguese interest in the west coast of North Africa had started back in the 12C, inspired not only by their compulsive urge for expansion and exploration but also by the quest for the gold-producing areas south of the desert and a desire to divert at least some of the gold trade northwards towards Lisbon.) El Wattas' son and successor, Mohammed, had developed a sympathy for the Portuguese during his enforced stay in Lisbon and he allowed them to settle in Mogador (Essaouira), Mazagan (El Jadida), Azemmour, Safi and Agadir. So, for a time, almost the entire west coast of Morocco became a separate Portuguese colony, to which the remaining castles, ramparts and huge bastions against the sea bear witness today. Chaos was evident throughout the country, with the Portuguese in the north and west, and rebellious Berber tribes trying to take control in the interior. The Merinides were confined to Fez and Marrakesh—the two traditional strongholds in time of unrest. The country was felt to need a new strong leader whose right to rule would appear incontrovertible, and holy men were asked to pray for such a man to come forward.

The Saadians. The Saadians, who were descended from the Prophet Mohammed, came originally from Arabia in the 12C and settled in the valley of the Draa in the south of Morocco. They had lived a quiet and isolated existence, with apparently no thoughts of expansion until the mid 16C when Morocco was manifestly crumbling away in the hands of the incompetent Wattasides. Their leader, Mohammed esh-Sheik (1540–57), was a much loved and brave man, and it was under his guidance that the Saadians first moved northwards in a bid to restore order and the observance of Islam, to oust the Christian invaders and to take the throne from the Wattasides. With their energy and singleness of purpose they achieved all this without much difficulty. By 1541 they had re-taken Agadir, and anyway the Portuguese were beginning to lose interest in Morocco and elected to withdraw from Mogador, Azemmour and Safi, leaving only Mazagan as a token foothold.

Mohammed marched on Fez and was given access quite easily by the last of the Wattasides who offered little resistance. But the people of Fez were shocked by these seemingly coarse and primitive people straight from the desert who paid scant respect to their traditional and cultured way of life. They were duly pacified by the Saadians who decided that they could not live in an atmosphere of profound hostility and in the 16C rebuilt the 12C Almohade town of Taroudant (just east of Agadir) as their capital. Mohammed was succeeded by two unremarkable sons and then by his grandson, Abd Allah (1574–76), a man described later as 'not a sultan but a saint', though it was noted that he did put ten of his 12 brothers to death as potential rivals. One of those who escaped being murdered—Abd el Malik—succeeded to the throne and marched victoriously on Fez in 1576, having enlisted the help of Turkish troops from neighbouring Algeria to do so. Fortunately the Turks were persuaded—with copious rewards no doubt—to return home promptly, and Fez became once more the rightful capital of Morocco, to the evident relief of all concerned, especially the Fassis themselves.

In 1577, another Saadian, a dispossessed nephew of the Sultan, was secretly applying to the King of Portugal for help in securing the throne for himself. King Sebastian did not need much persuasion as he already dreamed of regaining Portuguese territories in Morocco. He landed in Asilah with a massive force of soldiers including the cream of Portuguese aristocracy and, incidentally, some 700 English troops under Thomas Stukeley, who had been blown off course en route for Ireland and had landed in Lisbon. There followed a memorable battle in 1578 at Ksar el Kbir, which resulted in a decisive and terrible defeat for the Portuguese. It came to be known as 'the Battle of the Three Kings' because Don Sebastian, the Saadian Pretender, and the Sultan Abd el Malik died there. After this mortal blow for the Portuguese at the hands of the Moroccans, the whole of Europe began to take notice of the remarkably recovered Islamic country: ambassadors were exchanged and visitors poured into Morocco, returning home bearing exotic gifts and tales of unbelievable riches.

Glorious in their victory, the Saadians under their new Sultan, Ahmed (1578–1603), settled down in Fez to continue the process of extravagant embellishment their predecessors had started. As they modified their customs and interests they were gradually accepted by scholars, religious leaders and ordinary people alike. A period of peace and considerable economic expansion followed. But Ahmed was an ambitious and energetic man and began to look towards the gold-producing areas of the Niger. In 1590 he mounted an expedition of some 3000 men—many of them drawn from the ever restless Berber tribes—across the Sahara. The journey was a terrible one, across the desert and then through dense tropical regions. Many died on the way. The survivors had little difficulty in subduing the totally unsuspecting and defenceless black tribes who were deprived of both their gold reserves and their liberty. Not only gold but also ebony, rhino horn, ostrich feathers and slaves found their way northwards, and indeed it is the descendants of these slaves who form part of the Royal Guard today. Gold became a passion for Ahmed, who took upon himself the title 'Edh Dhahabi' (meaning 'the golden one'). The whole area of Western Sahara, Mauritania, Timbucktoo and southwards to the Niger became a Protectorate and was administered by Saadian 'pashas' from Timbucktoo whence, incidentally, tobacco was first introduced into Morocco. At this time many

British and Portuguese explorers were trying to work their way up the Niger from the coast, also trying to find the source of the gold. These expeditions usually failed as the sailors fell prey to disease or to hostile local tribes.

Not everyone was benefiting from the wealth of the Saadians. There was still great poverty amongst the ordinary people, especially in the south, and the Saadians paid far less attention to the plight of the mass of the population than the early Merinides had done. Most of the gold was spent on prestigious royal palaces such as the Badi in Marrakesh (begun 1580), for which 50 tons of marble was brought from Italy and which was later all but destroyed by the Alouites; and there was the ethereal mausoleum (les Tombeaux Saadiens) in Marrakesh built by Ahmed Edh Dhahabi to contain his own body and those of his descendants. By this time the Saadians had turned their attention away from Fez, which has only the resplendent pavilions in the court of the Karaouyine Mosque to show for all that incoming wealth. So total was the involvement of Ahmed in his quest for enrichment that he began seriously to neglect his domestic affairs and the people grew restless and started to look for alternative rulers. When he died in 1603 his three sons fought for the throne and countless pretenders appeared and joined in the fray. The army lost control and a period of civil war followed during which Fez was sacked again and again. Even the call to prayer from the minarets was suspended.

During this period, Fez, together with Meknes and the surrounding countryside, also had to contend with a politically ambitious religious sect known as the Dila. They were Berbers who had set up a zaouia near Khenifra in the Middle Atlas at the beginning of the 17C and who became quite ruthless in their efforts to take over and rule that part of the country. In the north even stranger things were happening: a large band of Spanish Muslims who had at one time been converted to Christianity, but had subsequently been expelled from Spain and so did not know where they belonged, settled on either side of the river Bou Regreg in Rabat and Salé. In 1627 they formed their own republic which they managed to hold on to for some 14 years. Their chief activity was 'trading', which was a polite term for piracy in which they successfully indulged for many years. Their exploits were primarily directed against Spain, but later they grew bold and extended their attentions as far as the English Channel. Despite this intrusion there were many Englishmen who considered using this wild but excessively brave gang of renegades against Spain, although King Charles I would not recognise the independence of the 'Republic of Bou Regreg'. The 'Republic' was eventually invaded and subdued by the dreaded Dila Berbers. Piracy continued however, much to the impoverishment of European traders, until action to put an end to it was finally concerted at the Congress of Vienna (1815).

Before the fall of the now decadent Saadian dynasty, there was just one enlightened ruler, who came to power in 1637. This was another Mohammed; he ruled for 18 years in Fez in a little pocket of comparative calm but could do little about the fierce rivalries raging elsewhere throughout the country. He was murdered in 1655 and his untimely end heralded the return of strife and killing in the city itself. No other capable Saadian leaders presented themselves and the people of Morocco were faced, once more, with the almost total disintegration of their state.

The Alouites. The Alouites were also descended from the Prophet. They had arrived from Arabia some three centuries earlier to settle near Rissani in the Tafilalet region of the south. (It is for this reason that they are sometimes referred to as the Filali.) Unlike preceding dynasties they did not move in and seize power but were formally invited in by the people of Fez to come to the capital and take over the throne of Morocco. Thus in 1666 the first Alouite ruler, Moulay Rachid, was welcomed into the city. He restored order with a firm hand, revived the life of the mosques and drove out all pretenders, including the Dila Berbers whose zaouia in the Middle Atlas he then went on to destroy. He also occupied Marrakesh and brought much of the south of the country under control. However his reign was short: he died in 1672. From all accounts it would appear that he was a brave and wise ruler intent on restoring some form of sanity and faith to the country as a whole; but he was also a cruel tyrant. His life ended abruptly when he was caught by the neck in the fork of an orange tree as he drunkenly spurred on his horse in the Aguedal Gardens of Marrakesh.

His brother Moulay Ismael (1672–1727) introduced a period of greater tyranny. He has been described both as a great and wise monarch and as one of the most cruel rulers that Morocco has ever known, the latter view emanating mainly from escaped slaves who were able to produce first-hand evidence of his excesses. It is indisputable that he made an indelible impression during his reign of 55 years and succeeded in creating stability out of chaos. He was tireless in his efforts to pacify the whole country, including its most isolated corners, and it was not long before every tribe paid him homage. He recovered Tangier from the British (it had been part of the dowry of the Portuguese Catherine of Braganza when she married Charles II in 1661); he also wrested back Larache and Mehdia from the Spaniards; he reduced the enclaves of Ceuta and Melilla to their present modest dimensions; and he made it crystal clear to the Turks occupying Algeria that they should not even consider moving any further westwards.

Undeniably Moulay Ismael made Morocco great again and ensured that the world knew about it, exchanging ambassadors with many leading powers. To reflect his glory and to have somewhere suitable to receive and impress foreign envoys he built 12 palaces in Meknes which he enclosed with 25km of ramparts to form 'the Imperial City', no doubt modelling it to a large extent on the Versailles of Louis XIV who was already on the French throne when Ismael came to power and by whose friendship and respect he set great store. It is interesting to speculate why he should have chosen Meknes, a town of only minor importance so far, rather than Fez, the traditional centre of cultural and spiritual matters. The answer is probably that he mistrusted the Fassis, and particularly the many hundreds of Saadians who still lived in and around the city, and anyway there would have been no space for him to build on such a massive scale. Today the miles of ruined walls, palaces, and stables bear witness to his enormous energy and ambition, and, to be fair, to the scale of his success. It is not so much the size of the buildings as the method for building them which shocks posterity: his labour force consisted of at least 2500 Christian slaves and some 30,000 Moroccan malefactors (including no doubt many Saadians and rebellious Berbers), hundreds of whom died horribly in the construction process. And yet Arab historians relate that he prayed hard and lived plainly, although the latter is a dubious judgement when we hear that he had a harem of around 2000 (which included at least one English woman), and we are indebted to the writings of an English prisoner in 'The Adventures of T. Pellow' published in London in 1890, for some colourful revelations. Pellow had escaped death by embracing the Muslim faith and by attracting the attentions of the favourite queen who put him in charge of her apartments and the 37 concubines who lived therein.

Moulay Ismael died in 1727 at the age of 81 and was succeeded by a series of quarrelling and incapable sons. The real power at this time was in the hands of the Black Guard, which the Sultan had built up for his own protection. They were descendants of slaves taken by the Saadians during their gold-plundering expeditions into the Timbucktoo area, and after the death of their master they felt they owed loyalty to no one. For 30 years they rampaged across the country, raising up and then destroying sultans for their sport.

In 1757 a wise and strong Alouite ruler came to the throne once more. This was Mohammed ben Abdallah, who by some means not fully explained brought the menace of the unwieldy Black Guard under control; probably by this time an excess of power was causing them to degenerate anyway. Mohammed was a good man and sought first to lift the spirits of the people of Fez who had been sorely tried by Moulay Ismael's cruel 'governors' to the point where many eminent citizens had left; he even built some new medersas, as effective a way as any of showing his goodwill. He also founded the modern town of Essaouira (where the Portuguese Mogador once was), inviting English, French and Jewish merchants to settle there, to import tea, cloth and other commodities in exchange for the exotic items such as ivory, ostrich feathers and gold still coming out of the sub-Saharan region.

Mohammed's son, Yazid, who succeeded in 1790, was a cruel ruler and undid much of the spiritual and material reparations undertaken by his father, until he was put down by his brothers two years later. Those two years were enough to plunge the country once more into misery, and a line of indifferent successors could do little to stop Morocco falling once more into a state of war with France and Spain. In 1844 Algiers was lost to the French, after the Moroccan army was humiliatingly defeated by General Bougeaud and whilst French ships were simultaneously bombarding Tangier. In 1860 the Spaniards entered Tetouan from Ceuta and were prevented from continuing to Tangier only by the British who were unwilling to tolerate any strong European force installed on that side of the Straits. Peace was achieved on terms proposed by the Spaniards, which involved payment of a huge indemnity by the Moroccans. At this time the European powers strengthened their diplomatic representation in Tangier and together set up and managed the Cap Spartel lighthouse.

This unsatisfactory state of affairs continued until 1873 when another acceptable monarch appeared. This was Moulay el Hassan, who tackled the awesome task of pacifying the tribes with undoubted skill and was the first monarch to enter the wild Souss area (inland from Agadir) where the tribes had not hitherto acknowledged the central authority of the State; to maintain control he built the town of Tiznit as a permanent centre for his garrison. He even went as far south as Goulimine and eastwards to the Tafilalet. But his methods were still those of his ancestors: he would mount an 'expedition of pacification and tax-collecting' keeping the destination as secret as possible and then setting forth equipped with battering rams and boulders (and sometimes dynamite) to bear down on some unsuspecting tribe. The unfortunate villages on his way would be utterly despoiled by the unruly entourage, and a wide swathe of countryside would be quite literally eaten up, as by a swarm of locusts. Sometimes the village caid would hear of the oncoming threat and manage to muster some gifts of slaves, cattle, camels and sometimes even his own daughters with which to meet and please the Sultan. Sometimes this worked well enough to save the village from total devastation and the expedition would turn away,

Alouite gateway, Rissani

satiated, to descend elsewhere. The immediate result would be despair and humiliation for the village, which sooner or later would turn into bitterness and a burning desire for retribution. Thus in the long term these primitive attempts at pacification were doomed to have the opposite effect. The methods had not changed or progressed in hundreds of years and it is tempting to conjecture how much longer they would have continued had the European powers not stepped in. Eventually the unceasing struggle to unite the country wore him out and he died in 1894 after a particularly exhausting journey across the High Atlas from Tafilalet.

Moulay el Hassan was succeeded by his 16-year-old son Abd el Aziz, who under normal peaceful circumstances might have achieved some success but who stood little chance with the rumblings of rebellion ever present, and growing louder. He was not helped by the sporadic but well-meant attempts by European governments to suggest ways of reforming the administration, such as fixed salaries for civil servants and a more structured method of tax collection, because although he supported those methods he was manifestly incapable of applying, far less enforcing them. After a few years he gave up the struggle and turned instead to his young university-educated European friends who tempted him away from affairs of state with expensive mechanical toys and extravagant games of polo. Meanwhile, European financiers and traders were moving in fast, anxious for the rich pickings which would surely soon come their way.

Attacks on foreigners were frequent and the tribes began to take power into their own hands. So did the Europeans. The British agreed that the French should occupy Tunis in return for their agreement to British occupation of Cyprus; later the British raised no objection to French action in Morocco, in exchange for British intervention in Egypt. Now it was the turn of the Spaniards who, for historic reasons, insisted on a share of 'influence' in Morocco and this was duly agreed. Not to be left out the German Kaiser visited Tangier and offered his help to the Sultan. In 1906 the Conference of Algeciras (30 nations) was called to put an end to all this uncoordinated interference which was potentially damaging to European peace as well as threatening to the sovereignty of Morocco. The resulting treaty had the effect of internationalising the whole affair and making it illegal for anyone to take bilateral action, whilst at the same time affirming the independence of the Sultan. It made Tangier into an international free port and granted France and Spain a mandate to restore order (thereby implicitly preparing the way for the Protectorate should it become necessary).

Morocco's own despair was exacerbated when the Sultan's brother, Moulay Hafid, Governor of Marrakesh, declared publicly that Abd el Aziz was unfit to reign, on the grounds that he had become an extravagant wastrel. The two brothers marched towards each other with their respective armies but, in the event, no battle ensued and the young Sultan fled to his French friends. Moulay Hafid took over the throne in 1908 but could do little to improve the general situation. The French occupied Casablanca, the Germans took a warship into the harbour of Agadir and similar incidents were occurring all round the coastline. In 1912, Sultan Moulay Hafid signed the Treaty of Fez which relieved him of his power to govern and declared the greater part of the country a Protectorate under a French Resident-General. Simultaneously, the Spaniards signed a treaty which allocated to them the protection of what was left—a small zone to the north. Tangier remained an international city (even though geographically it fell within the Spanish zone) and was controlled by the signatories to the Treaty of Algeciras through their diplomatic representatives. Even the Sultan was represented there by a delegate (Mendoub). Four months after the signing of the treaty Moulay Hafid abdicated, understandably appalled by what he had allowed to happen, and another of his brothers was placed on the throne by the French. This was Moulay Youssef (1912–27), a suitably virtuous and aquiescent man, who was allowed to live in the traditional style of a Moroccan sultan and was treated as the sole spokesman for the Moroccan people whilst retaining no governing power.

The first French Resident-General (later Marshal), Louis Lyautey, aimed not only to pacify but also to construct. His attitude towards the country he was sent to protect, and later learned to love, was positive. He was scrupulously careful not to undermine Islam or to destroy any of its monuments. He built the ports of Casablanca and Kenitra and the new towns of Rabat, Fez, Meknes and Marrakesh, whilst leaving the old medinas quite untouched. The French arrived in large numbers to live and work in this land of opportunity. A modern educational system was introduced, t̲ ̲ administration was modernised and the legal system reformed; ro ̲ds and railways were built, and phosphates were discovered in the area ̲outh of Casablanca and later exploited to become Morocco's main export. The list was impressive and the benefits incalculable; Morocco was pulled abruptly into the 20C. However, development was essentially along French lines and lessons in schools were always in French; French became the language of learning and of progress. The Spanish zone was not developed so rapidly, partly because it comprised the more lawless and remote parts of the country, including the Rif mountains, and partly because the Spaniards were preoccupied with their own domestic problems, which were to culminate in the devastating civil war. Fewer Spaniards settled in Morocco and there was greater tolerance of Moroccan culture, which was already so closely linked with their own.

For the first few years there was relative peace in the cities, as if people were stunned by what had happened and thought it best to bow to the inevitable. Not so in the dissident areas of the south where tribes were traditionally very rebellious. By c 1920 there were signs of the more structured resistance to come, particularly in the Rif mountains where the very adept Berber leader, Abd el Krim, a caid in the Melilla area and a highly respected scholar, gathered a huge following and won a massive victory against the Spaniards near Al Hoceima. El Krim then went on to proclaim an independent 'Rif Republic', with himself as president. He was a formidable adversary and it took the combined strength of the French and Spanish forces five years to put him down. He was seen as a potential focus for general national resistance and therefore a major threat to any hopes of peace.

The French began to drive a wedge between Arabs and Berbers by playing on their differences. They even persuaded the Sultan to sign in 1930 a decree upholding Berber law which it was hoped would perpetuate separation. But this was a serious miscalculation, for it served merely to draw the two races closer together, both fearing they were being manipulated by a common enemy. A new prayer was heard in the mosques: 'Oh God, separate us not from our Berber brothers'. When, after a few months, the decree was amended there was great celebration; the cause of nationalism had been well served.

In the cities, particularly in the new administrative capital of Rabat and the traditional capital of Fez, young intellectuals began to meet together to formulate plans for ridding Morocco of the foreign yoke, and a serious national independence movement was born. However, it had to contend with the powerful caids in the south, whose strength had if anything been increased by the French who saw them as a means of controlling the High and Anti Atlas tribes. These traditional leaders feared that a nationalist government would reduce them to size and so they favoured the status quo and did their best to discredit the independence movement.

In 1927 Sultan Moulay Youssef died and was succeeded by his son Mohammed. At 17 years old Mohammed V had a quiet and friendly disposition and the French assumed he would be as amenable as his father had been. In fact the modest exterior concealed an iron will. But it was not until after World War II that the independence movement really gathered momentum. Moroccans by this time held their heads high again; the troops they had provided for the French army had conducted themselves with honour; President Roosevelt had talked with the Sultan and Morocco was no longer the isolated and ungovernable country she had once been. At this time an official independence party was formed, called Istiqlal, whose first act was to send a memorandum to the Sultan and the French authorities asking for independence and a democratic constitution. The immediate reaction to the memorandum was the arrest of several Istiqlal leaders on blatantly trumped up charges, and the replacement of a mild Resident-General with the formidable figure of General Juin. The new Resident-General, whilst appearing to go along with some of the demands of Istiqlal, was actually stiffening French control throughout the land by allowing city councils to be elected but at the same time ruling that half their membership should be French.

The Sultan began to exercise the only power he really had and that was to refuse to sign any more decrees concerning his people. This seriously alarmed the French who invited him on a State visit to Paris in the hope of persuading him by flattery to be more co-operative. Not so however, and the Sultan took the opportunity to propose some very radical changes to the Moroccan-French relationship. These were not even considered, but the fact that they were publicly requested ensured a triumphant return home for the Sultan, now a national hero.

Istiqlal grew stronger by the week and the notorious Pasha of Marrakesh, Thami el Glaoui (1886–1956), accused the sovereign publicly of being Sultan of Istiqlal rather than Sultan of all Morocco. Already a powerful man, with the support of all those who lived off the fat of the land at the cost of the majority of the poor, el Glaoui plotted with the French Government to discredit Istiqlal and particularly the Sultan who openly supported it, even to the extent of collecting hundreds of signatures in support for the deposition of 'this dangerous man'; it was suggested that he was not only a bad sultan but a bad Muslim because he allowed his daughters to go out in the street unveiled.

In August 1953 the palace was surrounded by French soldiers and the Sultan and his family were deported, first to Corsica and then to Madagascar, and an elderly, frail, and completely harmless relative was put on the throne in his place. The reactions to this were predictable. In his absence Mohammed V rapidly became an idol, and sympathy for him crystallised into intense longing for his return. Moreover, there began a period of overt violence towards French officials, to the point where they no longer felt safe anywhere in Morocco. It is remarkable that the Spanish Government had not been consulted at all about the removal of the Sultan, and it was extremely irritated by this omission. A rift began to develop between the two 'protecting' powers.

Security within Morocco deteriorated fast over the next two years and there was a bloody massacre of French officials at Oued Zem. This led their Government to depose the ineffectual token Sultan with a view to replacing him with a Crown Council. It was whilst plans for this were being drawn up that Thami el Glaoui returned to centre stage. Realising the way events were inexorably leading, he publicly denounced the Crown Council as illegal and allied himself to the people's call for the return of the rightful monarch. Within a week the Sultan was taken to France, much to the relief of all concerned who had feared a prolonged period of rioting and bloodshed. There he signed a declaration promising that there would be a constitutional monarchy which would move towards a democratic state. This was in December 1955.

In March 1956 an agreement was signed by the French which granted full independence to Morocco. The following April a similar agreement was signed by the Spanish Government and the old frontier post between the two zones was destroyed. In October, the same year Tangier lost its international status and became just another independent Moroccan city looking towards its past rather than its future. The Sultan formed a government and French officials were gradually replaced by Moroccans, though many stayed on as advisers. The change-over was quick and smooth, and any dissident elements in the south who continued to attack French outposts were gradually absorbed into the new Moroccan army. Schools turned towards education in Arabic—though there was at first a desperate shortage of teachers, a university was established in Rabat, the Karaouyine in Fez was given more up-to-date premises, and newspapers in Arabic appeared almost overnight. Amongst the more dramatic innovations was the building, by volunteers, of the '*Route de l'Unité*' (begun 1957) which united Fez with the Mediterranean across the Rif, which had always been a dangerous and uncharted barrier between the two regions. The Sultan changed his title to that of King, an act intended to demonstrate his desire to rule along progressive lines; and he appointed a fully representative National Consultative Assembly. The country was divided into regions which were based on economic rather than tribal boundaries and these were represented by elected regional and municipal councils.

King Mohammed V died, unexpectedly, after a minor operation in 1961, and was succeeded by the then Crown Prince, the present King Hassan II of Morocco. In 1962 the new monarch presented a new constitution to the people which was ratified after a referendum. Its first clause states: 'Morocco is a Muslim sovereign state whose official language is Arabic. It is a social, democratic and constitutional monarchy.' The first elected parliament assembled on 18 November 1963.

Amongst the many events which have taken place within Morocco since that date there is one which dramatically joins the past with the present, and that is the 'Green March', commemorated as a public holiday on 6 November. On that date in 1975 the King led 350,000 unarmed Moroccans, preceded by the army, south into the desert in order to reassert Rabat's sovereignty over what was then the Spanish Sahara, a sovereignty which, it was claimed, went back to the conquests by the Saadian dynasty in the 16C. The Spaniards withdrew (General Franco was dying at the time) but the Polisario was formed (supported by Algeria and Libya) to oppose Moroccan rule and to fight for self-determination of the Saharwi. A vicious and costly war started with Polisario guerillas ranged against sometimes inexperienced Moroccan soldiers, and many lives were lost on both sides.

Much of the world was deeply affronted by this apparently imperialistic move, and Morocco left the Organisation of African Unity in 1984 because it had offered a seat to the Polisario. However, the war changed character and the killing almost stopped when the Moroccans completed a most astonishing 2092km defensive wall around the disputed territory as far south as Dakhla. This denied the Polisario access to the sea, which they had previously used for mounting attacks on shipping off the west Saharan coast, and meant that the inland area could be declared safe again and cautiously opened up. For a time in the late 1970s visitors were unable to go much farther south than Goulimine; now people are actually being encouraged to visit the new resorts of Laayoune and Dakhla.

Internationally, the incident diminished in importance though occasional skirmishes would bring it back into the headlines. Now the UN has decreed that the matter must be settled once and for all. Morocco, anxious to improve its trade with Europe and keen to increase international tourism, agreed to hold a referendum which would decide whether the Western Sahara should be Moroccan or independent. Those entitled to vote would be authentic Saharwi people who numbered 73,000 according to a Spanish census held in 1974. The referendum was scheduled for January 1992 but did not take place and the UN Secretary General noted that it would be necessary to delay it by some months because of administrative difficulties on both sides. In the other words, there has been a failure so far to agree the eligibility criteria. Officials are still hopeful however that these will be finalised and that the wishes of the people most concerned will be established—by an internationally organised referendum—within the year.

The Gulf War in 1991 had a devastating effect on Morocco's tourist industry—unjustly, Moroccans would claim, since theirs were amongst the first troops to stand alongside the Allies in the Gulf. The position of the populace was however different from that of the King and thousands of people marched through Rabat in sympathy with the Iraqi leader Saddam Hussein. One could argue that this was a sign of growing democracy since such a march would certainly not have been permitted 10 years earlier. Wisely or not, the mood of the country was perceived as potentially dangerous and westerners were advised not to go there.

Fortunately this has proved to be only a temporary setback, arising out of a situation which forged many strange alliances and swiftly destroyed many others. Morocco is a stable nation, on the edge of a troubled region, and has in the past been seen as a powerful mediating force in the Arab–Israeli conflict. Its position, but a few miles from the southernmost tip of the European Community, makes it an important link for Europe with both Africa and the Arab world.

Chronology

1200 BC	Phoenicians set up trading posts along north coast.
500 BC	Carthaginians arrive.
33 BC	Romans establish Kingdom of Mauritania under Juba.
44 AD	Direct rule from Rome.
250	Romans begin to withdraw.
3C–7C	Dark Ages: Vandals and Goths sweep through country.
683	Arabs arrive led by Oqba ben Nafi.
711	First Muslim invasion of Spain.
788	Arrival of Moulay Idriss, founder of Idrisside dynasty.
799	Foundation of Fez.
1062	Almoravides invade under Youssef ben Tachfine and found Marrakesh.
1147	Fez and Marrakesh surrender to Almohades
1195	Yacoub el Mansour extends Muslim conquest to Spain and starts to build El Hassan mosque in Rabat.
1212	Battle of Las Navas de Tolosa reverses Muslim fortunes in Spain.
1248	Merinides conquer Fez and found Fez Jdid alongside.
1399	Wattasides attempt to rule. Portuguese begin settling along west coast.
1492	Muslims finally expelled from Granada.
1540	Saadians arrive and found a new capital—Taroudant.
1578	Defeat of Portuguese at Ksar el Kbir. Saadians move capital to Fez and extend empire southwards to Timbucktoo.
1627	Spanish Muslims set up pirate 'Republic of Bou Regreg'.
1666	Alouites arrive under Moulay Rachid.
1672	Moulay Ismael begins to build imperial city of Meknes and creates the Black Guard.
1790	Morocco relapses into chaos. European powers attempt to intervene.
1873	Moulay el Hassan pacifies tribes in S and builds Tiznit.

1906	Conference of Algeciras affirms independence of the sultan and makes Tangier an international free port.
1912	Treaty of Fez declares most of country a Protectorate under France. A similar treaty grants northern zone to Spain. Rabat and Tetouan are respective capitals.
1953	Sultan Mohammed V sent into exile.
1956	Full independence granted to Morocco. Sultan returns and forms a government. Tangier loses its international status.
1962	King Hassan II accedes to the throne.
1975	350,000 unarmed Moroccans march into Western Sahara.

Chronological Table of Moroccan Dynasties

The Idrissides

788–791	Idriss I
791–804	Rachid (regent)
804–828	Idriss II
828–836	Mohammed I
836–848	Ali I
848–923	(sons and grandsons of Ali)

The Almoravides

1062–1107	Youssef ben Tachfine
1107–1144	Ali ben Youssef
1144–1145	Tachfine ben Ali
1145	Ibrahim ben Tachfine
1145–1147	Ishaq ben Ali

The Almohades

–1133	Ibn Tumart
1133–1163	Abd el Mumene
1163–1184	Youssef
1184–1199	Yacoub el Mansour
1199–1213	Mohammed al Nasir
1213–1223	Youssef al Mostansir
1223–1248	sons of Youssef
1248–	(Fez lost to Merinides)
1248–1266	El Murtada
1266–1269	Abu Dabbus
1269–	(Marrakesh lost to Merinides)

The Merinides

1244–1258	Abou Yahya
1258–1286	Youssef
1286–1307	Yacoub
1307–1308	Abou Rabia
1308–1331	Uthman
1331–1351	Abou el Hassan
1351–1358	Abou Inan
1358–1396	(sons and grandsons of Abou Inan)

| 1396–1398 | Abd Allah |
| 1399–1554 | *Wattasides* |

The Saadians

1554–1557	Mohammed esh-Sheik I
1557–1574	sons of Mohammed
1574–1576	Abd Allah
1576–1578	Abd el Malik I
1578–1603	Ahmed Edh Dhahabi
1603–1628	Moulay Zaidan
1628–1631	Abd el Malik II
1631–1637	El Walid
1637–1655	Mohammed esh-Sheik II
1655–1660	Ahmed el Abbas

The Alouites

1666–1672	Moulay Rachid
1672–1727	Moulay Ismael
1727–1757	sons of Moulay Ismael
1757–1790	Mohammed ben Abdallah
1790–1792	Yazid
1792–1822	Sulaiman
1822–1859	Abd er Rahman
1859–1873	Mohammed
1873–1894	Moulay el Hassan
1894–1908	Abd el Aziz
1908–1912	Moulay Hafid
1912–1927	Moulay Youssef
1927–1961	Mohammed V
1961–	Hassan II

Select Bibliography

Barbour, Neville. *Morocco* (Thames & Hudson, London, 1965).

Bovill, E.W. *The Golden Trade of the Moors* (second edition, Oxford, 1968).

Carrier, Robert. *A Taste of Morocco* (Arrow Books)

Forbes, Rosita. *El Raisuni* (Thornton Butterworth)

Gaillard, Henri. *Une ville d'Islam: Fes* (Paris, 1905).

Guillaume, Alfred. *Islam* (Penguin Books, London, 1954).

Harris, Walter. *Morocco that Was* (Eland Books)

Hassan II. *Le Défi* (Michel, Paris, 1976).

Landau/Swaan. *Morocco* (Elek Books, London, 1967).

Lane-Poole, Stuart. *The Barbary Corsairs* (London, 1890).

Le Tourneau, Roger. *Fes avant le Protectorat* (Casablanca, 1949).

Le Tourneau, Roger. *La vie Quotidienne à Fes en 1900* (Hachette, Paris, 1965).

Lévi Provençal. *La Fondation de Fes* (Paris, 1938).

Maxwell, Gavin. *Lords of the Atlas* (Longman, London, 1966).

Meakin, Budgett. *The Moorish Empire* (London, 1899).

Pellow, Thomas. *The Adventures of T. Pellow* (Brown, London, 1890).

Rogers, P. G. *A History of Anglo-Moroccan Relations to 1900* (London, Foreign & Commonwealth Office).

Rowth, Emily. *Tangier, Britain's Last Outpost* (London, 1910).

Sefrioui, Ahmed. *Morocco* (Hachette, Paris, 1956).

Trotter, P.D. *Our Mission to the Court of Morocco in 1880 under Sir John Drummond Hay* (Edinburgh, 1881).

BACKGROUND INFORMATION

Language

The official language of Morocco is classical Arabic but the spoken word is dialectical, similar to that of Algeria and Tunisia, and is known as Maghrebi Arabic.

Berbers, who form 60 per cent of the population, speak one of three Berber dialects—Rifian, Braber or Chleuh—which are said to be mutually incomprehensible. Most Berbers also speak some Arabic.

Nearly all Moroccans, with the exception of the very old, the very young or the very isolated (desert nomads for example), speak some French, a legacy of the Protectorate, since when it has been taught in all schools, even the most remote. However, many people in the old Spanish Zone around Tetouan prefer to speak Spanish as French has only been taught there since Independence in 1956.

All the larger hotels and most of the tourist shops and restaurants are equipped with English speakers but otherwise English will rarely be understood.

Although it is not strictly necessary for the short-term visitor to know any Arabic, an attempt to recognise and/or speak a few words of greeting can be rewarding and will undoubtedly give great pleasure. These might include the following:

Labas, hello (informal
Salaam aleikum, peace be with you (formal hello)
Ash h'barak?, how are you?
Mezian, very well
Marhaba, welcome
Shokran, thank you (informal)
Barak 'allah oufik, may the blessing of God be with you (formal thank you)
Bis m'allah, in the name of God (often said before starting a meal)
El hamdu lilla, praise be to God (upon hearing good news)
Insh 'allah, God willing (after expressing an intention)
B 'slama, goodbye
Sidi, sir
Lalla, madam
Waha, yes, ok
La, no

Other useful words:
mezián, good, nice, beautiful
chwiya, little, small, a few
bezzéf, a lot
kbir, big
sghrir, little
zid, more
Ma f'hemshi, I don't understand
Shnoo hada?, what is this?
Bish'hal?, how much?

wahad, one
juge, tnine, two
tleta, three
arba, four
khamsa, five

setta, six
sebta, seven
tmenya, eight
tse'ud, nine
acha, ten

Glossary

AGADIR, a fortified grain silo
AGDAL, garden
AID, feast
ÄIN, source, fountain, eye
ÄIT, sons, tribe (Berber)
ALLAH, God
BAB, monumental gate
BABOUCHES, leather slippers with pointed toes and no heels
BARAKA, blessing, mystical power
BEN (pl. BENI), son, sons
BIT, room
BLED, countryside
BORDJ, fort
CAID, government official, district officer
CALDARIUM, hot room in Roman bath (Latin)
CHERIF, descendant of the prophet Mohammed
COL, mountain pass (French)
DAR, house
DAYET, lake
DIFFA, traditional Moroccan meal, usually at a festival
DJELLABAH, long outer garment usually with a hood
DOUAR, village or group of tents
FANTASIA, colourful Berber display of horsemanship
FASSI, someone born in Fez
FONDOUK, lodging house with space for livestock
FRIGIDARIUM, cold room in Roman bath (Latin)
HADJ, pilgrimage to Mecca—also title for someone who has made the pilgrimage
HAIK, garment used by women to cover themselves in public
HAMMAN, public bath (Turkish-style)
IMAM, prayer leader
JAMAI, mosque or assembly; also Friday (as the day of prayer)
JBEL, mountain
KASBAH, a chief's residence; a fortified house (especially in the south)
KIF, hashish, cannabis
KORAN, the word of God, dictated to the prophet Mohammed by the Angel Gabriel
KOUBBA, small white domed building holding relics of a saint or holy man
KSAR (pl. KSOUR), fortified village—houses usually clustered round a kasbah (especially in the south)
KUFIC, Arabic script named after the town of Kufa, in Iraq

LALLA, term of respect for a woman
MAGHREB, West: often used to describe North Africa
MAKHZEN, government
MARABOUT, saint or holy man, or his shrine
MECHOUAR, assembly area; the space around a royal palace
MECHRA, dam
MEDERSA, religious boarding school or students' lodging house
MEDINA, town; now used for the original, pre-Protectorate town, often medieval
MELLAH, Jewish quarter
MENDOUB, representative of the sultan
MIHRAB, niche inside a mosque showing the direction of Mecca
MOULAY, descendant of the Prophet
MOUSSEM, festival and/or pilgrimage in honour of a saint or holy man
MUEZZIN, prayer caller (usually from minarets)
NYMPHAEUM, Roman pleasure-house, usually containing fountains and pools
OUED, stream or river
PASHA, governor of a city
PERISTYLE, continuous colonnade around a Roman courtyard or building
PISTE, rough track (French)
SHEIK, leader of a religious brotherhood
SIDI, term of respect for a man
SOUK, a stall in a market, or a whole market of stalls
TEPIDARIUM, warm room in Roman bath
TIZI, mountain pass
ULEMA, religious elder
VIZIR, prime minister
ZAOUIA, religious retreat or cult centre
ZELLIGE, mosaic made of intricate ceramic or enamelled shapes

Climate

Morocco is characterised by a great diversity of climates, as might be expected in view of its unique position facing two seas and backing on to the Sahara. The one thing all areas have in common is sunshine, and that in abundance. The country can be divided roughly into three climatic zones.

The Coastal Zone extends across the N and W of the country. Summers are moderately hot and winters are fairly cold. Rainfall is quite scarce in summer but plentiful during the rest of the year, and there is a high level of humidity at all times, particularly on the north Atlantic coast. The area E of Tangier has a typical Mediterranean climate with hotter, dryer summers but cool winters.

Best months for visiting this zone are from April to October, although Agadir, being so far south and protected by mountains, remains very warm even in winter and so can be visited at any time of year. Despite its southerly position it escapes excessive heat even in the high summer because it is open to the sea.

The Mountain Ranges include the Rif, the High Atlas, the Middle Atlas, the Jbel Ayachi, the Anti Atlas and the Jbel Sahro. All the mountain ranges have hard, cold winters, with heavy snowfall in the highest parts lasting for three to four months, and fairly hot, very dry summers. The best season for visiting depends on what you want to do there. For exploring, walking, fishing, wild flower collecting, mule trekking, April to September is best. The roads are often closed in winter by snowfalls, avalanches, floods, etc., although those leading to ski resorts are usually well maintained whatever the conditions. The best skiing months are December, January and February.

AVERAGE TEMPERATURES

	JAN	MAR	MAY	JUN	AUG	OCT	DEC
Agadir	20.3	22.5	24.1	25.0	26.9	25.9	20.6
Al Hoceima	16.3	18.2	22.6	25.5	29.2	23.3	17.3
Casablanca	17.2	19.5	22.1	24.1	26.7	23.9	18.0
Ifrane	8.5	12.9	18.3	24.8	30.1	18.7	9.5
Errachidia	17.2	22.8	30.3	35.7	39.1	26.9	18.2
Marrakesh	18.1	23.0	28.7	32.9	37.5	28.1	18.3
Meknes	14.9	19.1	24.5	29.6	33.7	25.0	15.5
Ouarzazate	17.3	23.0	30.8	36.0	38.4	27.0	16.7
Rabat	18.4	21.2	25.9	28.8	31.6	26.5	19.0
Tangier	15.4	17.4	21.4	24.2	26.8	22.1	16.0

AVERAGE HOURS OF SUNSHINE

	JAN	MAR	MAY	JUN	AUG	OCT	DEC
Agadir	249	302	319	319	326	251	205
Casablanca	163	214	289	303	300	329	175
Fez	157	235	289	339	336	237	137
Ifrane	57	235	284	364	342	236	129
Marrakesh	209	263	296	334	328	241	190
Meknes	160	207	301	309	337	238	168
Ouarzazate	214	292	343	360	283	239	207
Rabat	182	217	308	318	326	254	184
Safi	186	245	290	318	315	229	182
Tangier	165	215	311	327	344	252	160
Tetouan	153	230	294	354	338	235	134

The Interior includes the rest of the country and has a continental climate which gets drier the further S or E you go. The northern region, which includes Fez and Meknes, is very hot and dry in summer, rather cold and damp in winter. As you travel S, the summers become even hotter, the winters warmer. It is not advisable to go S of Marrakesh during the months of June, July or August when the heat can become intolerable to anyone who is unaccustomed to it. Even Marrakesh can overwhelm you at that time unless you are provided with air-conditioning and go out only in the early morning or at night.

The best season for exploring the Interior is during either March, April and May or September and October. Marrakesh itself and other southern towns are popular throughout the winter months but exploring the country-side around them can become difficult once the rain or snow has started to fall in the mountains. The dry river beds (*oueds*) which cross and re-cross the desert tracks and which frequently originate in the mountains can suddenly become rushing torrents and make the track quite impassable. This situation does not usually last very long as the water soon disappears into the thirsty river bed, but it can lead to delays.

Flora

With its great variety of climate and topography, from sandy desert to perpetual snow and from the low coastal plains to the giants of the Atlas, Morocco has a rich and varied flora, attractive to the layman because of the beauty of the vast spreads of colour painted by the meadow flowers in spring and early summer, and of interest to the botanist because so many of the species are narrowly endemic and often unique, particularly at high altitudes.

Meadows in spring and early summer look like oriental carpets, woven with species of *Calendula* (pot marigold), *Centaurea, Matthiola*, lupin, *Echium*, lavender and members of the chrysanthemum family. A taller accent is given by the asphodels, resedas, anchusas, fennel, and the century plant (*Agave americana*) which produces a magnificent spike of a flower from its prickly rosette once every 100 years. Many species of convulvulus decorate the roadside. In lightly wooded country there is a wealth of orchids. The narcissus family is represented, especially by some of its miniature members. The vast Euphorbia genus is there, particularly in arid areas, and the country is rich in prickly, thistly plants, such as *Echinops ritro*, a familiar sight in English herbaceous borders, and *Silybum marianum*, the holy or milk thistle, with its white-mottled, deeply cut leaves. The iris family is also widespread, especially in coastal regions.

Trees of particular interest are the cedars (*Cedrus libani* and *Cedrus atlantica*), especially the blue variety (*glauca*) found in the Middle Atlas and the Rif; the cork oak (*Quercus suber*), widespread in the regions bordering the N and NW coasts; ancient olive trees, particularly around Meknes; date palms (very beautiful in flower) in the pre-Saharan oases, and the curious argan (*Argania sideroxylon*) along the SW coast around Agadir, into which goats climb in search of the olive-like fruit, and later deposit the stones from which a useful oil is extracted.

Shrubs and small trees are mostly of the maquis type: many varieties of *Cistus* or rock rose with its crumpled petals and sticky aromatic foliage; brooms, of which one endemic variety, *Cytisus battandieri*, is now very popular in English gardens; the acacias, wattles or mimosas; oleanders (*Nerium oleander*) flowering from April to September along the dried-up water courses and, occasionally to be seen in some sheltered valleys, *Arbutus unedo*, the strawberry tree.

Sport

Shooting. There is first-class shooting in Morocco and a diversity of game, including snipe, duck, pheasant, quail, pigeon, and wild boar. The season is nine months long with staggered opening and closing dates between 1 October and the end of June, except for the month of April which is closed. There are now several well-organised reserves and territories which welcome tourists. The best known and largest of these is the *Arbaoua Game Reserve*, some 121,410 hectares of land between Ksar el Kbir and Souk el Arba in the north. It offers snipe, woodcock, duck, teal, partridge, pheasant, quail and wild boar in season. The area consists of a mixture of grain fields, marshes, wetlands and woodlands—an ideal environment not only for the snipe but for all the migratory species that winter here, including the Barbary partridge which is widespread within the area.

Other territories include:

Benslimane (E of Casablanca), 4047 hectares: mainly partridge and pheasant.

Marrakesh, a rugged scrubby terrain of arbutus trees and dwarf palms at the foot of the High Atlas: Barbary partridge, turtle dove and wild boar.

Agadir, a region of olive and orange groves in the Souss valley: quail and turtle dove.

Kabila, equidistant between Tetouan and Ceuta, this new 24,282-hectare area along the Mediterranean coast offers partridge, duck, snipe and wild boar.

Game is also plentiful in the Rif mountains around Ouezzane, in the Oulmes hills SW of Meknes and almost anywhere in the High Atlas.

Seasons are as follows:

Snipe: season opens first Sunday in October and closes first Sunday in March. A minimum of four guns is required. Bag limit is 20 snipe per gun per day.

Duck: as for snipe. Bag limit is 12 birds per gun per day.

Turtle Dove: season opens 1 May. Season closes 30 June. A minimum of four guns is required. Bag limit is 60 birds per gun per day. Shooting is permitted only on Saturdays, Sundays and Mondays.

Barbary partridge and pheasant: season opens first Sunday in October and closes end of January (partridge) last Sunday in March (pheasant). Estimated bag 20 pieces or more per gun; for driven shooting 300–500 pieces or more per group per day.

Wild boar: season opens first Sunday in October and closes 15 February. A minimum of eight guns is required. Driven boar hunting is practised with the full range of required personnel, beaters, porters, etc. The animals are very wild and hard to flush. The hunter must be a fast shot. Rifles are forbidden and a standard shot gun is recommended with brennecke or blondeau bullets. Estimated bag between four and six wild boar per group per day.

The Moroccan company *Sochatour* (72 Blvd Zerktouni, Casablanca; tel. 27-75-13) has been created in co-operation with the Ministry of Agriculture and the Department of Water Resources and Forestry (*Administration des Eaux et Fôrets*), and it is they who oversee all shooting in Morocco. They supervise the areas mentioned above, provide qualified staff, and dogs where necessary, make arrangements for your trip and will take care of such formalities as procuring a temporary import licence for guns, as well as a Moroccan licence to shoot. (Unlicensed importation of firearms or unlicensed shooting can lead to severe penalties.)

To effect the necessary formalities they need the following documents: three passport-size photos; a photocopy of your gun licence from your own country; a photocopy of the first page of your passport indicating date and place of issue; a statement of the make, calibre and registration number of your gun(s); written confirmation of the date, airport and flight number for your arrival in Morocco. (Shells, calibre 12, 16 or 20 can be purchased from Sochatour at a cost in the hunting areas.)

Arrangements for shooting trips can also be made through some travel agencies direct and some of the Inclusive Holidays may include such trips.

It is also possible (though rather uncertain) to be completely independent: acquire an import licence through the Police Department in Rabat (*Direction de la Sureté Nationale*, Rabat) and a permit to shoot from the local Prefecture (*Service de Chasse*) within the area.

Trout fishing. The numerous streams and rivers rising in the High and Middle Atlas mountains and the many lakes to be found on the high plateaux are naturally rich in trout. (There is no salmon fishing in Morocco.) The best stretches of water are often those which are the most difficult of access, for example, the headwaters of the river Oum er Rbia in the thickly forested area between Ain Leuh and Khenifra in the Middle Atlas, and the Lake Isly on the Imilchil plateau. If you can manage to get there, you will most certainly have worthwhile sport, probably in complete isolation and in beautiful surroundings. The local village shopkeepers and hotel patrons are often ardent fishermen themselves, and might be prepared to advise on routes of access and sometimes offer guides. There are tackle shops in Rabat and Casablanca but the fly fisherman would be well advised to bring his own supplies.

Trout fishing is very popular and the more accessible rivers and lakes are heavily over-fished. An example of this is the river Gigou which winds pleasantly alongside the road between Ifrane and Midelt. It has fast running water and good, deep pools, and is in such an attractive setting that the fishermen heavily outnumber the available trout. The Moroccans are aware of this problem and have created special artificially-stocked lakes known as *plans d'eau à permis spéciaux*. These lakes (most of them in the Middle Atlas) are open only for about three months each year, usually in the spring and summer, and fishing is strictly controlled, the fish being counted and weighed before you leave. The lakes are always easily accessible and usually equipped with car-parks and other facilities. For anyone who does not mind standing shoulder to shoulder with other enthusiasts and casting to music from transistors, the clicking of knitting needles and the squealing of children, this is the place to go, for you will almost certainly catch trout.

Course fishing. Pike, black bass, perch and other varieties are readily available in the natural and artificial lakes of the Middle and High Atlas and, notably, in the reservoirs of El Kansera (near Khemisset), Bine el Ouidane (near Beni Mellal) and Mouley Youssef (80km E of Marrakesh). This last named, set in glorious surroundings and easily accessible by car, was stocked with black bass only a few years ago, which have now multiplied to such an extent that there is no limit imposed on the number which may be legitimately fished. The average weight is 750 grammes. There are boats for hire but much of the lake can be successfully fished from the shore. There is a ring of natural lakes in the Immouzer–Ifrane area which are particularly rewarding as well as being in charming settings. These include Dayets Hachlaf, Ifrah and Aoua.

Permits are required for both trout and course fishing. These are cheap (for all except the specially stocked lakes) and can be bought either direct from the *Administration des Eaux et Fôrets*, 11 Rue Revoil, Rabat (tel. 253-35), or possibly from your hotel or from the local tourist office. Permits for the special lakes are bought on the spot and tend to be more expensive. The seasons vary from year to year and from region to region and are rigidly controlled by inspectors from the *Eaux et Fôrets*, but it is fairly safe to say that some form of fishing is possible somewhere at any given time of the year. A Decree is published annually which gives dates of opening and lists of fishable waters and everything else which it is necessary to know. This, too, is available from the *Eaux et Fôrets*.

Sea fishing. Bream, loup de mer, mackerel, and many other varieties are fished from rocky promontories and from boats along the Mediterranean and Atlantic coasts. Deep sea fishing with rod and line, and underwater fishing with speargun and aqualung are also possible off the great expanse of coast all the way from Al Hoceima to Dakhla and power-boats can usually be hired. This last named resort, some 900km S of Agadir and accessible by twice-weekly flights from there, is becoming popular for its superb sea bass fishing, with specimens reaching anything up to 75kg, caught by trawling from a boat. No permit is required for sea fishing.

Golf was first played in Morocco at Tangier in 1917. It is now one of Morocco's most popular sports and there are some excellent golf courses which can be used all the year round.

Rabat has a 45-hole course at Dar Es Salam (14km to the S on the Rommani road). It comprises the Red course—18 holes, par 73, 6825m (18 handicap minimum), a championship course; Blue course—18 holes, par 72, 6205m; Green course—9 holes, par 32, 2150m. Luxurious clubhouse facilities. The course is closed on Mondays. Green fees are 120 dirhams per day.

Mohammedia was Morocco's No. 1 course before Dar Es Salam was opened. It is located 25km N of Casablanca and lies partly along the seashore. It is an 18-hole course with a par of 72. It is closed on Tuesdays.

Casablanca: 10 minutes' drive westwards from the centre of Casablanca, the Royal Anfa Golf Club is set inside a race-track and is nicely planted with flowers. It has 9 holes and is used for 18, with a par of 67.

Tangier has an 18-hole course two miles SW of the city at the Royal Country Club of Tangier. This course was made in 1917 and then redesigned by the British golf architect, Frank Pennink. Par 72.

Marrakesh has an 18-hole course known as Royal Golf of Marrakesh 4km from the centre of town. The greens are kept in top condition by irrigation and are overlooked by the Atlas mountains. Par 72.

Agadir has a 9-hole course (par 36). An international championship course is nearing completion.

Meknes has a 9-hole (par 36) course sited within the ancient walls of the Imperial City.

Cabo Negro (near Tetouan) has a 9-hole (par 36) course with wonderful views of the Mediterranean.

Haouzia (N of El Jadida) has an 18-hole course nearing completion.

Skiing. *Oukaimeden* (2650m), in the High Atlas S of Marrakesh, offers the best skiing in Morocco, with one chair lift, two ski-tows and facilities for hiring boots and skis. Most of the runs are steep; and there is a giant slalom course which will challenge the most experienced skier. In general this is not beginners' skiing. There are two hotels—Chez Juju, and Hotel Imlil—both adequate and decorated in the traditional Alpine style. Marrakesh is only an hour's drive away and many people prefer to stay there and combine the joys of city life by night with those of the ski slopes by day. The official season is from December to April. However, the snow is not always predictable and it is not uncommon to see a ski-laden car of holiday-makers heading southwards from Oukaimeden towards the desert during the winter months because the snow has simply failed to arrive.

Mischliffen (2036m), a 20-minute drive from Ifrane, is the busiest skiing station of the Middle Atlas. It is a volcanic crater fringed with cedars, and skiing is confined to the one big bowl, or round the top amongst the trees. Nevertheless, there are two ski-lifts and the gently rounded slopes are always busy in the winter months because of their accessibility to Meknes and Fez and because of the spectacular beauty of the whole region. Facilities are poor to non-existent which is a pity because this is a wonderful place for family skiing. There is also skiing at Jbel Hebri (2104m)—a slope just beyond Mischliffen (coming from Ifrane). Skiing here is slightly steeper, with just one ski-lift and an auberge with camping facilities. Nevertheless, skiing amongst the cedar trees has a certain irresistible charm and both stations are easily accesible by road. The season is not defined but is roughly the same as for Oukaimeden.

Ketama in the Rif, sometimes called 'the Moroccan Switzerland', is beginning to develop its ski potential. The cedar-forested slopes of Mt Tidighine are a joy. There is one ski-lift and a good hotel: the Hotel Tidighine.

Watersports. Morocco has 2000 miles of coastline and much of it consists of unspoilt sandy beaches which are perfect for sea bathing, though dangerous outside the bays on the Atlantic side. Sailing, water skiing, windsurfing and sail-boarding are available at all the main seaside resorts and many new marinas are under development including those at Asilah, M'Diq, Agadir and Sables d'Or (near Rabat).

Other sports available include riding, both on the beaches and in the mountains, mule-trekking, and mountaineering, particularly in the Jbel Toubkal area of the High Atlas (see Rte 16). Most large hotels have tennis courts and swimming pools and there are municipal swimming pools in all the major towns which are clean and well kept.

What to buy and how to buy it

Traditional crafts, or *artisanat*, employ over seven per cent of Morocco's working population and are Morocco's fifth most important export (the other four being phosphates, agricultural produce, oranges and fish). These crafts, which reflect centuries-old skills and use local materials such as cedar wood, leather, wool, and vegetable dyes (to name but a few), are a huge attraction to the outside world. They are available in all medinas, and it is often possible to see them being made. Sometimes the abundance is almost overwhelming, but nevertheless the goods are all sold, and very profitably too as more and more visitors pour into the big towns in the high season.

There are two methods of acquiring these items: either by plunging into the medinas and bargaining, or by making for one of the Government-controlled craft shops or *Centres d'Artisanat* where the price is fixed, probably a little higher than you would pay in the souks, but where the quality is reliable and the atmosphere more peaceful.

Do not, however, be discouraged from entering the hurly-burly of the souks. The joy of a bargain cunningly and painstakingly acquired, and the satisfaction felt by both buyer and seller after the game has been well played, are experiences not to be missed. The rules for bargaining are: when asked to name the price you are prepared to pay, pitch it at about half the figure you would expect finally to pay, for the seller will quote you twice as much (at least) as he will settle for. He will no doubt tell you several times that you are ruining him but (in the end) that he will make an extraordinary concession *'parce que vous êtes mon premier/dernier client aujourd'hui'*. You, having exclaimed several times that you are *'un pauvre étudiant'*, will forage around and find the money somehow. If at any point this well-oiled ritual appears to stick, then simply turn to walk away, apparently no longer interested. You will undoubtedly be called back with the cry: *'mais qu'est ce que vous voulez payer?'*

In the medinas there are also increasing numbers of co-operatives making carpets, kaftans or jewellery, and presenting them for sale in a very professional way. The foot-weary visitor will be invited to sit down and take mint tea, and be regaled with a story (in English, French, German or Spanish) of how the items are made, whilst prime samples are put before his eyes. There is often high pressure salesmanship here and nothing is too much trouble, no export order too difficult to fulfil or too far to send. Co-operatives will always tell you that the price is fixed, but that is not necessarily so, particularly at the end of the day and most particularly if you happen to be a member of a large group. Quality is always high here and the process less of a strain than the one-to-one bargaining ritual.

Carpets form the most important part of Morocco's artisanat. They are priced according to their age, their place of origin and the density of the knotting. The most valuable and most beautiful are the Rabat carpets, which contain the greatest density of threads of any Moroccan carpets (10,000 per square metre). Based on a design introduced by the Turks in the 18C, they bear a central medallion and a wide border of intricate pattern—the wider the border the greater the value of the carpet. The colours are harmonious and range through reds, blues, yellow, greens and oranges: the most frequent ground colour being a soft, pinkish red. The quality of workmanship and the softness of the colours, particularly those of the old carpets which are made with vegetable rather than chemical dyes, is outstanding. They are on the whole hardwearing, but care should be taken when choosing an old one: look out for holes and worn places, and any fault or repair should be allowed for in the price. Old Rabats are expensive and becoming quite hard to find. New ones are priced per square metre, according to the quality of the wool and the amount of work which has gone into the making of them; the accuracy with which old designs have been reproduced also counts.

Apart from Rabat carpets and those known as 'royals' or 'orientals', which are quite similar in design and come in rich blues and reds (indigo and poppy flower dyes), all the others are Berber made. Each tribe produces its own carpets, the designs passed down through generations. There is an infinite variety of texture, colour and mood, and the expert can tell at a glance from which region a carpet comes. Those from the Middle Atlas tend to be worked in beiges and browns, often undyed natural sheep's wool with a simple design in one corner in deeper brown, reproducing exactly that of the tattoos worn by the women of that tribe on their face or hands to ward off illness or ill fortune. Those from the High Atlas are in reds and ochres; those from Ouarzazate in reds and blues. Some are very finely worked in a combination of wool and silk: a woven wool base with silk embroidery and sometimes sequins added. Some of these in soft reds and browns are very beautiful, others appear slightly garish to the untrained eye. They are really too thin to put on the floor; the Berbers would hang them in their tents. Others are made of camel wool, less attractive perhaps to Westerners,

Carpet vendor, Fez

particularly in the knowledge that it takes 15 camels to make one small carpet since only the wool from neck and hump can be used.

The best place to look for Berber rugs and carpets, old or new, is undoubtedly the Middle Atlas and the south, where they have been made.

You might find them in a souk by the roadside in some small High Atlas or desert town, where they will be cheaper but perhaps not as longlasting. Rabats and 'orientals' are best bought in the medinas of the main cities.

Jewellery. Moroccan women, whatever their means or social status, like to adorn themselves with jewellery at all times of the day. Indeed it is no uncommon sight to see a country woman working in the fields, her neck wound round with heavy necklaces of silver or of amber.

The most typical and most widely available jewellery is made of silver. Gold pieces—worn only by rich women in the towns—include the heavy, ornate dowry belts, often studded with emeralds, which are worn tight over the kaftan. Most of the old silver jewellery is heavy and primitive in design, much of it probably originating in medieval Spain: when the Moorish invaders were finally chased out of that country they brought back with them designs and inspirations which hugely enriched the Islamic repertoire at home. These were later assimilated into the already existing artistic traditions of the Berbers which had, in turn, been influenced to some extent by black Africa. The silver itself and the semi-precious stones with which the jewellery is frequently decorated are not of great value but the pieces have great charm and simplicity.

The heavy bracelets are worn by Berber women around their wrists or ankles. One kind, originating in the Draa valley, has protruding knobs and was undoubtedly used for self-defence. A good modern use for these is to take them to a silversmith and have a base put on them, turning them into quite original ash-trays.

Necklaces are also substantial, often making use of old coins and chains threaded with tiny pieces of coral. These can look most striking on a plain black dress but usually the fastening needs attention, if there is one at all. Sometimes there is just a piece of string which is entirely unworthy of the coins it supports. Even heavier are the necklaces made of huge amber beads, these are quite difficult to find now and you should beware of plastic imitations.

There are also brooches, ear-rings, pendants, and beautifully-worked fibulas often set in the traditional jackal's paw design to which magical qualities are attributed. These were used by women to pin cloaks or shawls at the shoulder but the pins are heavy and often blunt and can be ruinous to delicate modern materials. Silver 'hands of Fatima' can sometimes be discovered—always a sign of good luck and very suitable for wearing on a chain as a pendant.

Modern jewellery, using the same basic designs but tending to be over-ornamented, varies greatly in both quality of material and execution and therefore in price. Antique jewellery is more difficult to find, and more expensive. The best hunting grounds, for old and new alike, are the Fez and Marrakesh medinas and, to a lesser extent, Rabat, but all medinas have their stocks and will sometimes yield up treasures. Further afield, and perhaps more fruitful for that reason, is the little pre-Saharan town of Tiznit, famous not only for its silver jewellery but also for its vast assortment of traditional sabres and daggers. The filigree work is perhaps the finest in all Morocco and can be admired in the sabre scabbards, diadems and belts which are rarely seen elsewhere.

Pottery. Fez, Meknes, Marrakesh and Safi are the great pottery towns and have been for centuries. As in the case of the carpets and jewellery, it is the old pieces which have the softest colours and the simplest and most satisfying designs. Pieces range from tiny ash-trays to huge dishes used by Moroccan families for cous-cous. There are pots and urns in classic shapes, flower vases and jugs; the eye is dazzled by the colourful variety. On the whole the Safi pottery tends to be more heavily decorated and more fanciful in design than that of Fez, Marrakesh and Rabat.

Salé also has a pottery industry but on a smaller scale. The pieces are fresh and different and the designs go well in contemporary homes. The objects tend to be more utilitarian, less decorative. Particularly charming are the coffee services with tall, narrow jugs, and the soup bowls with conical lids.

The best places for seeing the potters at work are the Fez and Marrakesh medinas and the potters' quarter at Safi. Modern pottery, recognisable by its shiny glaze and bright colours, is really very cheap and sometimes rather tawdry as inevitably some objects are being specially designed for the mass tourist market. Old pottery, not so easy to find, is more expensive but open to negotiation. The new is to be found in all tourist shops; the old should be sought in the medinas of the towns of its origin and also in that of Rabat. Before attempting to buy old pottery it is a good idea to go to a museum such as the Maison de l'Artisanat in Rabat, or the Kasbah Museum in Tangier, or the Dar Batha in Fez, to decide what it is you want and thereafter to recognise it when it comes your way.

Leather goods. For centuries the tanning of leather has been an important part of the Moroccan economy. Traditional tanneries, such as those to be seen in the Fez medina, are beginning to disappear and the work is now being done on a more modern industrial scale. The quality of the finished skin is usually the better for that.

Sandals, babouches, saddles, bags and other such utilitarian objects have been part of the Moroccan scene for many hundreds of years. Since the beginning of this century, the repertoire has been extended to meet the taste of the Western world: cigarette boxes; desk sets; wastepaper baskets; wallets and pouffes (these last in astonishing variety, gold-tooled, if coming from Fez, embroidered with silk if from Marrakesh). Many of them are still made by hand. Quality of skins varies considerably: a desk set in fine black kid-skin, discreetly tooled in gold, can make a handsome present, and it is quite satisfying to see an exactly similar article for sale in a London department store for six times as much as you have had to pay, by dint of skilful bargaining. The medinas are the best places to look. Leather goods in tourist shops should be examined carefully for possible flaws: the more ornate the decoration, the less fine the quality of the skin is a fairly safe rule.

One prosperous branch of the leather trade is book-binding. This is done with great skill and precision and the finished product is something which few countries in the world can match. 'Bound in Morocco leather' is no idle term. With the increase in the sale of paperbacks throughout Europe, the Moroccan book-binder is finding his rare skills more and more in demand.

Miscellaneous: There are many other delightful objects which do not fall into the four categories above: big brass lanterns with insertions of coloured glass to reflect the light, or little ones which are meant to take a candle; heavy copper urns which make imposing flower vases; silver (or rather, silver-plated copper) six-sided caskets, which are part of the tea-making paraphernalia but which make attractive ornaments in their own right, ranging as they do from the very tiny egg-cup size to the big rectangular ones some 30cm long (these are to be found most readily in Marrakesh); trays in silver, copper and brass; loosely-woven woollen blankets in stripes of brown and black, or brighter colours, make spendid winter bedspreads; and of course kaftans, now made in the new European form: narrower, shorter and lighter. You can buy kaftans ready-made, or you can choose a length of silk from the sumptuous displays in the medinas and have it made up then and there.

Fez embroidery is remarkable for having no 'wrong' side, and tablecloths with napkins or traycloths to match make a worthwhile purchase.

Woodwork, particularly that of the soft and sweet-smelling cedar, is another traditional skill, and products vary from simple utilitarian dishes and salad bowls to superbly painted and carved chairs and inlaid chests. Essaouira is renowned for work in sandalwood (*Thuya*) and the inlaid jewel boxes, chessboards and small tables are delicate and most collectable. Sometimes old pieces can be found: dark painted panels rescued from some palace ceiling, or 'mouche arabes' taken from an old mosque (grilles with miniature columns of turned and sculpted wood, behind which women could see but not be seen), or even bridal chairs from Fez.

Morocco is also a treasure house of semi-precious stones: amethyst, topaz, cobalt, etc. These should be bought, if possible, in the High Atlas mountains where they originate. You do not have to search very far for they are displayed in stalls or on makeshift tables wherever there is space on all the high passes, but be careful of imitations and do not hesitate to apply a wet finger to a doubtful 'amethyst' to see if the purple paint rubs off.

Guides

It is an unfortunate fact that wherever you go in Moroccan towns, and particularly in the medinas, you will be accosted by aspiring guides—old and young, official and non-official, honest and not-so-honest.

However confident and independent you may be feeling, you will at some point decide it is better to take on a guide, if only to be left in peace by the other aspirants who will then recognise you as 'won' and magically melt away. Your chosen guide will also discourage the multitudes of children who hold out their hands for dirhams, 'stylos' and 'bon-bons', encouraged no doubt by the large tour groups with bulging purses. (It is noticeable that, as tourism has grown, more and more children have found it profitable to beg.) There are the official, badge-wearing guides who charge a set rate and are obliged to conduct themselves responsibly or they will lose their official status; and there are the 'unofficial' ones who have nothing to recommend them but their bright honest faces, and may be just as good. Both sorts tend to hang around outside hotels and near medina entrances. Here are a few golden rules which should help avoid disappointment and/or embarrassment on both sides.

1. Agree the price before you start the tour. Official guides in major towns ask 50 dirhams for half a day. Even if you just go out for an hour, they will still charge that unless you negotiate something better at the beginning. Best to negotiate a slightly lower rate with unofficial guides, promising something on top if you enjoy your tour. An acceptable rate in rural areas is 10 dirhams an hour. Never leave it open. '*C'est comme vous voulez*' usually leads to arguments at the end.

2. Do not be pushed around. Plan your trip beforehand with the aid of a guide-book or plan. Tell him what you want to see, what you want to buy (if anything) and what time you want to be back.

3. Do not be deflected from your original plan. The guide may try to take you to his own contacts, carpet co-operatives, etc. Fine if you have already said you want to look at or buy carpets, but remember he may have in mind the commission he will get from his friend should you be persuaded to make a purchase.

4. Do not let him hurry you. If you want to stop and look at something on the way, do so. He will always wait.

Consider sometimes taking a non-official guide (if he makes a good first impression). Moroccans are by nature very friendly people and when your guide tells you he wants to practise his English, he probably means it. He also of course needs your money to supplement his income (or lack of it). Young students often have interesting tales to tell, are more amenable and will sometimes invite you home to meet their families. On the whole, one need have no qualms about accepting such an invitation, though there have been one or two cases where visitors have been relieved of their valuables once inside the house.

Official guides, on the other hand, are occasionally quite obviously bored and blasé, making it plain that they deserve a better life. This is particularly so in big resorts like Tangier where they have evidently said the same thing to too many tourists too many times.

Best of all are the old men in country districts: friendly, dignified in their striped jellabahs and yellow babouches, and full of fascinating anecdotes, they unwittingly speak a unique mix of English, French and German. They are usually quite incapable of answering questions but their flow of information is well presented and the nuggets of wisdom they produce are often memorable.

A note on Islam

To come anywhere near understanding the Moroccans (all of whom are Muslims with the exception of a very small minority of Jews), it is necessary to know something of Islam, which to them is much more than a religion: it is a way of life. The word Islam in fact means 'submission to God'. It is believed by the Muslim that Mohammed, the last in a line of prophets, was visited by the Angel Gabriel who dictated to him the authentic word of God. This he wrote down in the Koran.

Today the Muslim can apply the principles of the Koran to almost every moment of his life. In particular there are the five 'Pillars of Islam'—five rules which he must keep if he is to be saved on the Day of Judgement. These are:

1. To believe and to testify that there is no God but Allah and that Mohammed is his prophet.

2. To say his prayers five times a day. This can be done wherever he happens to be but preferably in the mosque, and the ritual must always be preceded by purifying ablutions and accompanied by a fixed number of genuflexions and prostrations. When the hour of prayer is nigh (the first is at daybreak) the chanting voices of the muezzins ring out from the tops of the minarets

calling the faithful to the mosque; on Fridays the imams give sermons in the mosques which generally stick very closely to the text of the Koran.

3. To observe the fast of Ramadan. Ramadan takes place in the ninth month of every Muslim (Hegiran) year which means that it moves forward 11 days every Christian year as the Christian year is 11 days longer. The exact date is determined by the night on which the thin crescent of the new moon of Ramadan is first perceived by the Oulemas. On a cloudy night it may well not be seen at all so the date can never be fixed absolutely.

Fasting (no eating, drinking or smoking) begins in the morning when the sun rises and continues until darkness falls. This is quite bearable when the hours of daylight are short, but in the summer, when there may be 12 hours of burning sunshine, it can be a hard sacrifice indeed. The moments of beginning and ending the fast are announced each day by the firing of a cannon in large towns, elsewhere by the voice of the muezzin or by the head of the family. At the moment of sunset the streets throughout the whole country are empty because everyone is at home or in an eating-house breaking his fast with *harira* (see Food and Drink below). The night passes in prayer, feasting and rejoicing and, for those who must work next day, in sleeping. A last meal is usually eaten just before sunrise, until the moment when (as the Koran says) you are able to distinguish the difference between a white and a black thread.

Above all Ramadan is a holy month. The last and most holy night of all is the 27th—the Night of Destiny. Muslims believe that on this night there is a spiritual bridge between Heaven and Earth and the mosques are crammed with the faithful:

> The night of Destiny is worth more than a thousand months.
> In this night the angels of the Spirit descend to earth with the
> permission of God to settle all things. Peace accompanies this
> night until the break of day. (Koran)

The next day is one of family rejoicing, a national holiday, a day for giving gifts and visiting friends (known as *Aid es Seghir*). Feasting and rejoicing may continue for seven days.

4. To give a 40th of his income to support the poor and the mosques.

5. To make the pilgrimage to Mecca at least once during his lifetime. Nowadays, with the help of air travel, this presents few problems except financial ones. In the past it could mean a hazardous expedition by camel across Algeria, Tunis, Libya and Egypt and might take months. On his return from Mecca the Moroccan is given the title of Hadj. Thereafter, however lowly his social status, he is treated with the utmost deference, as if he had brought back with him some of the holiness of Mecca. Increasingly, a pragmatic attitude is taken towards those who cannot afford to go to Mecca. And five pilgrimages to Moulay Idriss are now said to equal one to Mecca.

These divine laws—and much else besides which the Koran dictates—are obeyed, in principle, by everyone from the King himself down to the most humble of his subjects. There are those of course who know how to adapt and modernise the more traditional 'Sayings of the Prophet', but on the whole, and most particularly during Ramadan, submission to discipline is unquestioning. The Moroccan does not feel the need to write or speak about religion; he observes its rules according to his degree of faith, his theological knowledge, and the time at his disposal. It could be said (and often is) that since every moment of his life is guided by the Koran, a devout Muslim can neither think nor act freely. But there is no doubt that the discipline imposed by Islam in Morocco, and particularly during the fast of Ramadan, builds a benign but unbreakable bond between all layers of society, rich and poor, young and old, Berber and Arab—a kind of solidarity and unquestioning unity which the rest of the world can only envy.

Souks, Moussems, Fantasias and Festivals

The word *souk* can mean a stall in a market or a whole market of stalls. Each market town within a given agricultural area has its souk (in this case a market) on a different day of the week. This day is fixed and it is often possible to tell from the name of a town the day on which it holds its souk: in Moroccan Arabic, the days of the week are called by numbers, i.e. Sunday is Day 1 or *el Had*; Monday, Day 2, is *et Tnine*; Tuesday, Day 3, is *et Tleta*; Wednesday, Day 4, is *el Arba*; Thursday, Day 5, is *el Khemis*; Friday is the only day which is not numbered; it is above all the day of prayer so it is called quite simply *el Jamai*, meaning 'the mosque'; Saturday, Day 7, is *es Sebt*. An example of this is the town of Souk el Arba on the Tangier–Rabat road, which does indeed have its souk every Wednesday.

These weekly country souks are most entertaining. Family groups, complete with children and donkeys, walk long distances to buy and sell. For them it is a social occasion as well as a commercial one. The tents are set up, often just outside the town, and the produce is displayed. Mint tea is brewed, and various unidentifiable delicacies are put to sizzle over the charcoal. You can buy anything from a couple of eggs and a kilo of oranges to a richly woven Berber carpet, or perhaps the latest thing in sun hats, made out of local reeds. Tailors set up their sewing machines and make kaftans out of customers' own materials; cobblers hammer soles back on to worn-out sandals; sometimes there are acrobats and musicians. It is always a scene of animation and colour.

A *moussem* is a religious festival (usually annual) in which a number of pilgrims collect together around the tomb of a saint to do honour to his memory and to ask his blessing on themselves, their families and their crops. The tombs, known as marabouts or koubbas, are contained within small, domed, square white buildings, which are to be found all over Morocco—sometimes isolated in the countryside, sometimes wedged in amongst the already crowded houses of the medinas. (As they are holy places close examination by non-Muslims may not be welcomed.) The pilgrims often travel many days to a moussem and bring with them their families, tents, animals and other possessions. The occasion is a joyful one—intended to break the monotony of daily life and provide relaxation for those who work hard—and devotions alternate with songs, dances and general merry-making.

This forms the core of the moussem. Other people from the neighbourhood will arrive with no particular interest in the saint but with donkeyloads of wares to sell: fresh meat and vegetables, pots, straw hats, carpets and cloth. Tents are pitched, cous-cous is made in industrial quantities and mint tea is brewed. Troops of dancers arrive in rich costumes and add to the colourful spectacle. Dances vary according to the region and some of the best are to be seen in the pre-Saharan area S of the Anti Atlas. Some moussems may be small affairs involving two or three villages only. Others may be of national importance. Indeed some get so big that the central theme of devotion to a saint is lost in the general festivities and folklore. Others, such as that at Moulay Idriss near Fez (the most famous of all), manage to retain their essential religious flavour because the onlookers are far outnumbered by the pilgrims. Needless to say all this frantic activity and exotic spectacle is very attractive to foreign visitors who are well tolerated as long as they show respect and are discreet with their cameras.

A *fantasia* is an important part of most traditional festivals and usually even the most modest moussem will manage to raise one. Lines of horsemen thunder across an open space, brandishing their rifles in the air, and, at a given signal (of which the onlooker is not aware), fire into the air. The riders, nobly and colourfully dressed on their magnificent horses, shout wildly with the intoxication of it all and charge over and over again, with no apparent object but to fire their rifles at precisely the same moment. The riders, seen through clouds of dust or sand, have inspired many Moroccan artists over the years, especially the contemporary Hassan el Glaoui whose atmospheric paintings are becoming justly famous throughout the world. Seen against a boundless desert landscape, this age-old Berber spectacle is quite breathtaking.

Anyone travelling extensively across the country, using side roads as well as principal routes, will probably come across at least a minor moussem and/or fantasia without even having to look for it. Here is a list of the important ones, followed by a list of miscellaneous festivals, which are really thanksgiving ceremonies but whose outward manifestations—with fantasias and so on—appear much the same to the visitor.

Moussems (the exact dates should be ascertained from the local tourist office or Syndicat d'Initiative).
Moulay Idriss (near Fez and Meknes): August.
Moulay Abdallah (on the coast 10km W of El Jadida): August.
Sidi Ahmed Ou Moussa (Tiznit, S of Agadir): end of August.
Side El Gandouri (near Khemisset, S of Rabat): August.
Tan Tan (S of Goulimine): end of May.
Goulimine: beginning of June.
Moulay Abdeslam Ben M'chich Alami, Beni Arous (near Larache): June.
Moulay Idriss Al Ashar, Fez: September.
Moulay Abdelkader (near Khemisset, S of Rabat): September.
Sidi Yahia, Oujda: September.
Festivals (exact dates available from the local tourist office or Syndicat d'Initiative).
Tafraout (near Agadir)—Almond Blossom Festival: February.
Kelaa des M'Gouna (near Ouarzazate)—Festival of Roses: May.
Marrakesh—National Folklore Festival: 5–14 June (varies slightly from year to year). This is truly a spectacular event, held in the grounds of El Badi Palace; it includes dancers, horsemen, singers and acrobats from all over the country, including the Atlas mountains, the Sahara, the Rif, and the 'Imperial' cities of Fez, Meknes, Marrakesh and Rabat.
Marrakesh—International Music and Dance Festival: 4–12 July. This includes musicians, singers and dancers from Europe, Black Africa and North and South America.
Sefrou (S of Fez)—Cherry Festival: June.
Immouzer-des-Ida-Outanane (near Agadir)—Honey Festival: July.
Asilah—Arts festival: August.
Imilchil—Marriage Fair: September.
Erfoud—Date Festival: October.

Food and Drink

Moroccans are amongst the most hospitable people in the world. Their heart-warming courtesy and the lavishness of the food provided, as much to a near stranger as to a family friend, is often quite out of proportion to their means. A guest in a Moroccan household is someone to be honoured, someone to partake of the best that can be offered. A Moroccan is deeply hurt if you refuse his offered hospitality, even if he can ill afford to give it to you. He will share his last crust with his guest.

Mint tea is the staple drink all over Morocco. It is drunk—very sweet—at any time of the day, before or after a meal. It is a refreshing and thirst-quenching drink in hot, dry weather, and a warming, revitalising one on cool, wet days. It is also an excellent digestive. The tea used is green tea and it comes from China. Tea as we know it is called black tea and is obtainable in the larger towns and hotels but otherwise may be difficult to come by.

The tea-making ceremony is an ancient and dignified one. The host usually invites a close friend or an important guest to prepare it. This fortunate man sits cross-legged on the most honoured seat in the room and is brought a round tray, usually silver or brass, about a metre in diameter and standing on its own legs. On the tray is a silver teapot with a conical lid, glasses, coloured and decorated to a high degree and usually far more numerous than the guests, and three silver boxes, one containing green tea, one irregular chunks of white sugar and one sprigs of mint. A steaming copper kettle is brought in, often with its own charcoal brazier. There is also a silver spoon and a sharp instrument for hacking the sugar into more manageable pieces.

Slowly, and in silence, a quantity of tea will be put in the pot. Boiling water is added. Then a large amount of sugar and a handful of mint are crammed in, the lid is pushed down and the mixture is left to infuse for some minutes. Then the tasting begins. The tea-maker, profoundly aware of his responsibilities, pours a little into his own glass, tastes it with all the concentration of a wine connoisseur, pours it back, perhaps adds more water, more sugar or more mint, leaves it a little longer, tastes it again, and so on until he is quite satisfied that it is good enough. He then pours a little into each glass, holding the pot high in the air and affecting a masterly flourish. The glasses are then filled and passed round on the tray. They are often so full and so hot that the only way to hold them is with the thumb on the brim and the second and third fingers underneath. Greatest pleasure will be given by allowing the glass to be filled at least twice more, unless you know that this is just the preliminary to a meal.

A full meal in a well-to-do Moroccan household can be a delicious and quite formal affair, and it is worth noting that appreciation of the food is on the whole deemed far more important than conversation. Indeed, a lack of conversation means that you are dedicating all of yourself to enjoying the meal and this is appreciated. Moroccans often eat in friendly silence. The time for talk is before or after. There is always an atmosphere of well-being and warmth and this is what matters.

You will be ushered to a seat on the narrow, padded divan, which lines the walls of all Moroccan living rooms, and cushions will be thrust behind your back to ensure your total comfort. A round low table will then be brought up to you, as yet with nothing on it but a richly embroidered linen tablecloth, or perhaps a more practical plastic one, and a number of very large napkins. Your host and those of lesser importance than yourself will group themselves around the table against the wall or on cushions and pouffes. A servant with a towel over his arm will then bring a kettle of warm water and a metal bowl with a raised disc in the middle which holds a cake of soap. You must wash your hands because you will be eating with your fingers—or, more precisely, with the thumb and first two fingers of your right hand.

After this procedure has been completed by all the first course is brought in, probably *mechoui*: a whole lamb, roasted in a special oven, standing up in all too realistic a manner on a heavy round platter. Or it may just be part of a lamb, according to the number of guests or the status of your host. Round loaves of delicious Arab bread, nutty and granular, are liberally scattered on to the tablecloth and little dishes containing salt and ground caraway seed are put around. There are no plates. The meat is so tender that it comes away easily in the hand. The fat, browned and crisp, peels away easily to reveal the succulent flesh underneath, and experienced mechoui-eaters know just where to look for the most tender morsels. Your host will murmur *'bis m'Allah'*, which means 'in the name of God', and invite you to start. If you appear at any time to hesitate or to have difficulty in extracting your meat, juicy portions will be held out to you by your host or anyone wishing to give you pleasure. This may well be the first of some four or five meat courses, but it is entirely up to you to take as much or as little as you like, although it is difficult in fact to avoid taking more. Do not be surprised if, after you have munched solidly for half an hour or so, your host says to you: *'mais vous ne mangez rien Monsieur/Madame'*; he does not mean it. He just needs you to reassure him that it is good.

A *pastilla* may come next, or it may come instead of the mechoui. This is the most calorific part of the Moroccan menu and should be eaten sparingly by the weight-conscious. It is wafer-thin layers of flaky feather-light pastry, usually made by your host's wife, and filled with a mixture of pigeon meat, almonds, hard-boiled eggs and an assortment of herbs and spices. It is served very hot and usually has icing sugar sprinkled on top. Hardened pastilla-eaters quite ruthlessly fold back the layers of pastry in order to get at the spicy meat inside, but be careful not to burn your fingers for the inside retains its heat long after the rim has cooled down. This is the glory of the Moroccan cuisine. If offered a pastilla, you know that you are being truly honoured. Countless hours will have been spent in the preparation of it; indeed it is said that a guest can measure his standing with a family by the number of layers of pastry in the pastilla.

Next may come chickens, slow-cooked with saffron and either salted lemons and olives, or dates and nuts, and served—usually three or four to a dish—in a delicious aromatic sauce. The chicken meat is easily removed from the carcass and the sauce can be mopped up with the bread. In the Mediterranean area, instead of chickens there might be a fish baked whole (usually bream or sea bass) and stuffed with either tomatoes and herbs or raisins, honey and almonds.

After all this there will probably be a *tagine*—a stew of tender mutton cooked with onions, prunes, and nuts, and often decorated with hard-boiled eggs, served in a heavy earthenware dish with a conical lid which is whipped off at the last moment so that the food can be served at maximum heat. (The dish itself is also called a tagine.) It is perfectly understood if, at this stage, you feel that you have eaten just about enough meat and prefer to soak your bread in the sauce, where much of the flavour is anyway, and pick at the prunes and the vegetables.

Finally comes the cous-cous, and when this appears you know you are approaching the end of the road. This is Morocco's national dish. It is served at all tables, from the richest to the poorest, and on all occasions. A veritable mountain of white granular semolina hides within it carrots, turnips, courgettes and, usually, pieces of mutton. The dish will probably be moistened by a thin piquant sauce poured over it at the last moment. The semolina may also be served plain, as a dessert, with milk, cinnamon and sugar. It varies widely from region to region and each of your hosts will think that his is the best. It is all a matter of personal taste and one can quite quickly become a cous-cous connoisseur while travelling across the country. Whichever way it is cooked, it is very light and digestible, and the right way to eat it is to pick up a small quantity of the grain in the fingers and, by applying gentle pressure, shape it into a perfect spherical ball. This is then tossed delicately into the mouth. Unless you have had time to practise in private, this can be a very messy business. Even with the protection of your napkin over your knees, cous-cous has a way of seeping down your chin and into your shoes or up your sleeves. Spoons will probably have been put around at this stage and it is not at all shaming to pick one up and use it. It will certainly be kinder to your host's carpet to do so.

Now you are nearing the end of the meal. You may be presented with a dish of typical sweetmeats including the famous *cornes de gazelle*: tiny croissants stuffed with ground almonds and honey and rolled in sugar and chopped nuts. Or you may go straight on to fruit: peaches; grapes; oranges; cherries; apples; bananas; dates; melons or iced watermelon, according to the season and where you are. Particularly look out for cherries in the Middle Atlas, bananas in the Souss valley around Agadir, and dates in the south. Fruit is cheap in Morocco, of high quality and plentiful.

The meal is over when the hand-washing apparatus reappears. Some of the guests may wash their faces as well. At this stage you can relax back against the cushions and even go to sleep if you wish. It is a relief to have room to spread out after the rather cramped eating position when you are bent over the low round table and your legs, if they should happen to be long, tend to be rather in the way. Tea, with a possible alternative of thick black coffee, will be served, and as soon as you have had your two or three glasses it is permissible to leave.

The meal described above is a formal, traditional Moroccan meal, called a *diffa* and served when a festival is being celebrated. The repertoire of dishes is fairly predictable and there is no reason to over-eat if you can master the technique of appearing to be permanently busy either choosing a morsel or consuming it. The custom of crouching over a low table around a common platter stems of course from earlier life in tents in the desert. The meal is taken very seriously but there is a warmth and friendly intimacy generated which is often lacking around the Western dinner table with its carefully positioned chairs and place-settings.

You will doubtless be surprised by the vast quantities put in front of you; seemingly far more than is necessary. In fact, there is no waste. Moroccan households take the form of large family conclaves and each dish, as it leaves the principal guests, goes straight on to other members of the family, or to the children, or to the servants. Moroccans do not normally eat on this scale. They live modestly and a simple meal of tagine or cous-cous with fruit to follow will suffice. The quantity and the general splendour of presentation is put on for you, the guest. It is quite unthinkable for a Moroccan to ask a guest to take pot-luck as Westerners might do if taken unawares by a sudden arrival.

Two more typical dishes deserve mention: one is the delicious *harira*, a soup which comes into its own during Ramadan when it is used to break the day-long fast. Imagine virtually the whole of Morocco poised around the soup tureen waiting for the magical hour of sundown when consumption may begin. It is an appetising and nutritious soup made of chick peas and haricot beans slow-cooked in stock, with or without mutton or chicken added, and flavoured with lemon and fresh tarragon. Then there are the ubiquitous *brochettes*—kebabs of grilled mutton; and spicy meat balls, known as *kefta*, which turn up on all occasions and in all settings, from road-side stalls to 5-star hotels, often smelling better than they taste.

A variety of drinks will be on hand to accompany the food, usually non-alcoholic. Coca-cola is universal, and so is locally-produced mineral water in still or fizzy form (*Oulmes, Side Harazem* or *Sidi Ali*), which is good and healthy. There will probably be fresh orange juice available and there may also be almond milk (made by adding milk to ground almonds): a dry, refreshing drink which blends well with the quantities of meat one consumes. In sophisticated households accustomed to receiving foreign guests, Moroccan wine will be offered. Wine is produced in three districts: Berkane (near Oujda), Boulaouane (Casablanca) and Meknes. The whites in particular are very drinkable, and the best of the reds is Cabernet du President (see list below).

The best way to enjoy Moroccan food is in a family home. Failing that the various dishes may be sampled in the traditional Moroccan restaurants, notably in the medinas of Fez and Marrakesh or, to a limited extent, in tourist hotels and restaurants. Moroccans themselves seldom eat out so the traditional restaurants (often occupying restored palaces) cater mainly for the tourists. A few combine dignity and elegance with the best that Moroccan cooking can offer; others pay more attention to the floor show than they do the quality of the food. If you hope to go through the full gamut of dishes, it is necessary to order in advance and to go in a party of not less than four.

A summary of typical dishes

Mechoui: whole lamb roasted in a special oven (or on a spit if outdoors) served with spices and Arab bread.

Pastilla: pie of flaky pastry containing pigeonmeat, almonds and hardboiled eggs.

Poulet au citron (can also be called *Tagine de poulet*): chickens casseroled with salted lemons and olives and saffron.

Tagine: stew, usually of mutton with either prunes and nuts, or dates and almonds; can also be chicken as above, or fish with honey, almonds and raisins. *Tagine* is also used to describe the distinctive earthenware dish with conical lid.

Cous-cous: granular semolina served in a mound and containing courgettes, carrots, turnips and, usually mutton. Can also be served without vegetables or meat but with sugar and cinnamon added.

Kefta: spicy meat balls, usually mutton but can also contain offal.

Harira: thick creamy soup of chick peas, haricot beans and either mutton or chicken, often flavoured with lemon and tarragon.

Cornes de gazelle: delicate pastries stuffed with honey and almonds.

Some local wines
Reds:
Cabernet du President
Guerrouane
Beni Snassen
Valpierre

Whites:
Coquillages
Valpierre blanc de blanc
Oustalet
Chaudsoleil

Rosé:
Gris de Boulaouane

PRACTICAL INFORMATION

Approaches to Morocco

Tourist Information. The Moroccan National Tourist Board has offices all over the world: in London the address is 205 Regent Street, W1R 7DE (tel. 071 437-0073); in New York it is 20 East 46th Street, Suite 1201, NY 10017; in Paris it is 161 Rue Saint-Honoré; in Montreal it is 2001 Rue Université, Suite 1460. These offices give general information but do not make bookings. In Morocco the head office is in Rabat at 22 Av. d'Alger (tel. 212-52); there are also offices in Casablanca (Place des Nations Unies); Marrakesh (Place Abd-el-Moumene-Ben-Ali); Tangier (20 Blvd Pasteur); Fez (Place de la Resistance); Meknes (Place Administrative); Tetouan (30 Av. Mohammed V); Oujda (Place du 16 Août); Agadir (Av. du Prince Heritier Sidi Mohammed). Staff usually speak English.

There is also a network of offices throughout Morocco known as *Syndicats d'Initiative* which give local information and are usually very helpful.

By Air. *Royal Air Maroc*, the national airline, has direct flights or connections from most major European cities, New York and Montreal, with regular scheduled service from London (Heathrow) to Tangier, Casablanca, Marrakesh and Agadir.
GB Airways operates a scheduled service from London (Gatwick) to Tangier, Casablanca and Marrakesh.
Charter flights are widely available from the UK to main resorts (usually Tangier, Marrakesh and Agadir) according to season.

By train. Standard tickets for all Moroccan destinations can be purchased from the station or via major travel agents. For those who qualify (usually by age/student status), Transalpino, Eurotrain and Inter-Rail tickets can represent a significant saving. Inter-Rail 91 offers one month's unlimited travel in Europe and Morocco to under-26s for £180; a new Inter-Rail 26+ card also includes Morocco in its one month offer for £260. Eurotrain: 52 Grosvenor Gardens, London SW1 (tel. 071-730 8518); Inter-Rail: tickets and information from British Rail Travel Centres; International Rail Centre, Victoria Station, London SW1V 1JY (071-834 2345).

By Car and Ferry. Whether travelling through France or Spain, a number of options are available.
SETE in France, to Tangier (38 hrs)—advance booking is recommended.
ALGECIRAS, in Spain, to Tangier (2½ hrs) or Ceuta (1½ hrs). Regular services throughout the day in high season. Ceuta (a Spanish enclave) has good road connections onwards into Morocco. Also hydrofoil, Algeciras/Tangier (1 hour).
ALMERIA & MALAGA in Spain, to Melilla (8½ hrs) the other Spanish enclave. A good springboard for Fez and Oujda and Saïdia.
TARIFA, in Spain, to Tangier (by hydrofoil ½ hour).
GIBRALTAR, via hydrofoil (1 hr) to Tangier.
PORTIMAO, (Faro at present) in Portugal, to Tangier (10 hrs)
There is no ferry direct from the UK.

Inclusive holidays. The following firms operate inclusive holidays to Morocco:

ABERCROMBIE & KENT tel. 071 7309600
BEST OF MOROCCO tel. 0380 828533
CADOGAN TRAVEL tel. 0703 332661
CLUB MED tel. 071 5811161
COSMOS tel. 081 4643477
CREATIVE LEISURE tel. 071 2350123
EMBASSY MANAGEMENT SERVICES TRAVEL tel. 0279 435423
EXODUS tel. 081 6755550
EXPLORE tel. 0252 319448
HAYES & JARVIS tel. 081 7485050
JASMIN TOURS tel. 06285 31121
KUONI TRAVEL tel. 0306 742500
MOROCCAN SUN tel. 071 4373968
SHERPA EXPEDITIONS tel. 081 5772717
SUNMED HOLIDAYS tel. 0293 519151
TRAVELSCENE tel. 081 4274445
TWICKERS WORLD tel. 081 8928164
WAYMARK tel. 0753 516477

Visa and passports. A full valid passport is required. No visa is necessary for nationals of the United Kingdom or of the United States. Visitors can stay for three months and should apply to the local police department (*Bureau des Etrangers*) if they wish to stay longer.

Customs regulations. The following items may be temporarily imported to Morocco duty-free: still and movie cameras with ten rolls of film for each; personal clothing and jewellery; binoculars; portable typewriters; camping materials and sports gear; radio; tape recorder; musical instruments. All kinds of foodstuff in reasonable quantities may be imported into Morocco, as long as the amount does not exceed the normal needs of the visitor. The visitor may bring in 400 grammes of tobacco, or 200 cigarettes or 50 cigars; one litre of spirits; four litres of toilet water.

Firearms and cartridges may be imported subject to a licence issued by the Police Department in Rabat, the *Direction de la Sureté Nationale*. Unlicensed importation of firearms can lead to severe penalties.

Money. The Moroccan unit of currency is the *dirham*, which is divided into 100 centimes. Its value fluctuates around 13.50 dirhams to £1 or 8.2 dirhams to 1 US$. Dirhams come in notes of 100 (dark brown), 50 (green) 10 red/brown) and 5 (dark blue); coins are 10, 20, 50 centimes and 1 dirham. Dirhams can only be bought within Morocco and it is illegal to import or export them. At all airports and customs posts there are banks ready to change your money, and it is necessary at that moment to obtain a receipt which you will need to show again on departure in order to convert back into sterling any money that you have left over up to a limit of 50 per cent of the total amount of the receipts. You will be required to declare all foreign currency, travellers cheques, etc., upon entry and exit. Dirhams are not accepted by duty-free shops.

Time. GMT plus 1 hour in summer months and GMT in winter.

Electricity. Generally 220 volt, occasionally 110 volt. 2 pin round plugs are the norm.

Accommodation and Restaurants

Hotels. The Moroccan National Tourist Board has classified all hotels from 1 to 5 stars and prices for grades 1 to 4 are controlled as follows:

(Rooms per night)	**Double**	**Single**
4-star A	400 dirhams	324 dirhams
4-star B	327	262
3-star A	237	196
3-star B	208	169
2-star A	155	133
2-star B	125	103
1-star A	110	95
1-star B	96	75

5-star and the few 5-star Luxe hotels (such as *Mamounia* in Marrakesh and *Palai Jamai* in Fez) are not controlled and can sometimes be very expensive. The best way to find out prices for these is to approach the Tourist Board direct or agencies such as Creative Leisure (tel. 071 2350123) or Best of Morocco (tel. 0380 828533) who will also make bookings. The Tourist Board can produce a full list of classified hotels showing their respective facilities, but not their prices.

There is also a plethora of small hotels and pensions to be found in the medinas which are 'unclassified' and often very cheap, though their prices can fluctuate with the season. They are usually noisy but clean.

A 'taxe de sejour' is payable per night at all hotels as follows: 5-star L: 30 dirhams; 5-star: 17 dirhams; 4-star A & B: 10 dirhams; 3-star A & B: 6 dirhams; 2-star A & B: 4 dirhams; 1-star A & B: 3 dirhams. This can vary slightly according to the region.

Youth Hostels. There are youth hostels at the following places: Asni (40 beds); Azrou (40 beds); Casablanca (80 beds); Chaouen (30 beds); Fez (60 beds); Maknes (50 beds); Marrakesh (90 beds). The rates for one night are about 10 dirhams per person, including use of sheets or sleeping bags. Age limit is usually 30 years. Further details are available from the Tourist Board.

Campsites. There are more than 50 campsites in Morocco and the Tourist Board will produce a list. On the whole those on the coast tend to be cleanest and most attractive, whilst those in large towns get dusty and over-crowded. A few are in particularly attractive or unusual environments, e.g. Meski (by a stream in the woods), Moulay Bouselham (by the lagoon) and Meknes (in the Imperial City). Cost is usually 5 dirhams per person, per tent and per car.

Restaurants. (See also Food and Drink above.) It is possible to eat very well for a reasonable price in Morocco, and there is a varied choice of cuisine especially in the larger towns. Some restaurants offer only Moroccan dishes, others a choice of Moroccan or international. Most of the larger hotels are open to non-residents for lunch and dinner.

There is a wide range in price and quality (and these are not necessarily connected); you can pay very dearly at a five-star hotel for an indifferent meal from a grandiose menu, or you can try out some of the hundreds of café-restaurants around town centres—which are often remarkably cheap—and discover gourmet food. Appearing on nearly every 'international' menu will be various salads (often huge and constituting a meal in themselves), steaks, brochettes and omelettes, followed by the ubiquitous creme caramel and fruit. Along the coast, and particularly the W coast between Casablanca and Agadir, there is a feast of fish restaurants, mostly good and some very good. Here again the cheapest can sometimes be ambrosial and it would be hard to beat a platter of grilled sardines straight out of the sea at, say, Essaouira for just a few dirhams. Moroccans rarely eat out except when on holiday themselves by the sea or at a resort such as Ifrane.

Traditional Moroccan restaurants are often housed in sumptuous palaces where a floor show may be included. For between 100 and 250 dirhams a head you can feast the night away (though often without alcohol) to the accompaniment of Andalucian or Berber music and exotic dancing. It is always necessary to book in advance (through your hotel) and it is not uncommon for such restaurants to be taken over by large tour groups, especially in Marrakesh. Guides are usually provided to take you there and back since the restaurants are often located deep in the medina.

Some traditional Moroccan restaurants
Fez (the first six are in the medina)
Palais de Fez, 16 Boutouil (tel. 347-07)
Dar Saada, 21 Rue Attarine (tel. 333-43)
Dar Tagine, 15 Ross Rhi Ras Jnana (tel. 341-67)
Palais des Merenides, 99 Zkak er Rouah (tel. 340-28)
Palais Mnebhi, 15 Zankat Ben Safi (tel. 338-83)
Restaurant Firdaous, 10 Rue Jenifour (tel. 343-43)
Ambra, Route d'Immouzer, Fez
Marrakesh
La Maison Arabe, Rue Fatima Zohra, 30 Derb Ferrana (tel. 226-04)
Dar es Salaam, Riad Zitoun Kedim (tel. 235-20)
Ksar el Hamra, 24 Rue Goundafi (tel. 252-37)
Gharnata, Riad Zitoun Jdid (tel. 236-35)
Riad, Arset el Maach (tel. 254-30)
Riad el Bahia, 1 Riad Zit un Jdid (tel. 236-53)
El Ambra, Arset el Maach (tel. 226-09)
Dar el Baroud, 275 Av. Mohammed V (opposite Koutoubia) (tel. 450-77)
Casablanca
Al Mounia, 111 Rue Prince Moulay Abdallah (tel. 222-669)
L'Etoile de Marrakesh, 126 Blvd Mohammed V (tel. 271-259)
L'Etoile Marocaine, 107 Rue Allal ben Abdallah (tel. 311-473)
Tangier
Hammadi, Rue de la Kasbah (tel. 345-14)
Ibn Batouta, Rue es Siaghine (tel. 345-27)
Meknes
Restaurant Zitouna, 44 Jamaa Zitouna (tel. 302-81)
El Jadida
Palais Andalous, Rue Curi (tel. 343-745)

Tipping. A tip is expected on most occasions for any service, however small. Restaurant waiters will expect approximately 5 dirhams per person, even though a service charge of 15 per cent has already been added to the bill; hotel porters expect between 5 and 10 dirhams for carrying your cases to your room; museum curators expect a tip as you depart, even though you have already paid an entrance fee; the *guardien* (whether an old man or small boy) will expect something for watching over your car when you park it in the city; children have learned to expect money for allowing you to photograph them (if they happen to catch you at it); and the ragged city child who gives you directions, will certainly expect a coin. A dirham or two can represent riches to him (or her) and should not be begrudged; the art is to make sure that you are talking to just one of them and not six.

Transport in Morocco

Motoring. A British or EC driver's licence is valid in Morocco and cars may remain in the country for six months duty-free. An international customs carnet is required for a caravan. Third Party insurance is compulsory and the International Green Card is valid so long as it has been extended to North Africa.

Car hire. There are numerous self-drive car hire agencies in Morocco and the big international companies such as Hertz, Avis and Europcar have representatives in the major cities and airports. Cars can usually be booked in advance through tour operators and a combined Fly Drive holiday is certainly cheaper than separate purchase of air ticket and car hire. Hire will include third party, fire and theft insurance but personal accident coverage should be carefully checked. Broken windscreens are usually covered but irreparable tyres (easily caused by mountain tracks) must usually be replaced at hirer's expense.

Petrol is slightly cheaper than in the UK and a litre of *Super* currently costs 7.11 dirhams.

Morocco has the best road network in North Africa. The trunk roads are exceptionally good and uncluttered. Secondary roads are narrower but usually well maintained. Third class roads, to be found in mountains or desert areas, are often unsurfaced tracks and fall into three categories: those which are passable all the year round in any type of car; those which are open to saloon cars in the dry summer season only, although they may be passable by four-wheel drive vehicles in wintry weather; those which are feasible only by a four-wheel drive vehicle at any time of year. Information as to the state of these third class roads is always available from local authorities or tourist offices.

Trunk roads are straight, and often empty. Driving for anyone coming from the congested European roads is sheer pleasure and often very fast. However, as nearly all fields and forests are unfenced there is a danger of untended cattle or donkeys (or even camels) straying on to the roads. You are also likely to come across heavily laden horse-drawn carts creeping slowly along in the middle of the road. Moroccan country people seem blissfully unaware of danger and their children will dash out without so much as a glance.

The French rule of priority for the car coming from the right-hand side is ruthlessly enforced. For the British accustomed to driving on the left-hand side this takes some getting used to, but it is completely logical—there can be no arguments as to who has the right of way, only a collision if your reaction is not quick enough. Main roads carrying priority even over right-hand turns have signs showing a thick arrow crossed by a tiny line;

DISTANCE CHART

	Agadir	Al Hoceima	Azilal	Casablanca	El Jadida	Essaouira	Fez	Laayoune	Marrakesh	Meknes	Ouarzazate	Oujda	Rabat	Safi	Tangier	Tetouan	Zagora
Agadir		1091	515	511	417	173	756	649	273	740	375	1099	602	294	880	892	543
Al Hoceima	1091		650	536	632	887	275	1740	758	335	992	293	445	792	327	278	1182
Azilal	515	650		275	336	418	375	1164	242	364	445	1233	325	399	603	622	625
Casablanca	511	536	275		99	351	289	1160	236	229	442	632	91	256	369	385	611
El Jadida	417	632	336	99		252	388	1066	197	328	399	731	190	157	468	484	575
Essaouira	173	887	418	351	252		640	822	176	580	380	983	442	129	720	736	555
Fez	756	275	375	289	388	640		1396	483	60	687	343	198	545	303	281	849
Laayoune	649	1740	1164	1160	1066	822	1396		922	1389	1024	1748	1251	943	1529	1541	1314
Marrakesh	273	758	242	236	197	176	483	922		487	204	826	321	157	588	615	379
Meknes	740	335	364	229	328	580	60	1389	487		652	403	136	485	267	258	769
Ouarzazate	375	992	445	442	399	380	687	1024	204	652		820	528	361	811	820	168
Oujda	1099	293	1233	632	731	983	343	1748	826	403	820		541	888	609	555	962
Rabat	602	445	325	91	190	442	198	1251	321	136	528	541		347	276	294	700
Safi	294	792	399	256	157	129	545	943	157	485	361	888	347		625	641	557
Tangier	880	327	603	369	468	720	303	1529	588	267	811	609	276	625		57	979
Tetouan	892	278	622	385	484	736	281	1541	615	258	820	555	294	641	57		1110
Zagora	543	1182	625	611	575	555	849	1314	379	769	168	962	700	557	979	1110	

if the junction is marked by a cross, then the driver must still give priority to any car coming in from his right.

Railways. A railway network of about 2500km links the major towns of Tangier, Rabat, Casablanca, El Jadida, Safi, Meknes, Fez, Marrakesh, Taza and Oujda. The trains have first, second and economy class carriages. If you are travelling in the hot season it is certainly worth paying the small amount extra for first class in order to benefit from the air conditioning. The fast trains have restaurants or buffet cars and at night sleeper or couchette facilities are available. Trains are modern, clean and comparatively cheap (economy class is usually cheaper than travelling by coach).

There is an excellent inter-city service between Rabat and Casablanca which takes 60 minutes and runs 20 times a day. It takes approximately 6½ hours to get from Casablanca to Fez, and 7 hours from Casablanca to Tangier (both via Rabat). Casablanca to Marrakesh takes 4 hours.

Coaches. Two national coach lines link virtually the whole country. CTM/Lignes Nationales operate services to most towns of any size whilst ONCF (the rail company) run express services to a number of towns connecting to the rail network. Private companies such as SATAS supplement these networks and it is possible to travel all over the country using these lines which have offices in all the main cities. For anyone who seeks excitement and local colour, and is not in a hurry, this is the way to see Morocco. The coaches travel fast but they will also stop at every little town for anything between five and 30 minutes, and always at a café. In the more remote areas the arrival of the coach is a great event for local people, and they are liable to produce singers, dancers, acrobats, as well as anything from whole sheep to sticky cakes for sale. Life is never dull and time is of supreme unimportance.

Air Services. For those who are really short of time, Royal Air Maroc operates regular services between Tangier, Casablanca, Marrakesh, Ouarzazate, Agadir, Al Hoceima, Oujda, Fez, Meknes and Rabat. To this list has been added a service between Agadir and the coastal resorts Laayoune and Dakhla in the far south.

Taxis. These are plentiful, particularly at railway and coach stations. The yellow *petits-taxis* are preferable on short trips because they are very cheap; but they will usually only take up to three people. *Grands-taxis* will cover long distances and bigger groups; they are usually clapped-out Mercedes whose drivers will ask very high prices of unsuspecting tourists; therefore it is essential to negotiate the price in advance. In country districts grands-taxis act like mini-buses and have specific collection points, usually insisting on 6 people before they will move at all. It is not customary to tip taxi drivers.

Health Care

Innoculations are not obligatory unless you are arriving from a declared infected area. It is however wise to have your typhoid, cholera, tetanus and polio immunisation up to date; some people consider a hepatitis jab is advisable.

Morocco is on the whole a healthy country and standards of health care

are high. There are plenty of French-speaking doctors around and hotels, tourist offices and pharmacies will have lists. Pharmacies should be your first port of call if a problem arises; their staff are well trained and their shelves well stocked with drugs, many of which would be available only on prescription in UK. They will also recommend doctors if necessary. Modern, privately-owned clinics and state-run hospitals are available to visitors should the need arise.

The most likely ailment to befall foreign visitors is diarrhoea, so always take supplies of your own preferred remedy. Even this can be avoided if you make it a rule never to drink, or brush your teeth with, water from the tap, even in the north. There are three types of mineral water (still and fizzy) which are cheap, especially if you stock up with big bottles at the corner shop. These are *Sidi Ali*, *Sidi Harazem* and *Oulmes*. Top hotels provide complimentary bottles in the rooms. Change of diet, or quite simply over-indulgence, can also cause problems at first. Hotels and restaurants tend to produce full and tempting menus for lunch and dinner. It takes a degree of will-power to insist on just a salad, or just an omelette for lunch, but this is certainly a good idea, especially if travelling in the heat of the day. Charcoal-grilled meats and fish from market stalls, ice-cream from street vendors, fly-blown dates and other fruits which have no peel, are best avoided, at least until you have had time to adjust.

Aids is not yet a problem in Morocco and public health education is low key.

There are mosquitoes in the south but they are said not to be malarial. Insect-repellent creams or sprays and some form of anti-histimine cream are however useful (and available locally if needed).

Bilharzia is believed to lurk in pools and streams in the south, so it is best not to have any contact with water in the oases, however tempting it looks.

Your own travel insurance is of course advisable (either through a travel agent, bank or at the airport).

In emergency, dial 15 for an ambulance.

Women travelling alone

Women need not feel threatened when travelling alone in Morocco as long as they respect local customs. Firstly, this means dressing suitably and not wearing shorts or mini-skirts or miniscule singlets. This is particularly important if you are anywhere near holy places (as in Fez or Moulay Idriss). Trousers or jeans are acceptable but people will respect you more for wearing a skirt. The beach is a different story and anything goes; but for getting there and returning from there, the above rule applies. Secondly, it is not the custom when speaking to unknown men (particularly older men) for women to look them directly in the eyes. This is difficult perhaps for Westerners, constantly reminded of the need for eye contact, but in Morocco, as in other Arab countries this could be treated as a 'come on' by men.

Moroccans, particularly young ones, are naturally inquisitive. They may call out questions as you walk past: 'what's your name' or 'where are you staying' or 'where are you from?'. This is usually just curiosity and has little to do with the fact that you are a woman. Just walk past and, if necessary, tell them sharply to go away. In town, older men will very often move forward and see off the questioners in no uncertain terms, but rarely hang around to be thanked.

It cannot be denied that Morocco is a man's country. What else can you expect when the Koran says that men are superior to women (Sura 414) and instructs men to bless God for not having made them women? No wonder women are not allowed in the holiest places of the mosque but are confined to their own special area; no wonder the cafés are all full of men with never a woman in sight (unless she is a foreigner); and no wonder it is still quite common in country districts to see a man riding a donkey and the woman (with a load of firewood on her back) walking along behind.

This is their culture and we should not presume to interfere. Moroccans will always say, if challenged, that they have the greatest respect for women (especially their mothers) and this is certainly true, even if their way of showing it is somewhat strange.

Moroccan women (who usually go around in groups of two or three) love to talk with foreign women (if not accompanied by men) but are probably too shy to approach you, and may only speak Arabic. A smile and a phrase such as 'your kaftan is beautiful' will amuse and delight them and they will possibly invite you back for tea in their homes; there will be lots of children and other women will appear, as by magic, to meet you, manifesting the very same curiosity about your life style as the men but in a gentler and less irritating way. If you have time and are keen to know more, show an interest in their cooking, which is their pride and joy. You may even learn to make a pastilla!

Ironically, there are occasions when travelling with a man can be more frustrating to the modern Western woman than going it alone, or travelling with another woman, insofar as all decision-making and serious conversation will automatically be directed at *him*, even if the question emanated from you, the woman, in the first place. *Plus ça change...*

Public Holidays and Opening Hours

Public holidays. There are public holidays on the following dates: 1 January, New Year's Day; 3 March, Feast of the Throne (anniversary of King Hassan's accession to the throne in 1961); 1 May, Labour Day; 14 August, Allegiance Day; 6 November, Day of the Green March (anniversary of the march into the Western Sahara); 18 November, Independence Day (anniversary of King Mohammed V's return to the throne in 1956).

In addition there are the following religious public holidays (as these are based on the Lunar calendar, which is 11 or 12 days shorter than the Gregorian Christian one, depending on whether there is a Leap Year or not, these events move backwards against our calendar by 11 or 12 days): Aid es Seghir ends the fast of Ramadan; Aid el Kebir (literally 'the great feast') commemorates Abraham's sacrifice and is marked by the ritual slaughter of a sheep by the head of each family; Mouloud is the anniversary of the birthday of the prophet Mohammed; First Moharram is the first day of New Lunar year.

Opening hours can vary, especially in rural areas, but for the main cities and towns they are approximately:

Banks: Monday to Friday, 8.15–11.30 and 14.15–16.30.

Shops: Monday to Saturday, 8.30–12 noon and 14.00–18.30. Shops in the medinas make their own rules, frequently closing on Fridays for religious reasons, sometimes opening on Sundays, and often staying open till very late in the evenings. Food shops in the medinas will usually open on Friday mornings only.

Offices: Monday to Thursday, 8.30–12 noon and 14.30–18.30; Friday, 8.30–11.30 and 15.00–18.30.

Museums are generally open every day except Tuesday. A few are open every day. Their hours are roughly the same as those for banks, with a long period of closure in the middle of the day. A standard charge of 10 dirhams is now charged for entry to all museums throughout Morocco.

The principal museums are as follows:

Rabat: Museum of Antiquities, rue el Brihi.

Tangier: Dar el Makhzen, Place de la Kasbah.

Meknes: Dar Jamai, Place el Hedim.

Fez: Dar Batha, Bab Bou Jeloud.

Tetouan: Archaeological Museum, Place el Jala.

Marrakesh: Museum of Moroccan Art, Palace of Dar Si Said.

Medersas usually keep the same hours as museums, but they are not open on Fridays (though they may be open on Tuesdays). Those which have been restored charge 10 dirhams per person. Others are unattended and therefore free.

Photography

As in most countries, photography anywhere near a military installation is highly unwise. On the whole, Moroccans are getting used to the sight of camera-laden visitors and some do not hesitate to profit from it, coming up and demanding dirhams if they feel the camera has been pointed in their direction. Water-sellers, bedecked with brass cups and colourful robes, probably make more money from posing than they do from selling water. Camel and goat boys also have the whole business refined to a delicate art and should not be begrudged their few coins.

Ordinary people going about their business should always be asked if they mind being photographed and this applies especially to women in rural areas who often cover their faces and run away in fear.

Photography of holy places such as the white-domed marabouts can cause offence and one should firmly resist the temptation to point a camera towards the interior of a mosque, however inviting the open doors may appear.

THE NORTH AND WEST COASTS: THE RIF MOUNTAINS

1 Tangier to Rabat

Total distance 277km. **Tangier**—46km **Asilah**—41km **Larache** (LIXUS)—36km **Ksar el Kbir**—37km *Souk el Arba du Gharb*—77km **Kenitra**— 40km **Rabat**.

TANGIER (280,000 inhab.), so close to the southernmost tip of Europe, is for many the first point of contact with Morocco. Its eventful history and its years as an International Zone have left it the most cosmopolitan and atypical of Moroccan cities. No longer the centre of political intrigue, Tangier dedicates itself to tourism. Its advantages are: a climate that is exceptionally temperate and sunny; beaches that face both the Mediterranean and the Atlantic; a modern town and an atmospheric medina. Its disadvantages are a somewhat bored attitude on the part of some hotel and restaurant staff who all too frequently give the impression that they have long since stopped trying to please. Tangier is a good starting-point for journeys to Fez and Meknes in the S and the Rif mountains in the E.

Information. Moroccan National Tourist Office and Syndicat d'Initiative both in Blvd Pasteur.

Post Office. 33 Blvd Mohammed V.

Transport. Airport 15km W of the town. Flights to London, Paris, Madrid, Gibraltar, and internal flights. Railway station: Av. d'Espagne (in the port area). Trains to Rabat, Casablanca, Meknes, Fez, Marakesh, Oujda. Ferry terminal very close to railway station. Sailings to Gibraltar, Algeciras, Tarifa (Spain); Portimao (Portugal), Sète (France). Bus station: W of the railway station, just outside the port. Buses to Rabat and Casablanca, Tetouan, Ceuta, Meknes, Fez, etc.

Hotels. Four 5-star, five 4-star A, four 4-star B, six 3-star A, one 3-star B, six 2-star A, three 3-star B, seven 1-star A, two 1-star B. Holiday village: Club Mediterranée.

History. Tangier's origins are steeped in legend. One of the Labours of Hercules was to fetch a golden apple from the Garden of the Hesperides (believed to have been near Lixus) which was guarded by the daughters of Atlas. In doing this Hercules managed to kill the evil giant Antaeus and then married his widow Tinge, in whose honour he built a city, which he named Tingi after her.

Tangier is one of the oldest urban settlements in Morocco. It was probably founded as a trading post by the Phoenicians in c 1100 BC—along with Liks (Lixus), Russadir (Mellila), Tamuda, Chellah, and others. The Carthaginians turned all these into prosperous colonies, and some of them, Tingi in particular, built up sizeable fish-salting industries.

The Romans arrived after the destruction of Carthage in 146 BC and Tingi became TINGIS. In AD 40 Tingis was made the capital of the province of Mauritania Tingitana, which was named after the city. Later, the seat of provincial government was moved to Volubilis, where it remained until the end of the 3C when the Romans returned in force to Tingis after abandoning Volubilis: probably in order to distance themselves from increasing pressure from Middle Atlas Berbers. This was in fact the first stage in their complete withdrawal from the province.

In the 7C Tingis was one of the first towns to fall prey to the great unstoppable wave of Arab invaders who, in 683, under the leadership of Oqba ben Nafi, began surging into Morocco from Kairwan in Tunis. It was from Tingis, now renamed Tangier, that Muslim armies departed soon after to begin the conquest of Spain. They were commanded by the man who was to give his name—Tarik—to the rock that stood between him and the mainland, and which is today known as Gibraltar (deriving from 'jbel', which means mountain, and Tarik). In the 11C the Almoravide sultan Youssef ben Tachfine (1062–1107) also used Tangier as a base from which to cross the straits in order to pacify Andalucia. Four centuries later, Arab refugees chased out by the now victorious Spaniards came back through Tangier.

At the end of the 15C Tangier became Portuguese, then it was Spanish, then Portuguese again until Princess Catherina of Braganza married Charles II of England, at which point the city was handed over, as part of her dowry, to England. From 1661–83 the British flag was raised over Tangier, though the Alouite sultan Moulay Ismael tried, without success, to storm the city in 1679 and repeatedly thereafter. By 1683 the English soldiers had become so weakened by poor diet, insanitary conditions, lack of money and, above all, the frequent and determined attacks by Moulay Ismael, that they withdrew; but not without first destroying a large part of the port installation and the famous mole, the remains of which can still be seen, it is said, at low water. For a fascinating account of this period, read Emily Rowth's book, 'Tangier: Britain's Last Outpost' (1910); also 'A History of Anglo-Moroccan Relations to 1900' by P.G. Rogers.

In 1906, under the Treaty of Algeciras, Tangier was once again separated from the rest of the country and made an international port. It was governed by a legislative assembly of 27 members, of which only six were Moroccan and the rest Europeans (each country bringing with it its own currency and banks). It followed that Tangier gained a reputation—a shadow of which still remains thanks to the cinema—for smuggling, political intrigue and espionage. It also became exceedingly prosperous. The international status continued until 1956 when the French and Spanish Protectorates ended. Its prosperity diminished but it became an attractive bolthole for the slightly tarnished élite of many nations. Now once again Tangier flourishes: this time it is the tourists who are bringing prosperity and hotels are springing up everywhere to accommodate them.

The best place to begin a tour of Tangier is the GRAND SOCCO—a large and very busy open square which is supposed to have been the site of the Roman forum and now occupies a strategic position between the modern town and the medina. There are two main objects of interest: one is the distinctive multi-coloured minaret of the *Sidi Bouabid Mosque*; the other is the extraordinary *banyan tree* just inside the Mendoubia gardens, which is thought to be 800 years old. The *Mendoubia Palace*, once the residence of the Sultan's representative (Mendoub), is now the tribunal (law-courts) and cannot be visited. The gardens however are open when the court is not in session—all day on Sundays, not at all on Fridays, and after 15.00 hours on other days. It is worthwhile going in to take a look both at the tree and at the broad view of the medina and fishing port from the terrace. All but two of the fine ornamented cannons which once rested here are now scattered about the town.

Djellabah making in a souk, Tangier

To enter the **Medina** go down the Rue Semmarine, which is to the left of the entrance to the Central Market. Turn immediately right and continue downhill along the Rue Siaghine (street of the silversmiths) to a small and busy square flanked by café terraces and known as the PETIT SOCCO. This has become a place for enterprising street traders who creep up behind as you sip your expensive coke and whisper 'Look—Woolworth's price' in perfect English. Just go a few yards up one of the narrow side streets to escape them. These side streets contain the cheaper and more authentic restaurants (such as the *Restaurant Andalos* in the Rue du Commerce) where freshly-caught fish will be charcoal-grilled to perfection and served up with a crisp green salad at less than half the price you would pay at one of the more sophisticated fish restaurants in the centre or by the beach.

If you cross the Petit Socco and take the Rue de la Marine NE you will find the **Great Mosque**, with its fine green-and-white minaret. It was built by Moulay Ismael at the end of the 17C. Continue down this street and you come to *Bab el Moussa*, where the terrace has a very fine view over the port towards Cap Malabata.

Return to the Petit Socco and turn up one of the narrow and enticing alleyways which lead towards the heart of the medina. These streets are crammed with every kind of shop and bazaar, selling ornaments in silver, gold, brass and copper, or silks and wools, or leather goods. Here and there, in quiet contrast with all the commercial bustle, are Berber women wearing traditional costume—red-and-white striped skirts and straw hats decorated with plaited wool and pom-poms—sitting alongside their wares of goat cheese, brooms and onions, which they have brought by donkey from the

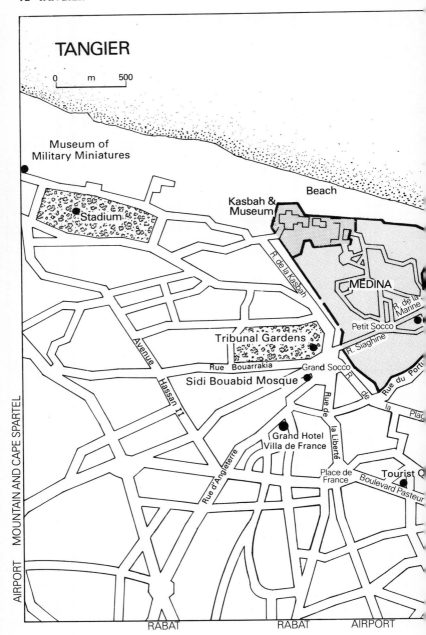

TANGIER

0   m   500

Museum of
Military Miniatures

Stadium

Beach

Kasbah &
Museum

R. de la Kasbah

MEDINA

R. de la Marine

Petit Socco

Tribunal Gardens

R. Siaghine

Rue Bouarrakia

Grand Socco

Sidi Bouabid Mosque

Rue du Port

Rue de la Liberté

Avenue Hassan II

R. de la Plage

Grand Hotel
Villa de France

Rue d'Angleterre

Place de
France

Tourist O

Boulevard Pasteur

MOUNTAIN AND CAPE SPARTEL

AIRPORT

RABAT   RABAT   AIRPORT

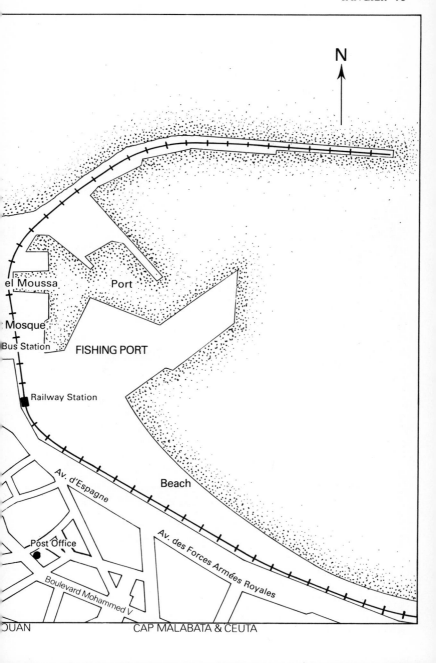

N

el Moussa

Port

Mosque

Bus Station

FISHING PORT

Railway Station

Av. d'Espagne

Beach

Post Office

Av. des Forces Armées Royales

Boulevard Mohammed V

OUAN

CAP MALABATA & CEUTA

Approach to the Place de la Kasbah, Tangier

mountain villages. Then there are bakers crouching in the shadows over their wood-fired ovens: customers bring their own dough to be baked; the round flat loaves are quite delicious and the ideal accompaniment to Morocco's rather spicy food. You will also notice old men sitting against the walls twisting strands of brightly coloured silk or wool, ready to be woven into kaftans.

One of the great charms of the medina is the opportunity it affords for glimpses of bright blue sea through white and shadowed walls; another is the preponderance of very beautiful old mosques (the one in Place Aissaoua dates back to 1263), with minarets that are miniature replicas of Sidi Bouabid on the Grand Socco.

If you keep on going uphill, you will eventually arrive at the **Kasbah**—the fortified part of the medina and now one of the most sought-after residential areas of Tangier, where traditionally-styled modern mansions, looking almost too perfect to be true, are packed quite comfortably in amongst older buildings. The PLACE DE LA KASBAH is the highest point in the medina, and its terrace faces the sea with good views of Jbel Tarik (Gibraltar) and the Spanish coast. The place is dominated by the great white bulk of the Royal Palace **Dar el Makhzen** (built by Moulay Ismael). It was occupied earlier this century when the ex-sultan Moulay Hafid was allowed to live here after signing the Treaty of Fez in 1912. It now houses a *Museum* (open every day except Friday). It has good examples of 17C and 18C craftsmanship and in the courtyard are marble columns from Volubilis. The rooms around the courtyard contain the museum and have some particularly fine hand-carved cedarwood ceilings painted in soft colours. The mosaic floors, marble columns and bare white walls are a perfect background to the display of old carpets, traditional furniture from Fez, ceramics, jewellery, leather, and ornamented daggers. Behind the Museum, the Sultan's garden is open to visitors and is full of orange and lemon trees, jacarandas, palms and strongly perfumed datura. Overlooking the garden there is a café-restaurant which offers exceptional views of the sea on one side and of the medina on the other.

Next door to the Museum and accessible from the Place de la Kasbah through a separate entrance is the former Treasury (*Bit al Mal*), very recently restored and containing a number of large wooden chests, an 18C balance and a heavy door with three separate bolts.

For a different—and quicker—route back to the Grand Socco take the Rue de la Kasbah (left and left again as you leave the restaurant) which skirts the medina. The street descends in steep steps and becomes the Rue d'Italie, which has more fine sea views and glimpses of ancient minarets. It is lined with typical Mediterranean houses with wrought-iron grilles over the windows.

To reach the old fishing port, leave the Grand Socco by the steep and narrow Costa de la Playa (Rue de la Plage). This animated street is packed full of restaurants and cheap *pensions*. The elaborate façades of the *Hotel Familiale de Talavera* and the *Gran Teatro Cervantes* (1913) give it an unmistakably Spanish flavour. The port is extremely colourful and lively, often crowded with hundreds of small craft, particularly at 5.00 am when the boats come in, or at sundown when they prepare to leave.

Next to the port is the town beach—a vast expanse of fine clean sand—which is very safe because it is in a bay. During summer it becomes very crowded. It is backed by a seemingly endless complex of cafés, changing cabins, casinos, etc. In the season you are obliged to change in a cabin (and there are policemen who check that this rule is complied with). Behind the line of cafés is a promenade, behind this the railway line, then the road and then the hotels—tall white giants, impersonal and rather expensive. For more isolated bathing you can go W or E and still benefit from the calming influence of the bay. Out of the bay, however attractive and peaceful the beaches look, the Atlantic becomes a treacherous enemy with strong unpredictable currents, and undertows and rough breakers. Never swim off a deserted beach.

Behind the beach is modern Tangier, a white and flourishing city, with its many large hotels, wide, flower-lined boulevards, good shops and restaurants. A medium-priced hotel, a one-time palace set in romantic gardens, is the *Grand Hotel Villa de France*, with a swimming pool and within easy walking distance of the Grand Socco. It is a little faded now as the jet-set prefer to be nearer the sea, but it has a certain wistful charm and a quality of peace which can be highly desirable after the pressures of the medina or the sophistication of the beach restaurants.

Opposite the hotel is the Anglican Church of St. Andrew, also a haven of tranquillity and final resting place of Walter Harris, *Times* correspondent at the turn of the century and leading authority on pre-Protectorate Morocco. Here too is the grave of Sir John Drummond Hay, distinguished Consul General from 1845 to 1886. Just up the road (Rue d'Angleterre) is the old British Consulate General which was recently closed and now contains a Museum of Contemporary Art. An unusual museum of somewhat specialised interest is that of Military Miniatures, which contains the publisher Malcolm Forbes' collection of 100,000 toy soldiers. It is housed in the Palais Mendoub in Av. Shakespeare in the *Marshan* sector, a short distance along the coast road going W from the Kasbah. Alternatively, it can be reached by turning right up Av. Hassan II at the end of Rue d'Angleterre and keeping going as far as the coast road.

The centre of the modern town is the PLACE DE FRANCE; and Blvd Pasteur leading E into Blvd Mohammed V is the main street. But the most fashionable and sought-after residential quarter is slightly outside the centre and is known as 'the Mountain'. Here are elegant houses built to every kind of fantasy and design, well spaced out between masses of shrubs and beautiful gardens. The Mountain is in fact just a small hill with a superb sea view. Many Europeans retire here. Amongst the many sumptuous residences are the palace of King Hassan II and a newly created palace of King Fahd of Saudi Arabia, both heavily guarded and unapproachable.

A road winds to the top of the hill and then continues on 11km towards *Cap Spartel*, at the extreme north-westerly point of Africa. Known in Roman times as AMPELUSIUM or 'Cape of the Vines', Cap Spartel now has a fine lighthouse (entry prohibited) with an 80km beacon range. Some of the rocky coves a little further on are perhaps more beautiful and make better photographs than the grass-covered Cap, which is fast growing a layer of stalls selling assorted tourist trivia. A Spanish restaurant completes the picture. One kilometre further along the road are two fine sandy beaches and a somewhat livelier restaurant (Bar Sol). Another 4km brings you to the Caves of Hercules—a series of natural caves famous for the production of millstones which have been quarried there since prehistoric times. Despite the name, these caves have nothing to do with the mythical 'Pillars of Hercules': it is now commonly held that the two 'pillars' are the Rock of Gibraltar and Monte Hacho at Ceuta, although some identify Jbel Moussa as one of them, especially as it has a similar form to the Gibraltar Rock. It is possible to enter these caves—with a guide—to study the weird formations of stalactites and stalagmites and to gaze into the deep pools of black water far below. It is all rather eerie, and sometimes beautiful as you catch a glimpse of the raging sea through a jagged opening. There are men outside the caves chipping at hunks of stone and fashioning crude shapes of animals and birds for sale. Quite a little resort is growing up around the

Caves, with shops, hotels, apartments, a campsite and even a health farm.

A little further along the road a track goes off right towards the beach and the ruins of *Cotta*, a 3C Roman settlement built over a Phoenician fish salting factory. (It is 15 minutes' walk in all from the car park at the Caves.) Like so much of Morocco's earliest heritage, this site stands neglected, seriously overgrown and not signposted. Little boys will undoubtedly appear out of nowhere to indicate a temple arch (lying on the ground), a small courtyard, an olive press, fish storage tanks and a water course.

Continuing along the road and then turning left back to Tangier will have made a round trip of about 30km. Alternatively, Cap Spartel and the Caves can be visited as a short detour from the main road between Tangier and Rabat.

About 14km on the other side of Tangier lies *Cap Malabata*. This, too, makes a pleasant EXCURSION and the views are exceptional of the Rif mountains on the one side, of the Spanish coast and the rock of Gibraltar on the other, and back towards Tangier nestling in the bay. From the café out on the point, there are rough paths winding through the gorse that lead right down to the sea, which is here partly the Atlantic and partly the Mediterranean.

The main road (P2) leaves Tangier from the Place de France, passing turnings to both the international airport and the Cap Spartel coast road mentioned above.

After 46km you come to **Asilah** (16,000 inhab.), built on the foundations of the old Phoenician city of SILIS. Today it is a charming white town by the seashore. The old part is enclosed within 15C Portuguese-built walls with two fine gates: *Bab el Bahar* (Sea Gate) and *Bab el Jbel* (Mountain Gate). If you follow signs for *Centre Ville* you will come to *Bab el Bahar* where there is a convenient car park. Walk through the Bab and the path will follow the shore as far as the pier from which there is a good view back over the ramparts with, in the foreground, the ancient cemetery and koubba of a local saint, *Sidi Marzouk*. Before reaching the pier, you will pass on the left the *Palace of the Caid Ahmad ar Raisuni* (who was also known as Raisuli), built in 1908 and overlooking the sea. It has two storeys of richly decorated rooms built around a central courtyard. Raisuli was a legendary figure in his time. He was so powerful that the Spaniards, at the beginning of their Protectorate, deemed it wise to leave him alone and allowed him to retain his authority over the wild Berbers of the Western Rif, who without him would doubtless have become quite uncontrollable. He was a very cruel leader and allegedly forced malefactors to jump to their death from the windows of his palace on to jagged rocks 30m below. One of his victims is said to have cried: 'Your justice is great Sidi, but these rocks will be more merciful'. Raisuli was eventually taken prisoner by the much more progressive and less self-indulgent leader of the Rif Berbers, Abd el Krim, who for a time seemed to be succeeding in forcing the Spaniards back into the sea.

Now the Palace is used every August for an Arts Festival—music, painting and poetry. The murals which somewhat surprisingly decorate much of the Medina have been created in the past by grateful artists. The Medina (which stretches behind the Palace) is charming: small, clean and full of local activity; the *trompe l'œil* effect of doors and windows painted on blank white walls is an added bonus.

The beaches of Asilah are tempting, with immense stretches of sand as far as the eye can see, and there are numerous organised campsites.

16km S of Asilah a road branches off left to Tetouan. A short distance along this road is a left-hand turn signposted to *Souk el Tnine Sidi Yamani*.

Roman mosaic amidst Phoenician ruins, Lixus

This village (6km left and 3km left again) lies near the *Cromlech of M'Zorah*—a remarkable circle of prehistoric standing stones, one of which is over 6m tall. The rough track which leads there from the village is not all that easy to find, but local people are usually happy to take you there.

Back on the main road, the next sizeable town is Larache which lies at the mouth of the river Loukkos (41km from Asilah). After 36km you will come to a right-hand turn, signposted *Plage Ras R'mal*, which leads to the important archaeological site of **LIXUS**, one of the best preserved of the trading posts set up by the Phoenicians around 1100 BC along the coast of North Africa. Lixus (or *Liks* as it then was) developed a thriving fish-salting industry. The Carthaginians later refined the salting process and produced a fish paste known as garum. The Romans came in the 1C BC, chased the Carthaginians into the sea, and probably took over the factories, the remains of which can be seen today right by the road, comprising 147 storage vats and sundry wells and water cisterns. Below would have been the port (with the sea, in those days, coming right up to that part of the promontory).

The main evidence of Roman occupation lies up the hill, and it is well worth scrambling up the rough path to see it. (It takes about an hour to cover all the sites.) There are traces of Phoenician building—huge, very carefully cut rectangular stones—and the Roman remains include, notably, an amphitheatre and a bath with a well-preserved mosaic depicting a wild and glaring figure of Neptune. The *amphitheatre* (which is the only known example in Morocco) would have been used for gladiatorial contests either between man and man or between man and wild beast, probably including lions from the Middle Atlas. Above the amphitheatre is a confusion of walls and foundations which seem to include a forum (with stumps of columns), several temples, a single-naved Christian church and a mosque. A few solitary cypresses give the picture a romantic look but one is struck by the all too obvious neglect of this interesting site. Many of the artefacts have been taken to museums, in particular the Archaeological Museum in Tetouan, but there must be much more to discover. Lixus lies uncared for, except by a couple of devoted but very nearly incomprehensible 'guides' one of whom will certainly appear the moment you arrive. He will at least ensure that you leave nothing out.

Like Tangier, Lixus is also connected by legend to Hercules, for somewhere in this fertile region behind the site is thought to be the Garden of the Hesperides, to which the god was sent in search of the Golden Apples (tangerines?) as his penultimate labour.

Larache is a pleasant fishing town with strong Spanish overtones and a stormy history. Today it is an important port for tuna fish, but once it prospered from the construction of pirate ships for the infamous 'Sallée Rovers' (based in Rabat and Salé), using wood from the forest of Mamora to the south. The Spaniards occupied Larache for a time in the 17C, and they built the *Château des Cigognes* (castle of the storks) which so picturesquely dominates the town.

The Alouite sultan Moulay Ismael reclaimed the town in the early 18C and much of the small medina was built at that time, as was the kasbah which crowns the town on the seaward side. When the Spanish returned in 1912 it became an important port for the Protectorate and it was at this time that much of the Spanish character was added, including many hotels and bars, the cathedral and the main square: once Plaza de España, now Place de la Libération.

From Larache the road turns inland 36km to **Ksar el Kbir**, built on the foundations of the Roman OPPIDUM NOVUM by the the Almohade sultan Yacoub el Mansour in the 12C. He gave it its Arab name which means 'Great Fortress'. Both Spaniards and Portuguese coveted this town, and the famous Battle of the Three Kings took place here in 1578 in which the Portuguese suffered a major defeat. The town flourished proudly until, in the 17C, Sultan Moulay Ismael was annoyed by the local caid and sent his troops in to destroy the walls, a sad insult to a town which for centuries had held an honoured place in Morocco's history.

It never prospered again though the Spaniards injected fresh life during the Protectorate. Today it is an active market town living off the produce of the fertile agricultural land which surrounds it. The main street is always animated and full of heavily laden donkeys, of men arguing about prices, and of women moving stealthily, covered from head to foot in white robes, often with only one eye showing. The main Tangier–Rabat road used to pass through the centre of town, with predictable traffic chaos especially on Sunday, which is market day. Now a by-pass has been built but, if time permits, the town makes an interesting stopping place on the long journey between Tangier and Rabat.

9km out of Ksar el Kbir is the old frontier post which used to separate the two zones—French and Spanish—during the years of the Protectorate. It was only partially destroyed in 1956 when Independence was granted to Morocco and it stands as a depressing monument to those difficult days, surrounded by a posse of basketware and pottery stalls. It really should be completely removed or else disguised and turned into a roadside café.

Arbaoua, 12km S, is almost exactly half-way between Tangier and Rabat. The hotel-restaurant which stands a few kilometres up the hill to your right—*Hostellerie Route de France*—is pleasant, provides hearty, reasonably priced food and exudes a strong French hunting-lodge atmosphere with dark panelled dining-room and trophies all around. It has 13 rooms and there is also a campsite. A game reserve (34,804 hectares) has recently been created on land between Arbaoua and the sea, and about a third of it is available to tourists. There is wild boar, hare, pheasant and, above all, snipe; locals claim that this is some of the world's best snipe shooting.

W of Arbaoua, and accessible by simply continuing along the minor road past the Hostellerie, is the splendid sandy beach of *Moulay Bouselham* which lies next to a lagoon—Merja ez Zergha—cut off by a sandbank. The beach produces spectacular Atlantic breakers. This might be good for surfers, but serious swimmers will prefer the lagoon. Moulay Bouselham is a quiet, single-street village which comes to life every June and July for the annual pilgrimage. There is one small hotel (*La Lagune*), several fish restaurants and a new mosque in front of which are seven koubbas. There is also a campsite on the shore of the lagoon.

16km S of Arbaoua, continuing on the main road, is a left-hand turning (the P23) to Ouezzane (53km; see Rte 7). By now you are crossing the great Gharb Plain—one of the most fertile areas in the whole of Morocco, producing cereals, oranges, olives, rice and tobacco. *Souk el Arba du Gharb* (37km S of Ksar el Kbir) is a sprawling market town, particularly busy on Wednesdays when (as its name implies) it has its weekly souk. From here there is a left-hand turn to Meknes (107km; see Rte 8).

18km S of Souk el Arba the road begins to run alongside the Sebou river, and just after the small village of *Souk el Tleta du Gharb*—on the opposite bank of the river from the road—are the rather sparse ruins of the Roman settlement of BANASA, with traces of earlier Phoenician occupation.

The last major town before Rabat is **Kenitra** (180,000 inhab.). Developed and modernised by the French at the beginning of the Protectorate, and known then as Port Lyautey, it is now very much second in importance to Casablanca as a port. It is a noisy, rather untidy, industrial town with little of aesthetic or historical interest. Its main function is as an outlet for the produce of its hinterland—fruit, wine (from the Meknes region), vegetables

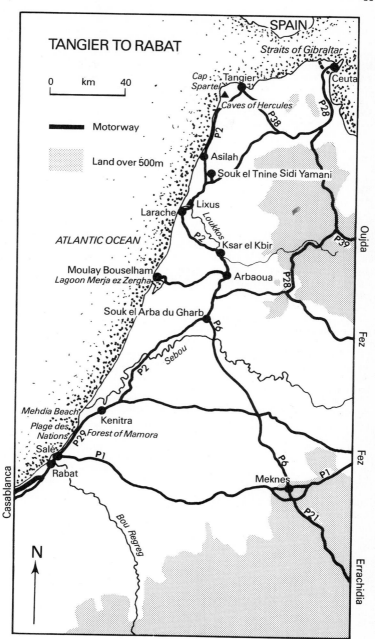

TANGIER TO RABAT

0   km   40

▬▬▬ Motorway

░░░ Land over 500m

SPAIN

Straits of Gibraltar

Ceuta

Cap Spartel

Tangier

Caves of Hercules

P28

P38

P2

Asilah

Souk el Tnine Sidi Yamani

Lixus

Larache

Loukkos

ATLANTIC OCEAN

Ksar el Kbir

P2

Oujda

P39

Moulay Bouselham
Lagoon Merja ez Zergha

Arbaoua

P28

Fez

Souk el Arba du Gharb

P6

Sebou

P2

Mehdia Beach

Plage des Nations

Kenitra

Forest of Mamora

P29

Salé

P1

Rabat

Casablanca

Bou Regreg

Meknes

P6

P1

Fez

P21

Errachidia

N

and cereals. It is served by *Mehdia Beach*, 7km away, which is not as attractive as Moulay Bouselham and does little for visitors. Mehdia was undoubtedly a Phoenician site originally and there are also vestiges of Roman occupation. It is now dominated by a crumbling 17C kasbah built by the Sultan Moulay Ismael to keep out Spanish and Portuguese invaders. The minor road from Kenitra to Mehdia continues past a lagoon—*Lac de Sidi Bourhaba*—and rejoins the main road after 11km.

En route you will pass right-hand turnings to 10km *Plage des Nations* and 5km *Les Jardins Exotiques* before going under a rather fine aqueduct to enter the town of Salé and, finally, Rabat (see Rte 2).

2   Rabat and Salé

RABAT (800,000 inhab.) is both an ancient Imperial city and a modern administrative capital, and manages to combine the trappings of both with remarkable success. It is the permanent residence of the monarch, the seat of government and home to over 80 foreign embassies. Its remarkable historic treasures, which are to be found both inside and outside the ancient ramparts, are well cared for, and from the visitor's point of view Rabat is small and easy to get around.

Information. Moroccan National Tourist Office: 22 Av. Al Jazair (also known as Av. d'Alger). Syndicat d'Initiative: Rue Patrice Lumumba.

Post Office. Av. Mohammed V.

Transport. Airport just outside Salé for domestic flights only. International flights from Mohammed V airport, Casablanca (6 airport buses daily from Hotel Terminus on Av. Mohammed V). Railway station: Av. Mohammed V. Trains to Tangier, Casablanca, Meknes, Fez, Marrakesh, Oujda. Bus station: Place Zerktouni (Casablanca road). Buses to Casablanca, Tangier, Meknes, Fez, Ifrane, Azrou, Kenitra.

Hotels. One 5-star L; two 5-star; two 4-star A; four 3-star A; two 3-star B; seven 2-star A; one 2-star B; five 1-star A; one 1-star B. (See page 93.)
   There are few notable restaurants within town except for those of the hotels themselves. Rabatis do not often eat out and most restaurants depend to a large extent on foreign residents and tourists for their trade. The same applies to night-life and by 22.00 hours the town is almost empty.

History. Rabat, the administrative capital of Morocco since 1912, was founded in the 12C when the first Almohade sultan, Abd el Mumene (1133–63), chose the left bank of the estuary of the Bou Regreg river (the site today known as the Oudaias) to build a large fortified camp (ribat), from where he could conduct his campaigns into Andalucia. His grandson, Yacoub el Mansour, later made the ribat his capital, extending it and erecting ramparts around it, some of which still exist, and the town became known as *Ribat el Fath* (camp of victory). But there had been a town here before, and archaeological discoveries indicate that the area had probably been occupied since prehistoric times. Certainly there is evidence of Phoenician occupation, probably dating from the 8C BC, on the site today known as Chellah.

In the 1C AD the Romans built a port here, which they called SALA COLONIA and which became one of the southernmost outposts of their empire in North Africa. Sala Colonia continued to function as a port even after the departure of the Romans.

In the 8C it was besieged and captured by Moulay Idriss I, but the Idrisside and Almoravide dynasties were to show little interest in Sala Colonia, and in 1154 it was abandoned. Subsequently, the inhabitants moved across the river to a better site and founded a new city which they called Salé. It was shortly after the mid 12C that the Almohades arrived and built their ribat at the mouth of the river.

In thankfulness for his splendid victory over the Spaniards at Alarcos in 1195, Yacoub el Mansour (el Mansour means 'the conqueror') started to build a mosque which was to have been of such vast dimensions that his whole army could pray inside it at one time. But he died before it was finished and today only stumps of the columns bear witness to the enormity of his dream. However, the minaret, known as 'le Tour Hassan' (the beautiful tower) remains a worthy and impressive monument to this great sultan. The minaret was not completed either, it lacks a top storey; but despite its rather squat appearance it has great charm and commands a superb view.

With the death of Yacoub el Mansour in 1199 the Almohade dynasty began to decline and Rabat dwindled in importance, particularly when the succeeding (Merinide) dynasty chose Fez as their capital (although they did build a necropolis and a zaouia alongside the original Roman site of Sala Colonia which they called *Chellah*).

Rabat and Salé became a haven for pirates who infested the northern waters for over three centuries, lying in wait for Christian ships and particularly Spanish and Portuguese men-of-war returning from the New World laden with gold and silver. Their adventures also provided Morocco with an almost unlimited supply of Christian slaves—a cruel irony (and satisfying revenge) at a time when Muslims were being driven out of Christian Spain.

At this time Rabat became second in importance to Salé: it even came to be known as Salé el Jdid (New Salé) to distinguish it from its more prosperous neighbour across the river. Many of the persecuted Muslims settled in Rabat and Salé (as they did in other northern towns). They brought new life to the towns and rebuilt much of Rabat's medina and Oudaias, replacing crumbling Almohade buildings with their own.

Rabat became the capital, for a short time, under the Alouite sultan Mohammed ben Abdallah in the second half of the 18C. It has been Morocco's capital city again since 1912, when the French Resident-General, Louis Lyautey, made it his administrative centre and built what is now known as *La Ville Moderne* alongside the old town.

The Kasbah of the Oudaias

The oldest part of Rabat—the point on the bank where Abd el Mumene first pitched his camp—is that which is known today as the *Kasbah of the Oudaias* (Oudaias was the name of one of the Arab tribes that invaded North Africa in the 11C). This is visible from the general area of the Hassan Tower as a promontory, a mass of flat-roofed houses and occasional

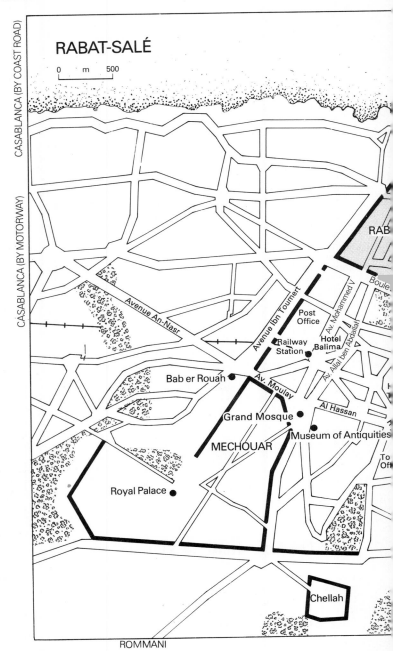

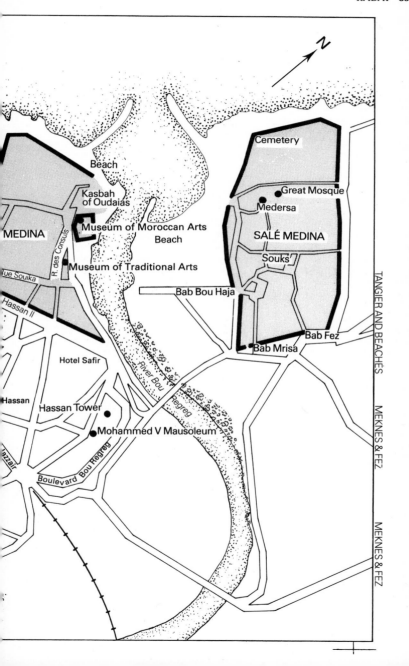

N

Beach

Kasbah
of Oudaias

MEDINA

Museum of Moroccan Arts
Beach

R. des Consuls

ue Soulka

Museum of Traditional Arts

Hassan II

Hotel Safir

Hassan

Hassan Tower

Mohammed V Mausoleum

azzal

River Bou Regreg

Boulevard Bou Regreg

Cemetery

Great Mosque

Medersa

SALÉ MEDINA

Souks

Bab Bou Haja

Bab Fez

Bab Mrisa

TANGIER AND BEACHES

MEKNES & FEZ

MEKNES & FEZ

minarets, held up out of the sea by massive ramparts. You enter it just before a monumental archway at the top of some steps; the arch is *Bab el Kasbah*, the work of Yacoub el Mansour in the 1190s. This is all that is left of the Almohade kasbah, the rest having been destroyed by the Alouite sultan Mohammed ben Abdallah in the late 18C.

Turn right and you find yourself on a straight, narrow street. Follow one of the alleyways on your left uphill and you are immediately in a different world, where little has changed for centuries—a world of white walls and deep blue shadows. The buildings are largely the work of Moriscos—Muslims forced to leave southern Spain by intolerant Catholic monarchs in the 15th and 16C—which accounts for the distinctly Andalucian appearance of the place. Today it is inhabited by some 3000 people, a few of whom are foreign artists or teachers who have chosen to immerse themselves in this uniquely evocative atmosphere.

Returning to the main street (Rue Djmaa), continue seawards until you come (after a 5-minute walk) to a wide jetty, high above the open sea, with an exhilarating view of Rabat and Salé to your right. There is a tiny carpet factory at the end of the jetty where very young girls with nimble fingers make carpets of modern or traditional design. You are welcome to look around and comments that these children should really be in school or at play are met with inscrutable smiles and assurances that they do have time for that too, although the children's tired eyes belie this. There is usually a good stock of carpets for sale, but the medina is a better place to find an old Moroccan carpet.

If you go back along the Rue Djmaa and take the last turning left (before the great archway), down a winding alley, you reach an open-air Moorish café looking out over the estuary. Painted a soft blue and decorated with colourful mosaics, it provides a delightful setting for mint tea and pastries stuffed with almonds and honey. From the far side of the café you can look back up at the vertical cliff into which houses of all shapes have been wedged.

Continuing your tour of the Oudaias, leave the café through a small archway and you will find yourself in a walled garden of great peace and enchantment, with paths that wander through beds of hibiscus, roses, lilies, poinsettias and plumbago. Rabatis love to come here to walk and meditate, watched by the storks who build their nests on top of the walls. The storks spend spring and early summer in Morocco and are generally regarded with much affection. Their untidy nests can frequently be seen crowning minarets in the city.

On the opposite side from the café, withdrawn into the niches in the wall, are old men working in wrought iron, tooling in leather, painting intricate designs on wood or shaping mysterious musical instruments. Behind them, in rooms set in the wall, is an exhibition of traditional costumes and pottery. Just outside the gardens, through the exit and to the right, is a small *Museum* which occupies a 17C residence. This was one of the many palaces that Moulay Ismael built in Rabat. Although he created Meknes as his capital, Moulay Ismael kept a garrison in the kasbah of Rabat in order to exact tribute from the pirates whose infamous trading he publicly condemned but privately espoused for his own ends; for example his palaces in Meknes were almost exclusively built by Christian slaves brought in by pirates. The museum contains rugs, musical instruments and jewellery; there is also an elegant reception room laid out just as it would have been in the 17C.

A second museum, the *Maison de l'artisanat* occupies a converted cus-

Entrance to the Kasbah of the Oudaias

toms house a few metres on the right of the road which forks left as you look down from the Oudaias entrance. The entrance to the museum is down some steps on the right. The exhibition proves the richness of Morocco's folk art, past and present. Here are carpets, leather-work, pottery, jewellery and embroidery.

Return to the Almohade gate, through which you left the Oudaias gardens, and you will find yourself looking down towards the **Medina**, still within its original ramparts. This maze of narrow winding streets and whitewashed houses was also created largely by Muslims returning from Spain. It, too, has a distinctly Mediterranean atmosphere: its small buildings, tightly packed together, with few windows but sometimes offering tantalising glimpses of flower-filled patios within. This delightful place is dotted with mosques and fountains, and is so small that the visitor can wander round without fear of getting lost.

The commercial area of the medina is more lively than the residential part, and the best street for shopping is the Rue des Consuls. It is so called because in the days before New Rabat was built by the French it was the diplomatic quarter. Now it contains the best shops. They often appear dark and dingy inside but contain a vast collection of old carpets, pottery, brass, copper and silverware, every kind of antique jewellery, jewelled daggers, dress materials and ready-made kaftans. There is much less pressure to buy here than in the popular tourist areas of Fez and Marrakesh. Notice particularly the fondouks, ancient courtyards which once provided overnight lodging for merchants and their livestock and are now often used by groups of artisans: some are full of cobblers, others of carpenters, others of goldsmiths; some are simply in use as food markets decorated with brightly coloured mounds of spices or olives or dates. The smells are wonderful.

This is as good a place as any to learn the skills of bargaining. If you are interested in something, ask the price and then offer a good deal less than you expect the merchant to accept, for he will have asked you for a much more than he expects you to pay. You will compromise at some intermediate sum. It is a ritual which Moroccans expect and enjoy. They are apt to look quite disappointed if some unwitting tourist offers the full asking price straightaway. If you are seriously looking for an old Rabat carpet (the most beautiful and most sought after of all Moroccan carpets) you should accept the invitation to sit down—on a pile of rugs—and talk of anything and everything except the one subject which interests you most: you will probably be offered a glass of mint tea which you must certainly accept; crumpled photographs of relatives studying in Europe may be produced. Only after these courteous preliminaries will the merchant seriously begin showing you carpets. You may not be impressed at first but, as time goes on, they will become older, rarer, more soft and delicate in colour. The carpet-seller will be enjoying the whole process and savouring your growing appreciation, and he will not be too unhappy if, after an hour or so spent in this delightful way, you thank him and gracefully withdraw without buying anything at all. For a more speedy but less rewarding method of acquiring a carpet, there is a carpet auction once a week in the Rue des Consuls. There is always a surprising variety of carpets which are thrown down and unrolled on the street with amazing skill and speed, sold and whisked away almost before you have time to draw breath. It is amusing to watch but you are unlikely to find any real treasures this way.

If, towards the end of the Rue des Consuls (going SE from the kasbah), you turn right down the Rue Souk Sebbat, you will find hundreds of tiny shops specialising in modern wares and artisanat, particularly leather goods. The prices are lower here and so, usually, is the quality. This street becomes the Rue Souika, with more utilitarian goods and fewer handicrafts for sale. Also on this street is the **Great Mosque**, which dates from the Merenide period but has been many times rebuilt. Beyond the mosque, down Rue Souk Semmara, a sizeable area which was once the Flea Market is now being completely redeveloped. You emerge past this on to one of Modern Rabat's principal squares—*Bab el Had*, with the Central Food Market on the Medina side of it. The market is worth a look for its magnificently displayed meat, fish, vegetables and fruit. There are piles of luscious peaches, apricots and melons in early summer and different kinds of grapes later on; as well as globe artichokes, aubergines, and red and green peppers. It all seems ridiculously cheap, and, because the climate over the vast area of Morocco is so varied, the seasons are long.

One of the most distinctive landmarks in Rabat is the **Hassan Tower**, which is 15 minutes' walk (or a short bus ride) along the outside of the Medina ramparts down the broad, animated Boulevard Hassan II. The Tower is almost all that remains of the mosque started by Sultan Yacoub el Mansour in 1194 but never finished. Not only time but also the Lisbon earthquake of 1755 has exacerbated the deterioration of the surrounding mosque walls (a few uneven chunks remain to mark the perimeter, now wisely protected by a modern wall). There are some 350 stone column stumps surviving, sadly bearing witness to what might have been the greatest mosque in the world, but which has ended up a roofless space. The site forms a rectangle of 180m by 140m, and the mosque, with 21 aisles, is believed to have had 14 entrances. The tower of warm red stone stands 44m high, but it should have been as high as 80m, roughly the height of the Koutoubia minaret in Marrakesh, which it closely resembles but which it is considered to exceed in fineness of detail. Each of the four sides of the minaret is decorated differently. Certainly the delicate almost lace-like tracery over the windows is comparable with and possibly finer than the Giralda in Seville, which was completed by Yacoub el Mansour to celebrate his successful campaigns in Andalucia. Inside the tower are six storeys, each comprising one room with a domed ceiling, and these are all joined by a wide ramp by which the sultan had planned to reach the top and address his people without getting off his horse. Until recently visitors were allowed to walk up the ramp to the top of the tower for an inspiring view of both Rabat and Salé, but the passage of so many feet was found to be causing damage to the 800-year-old structure, and it is now permanently closed.

At the opposite end of the mosque site (and actually occupying a portion of it) is a great complex of gleaming white buildings. In front, nearest the road and approached by a flight of steps, is the *Mausoleum* (begun 1961) which King Hassan II had erected in memory of his father, Mohammed V. No expense has been spared in the creation of this unique edifice which took over 10 years to build by more than 200 of Morocco's finest craftmen (mainly from Fez) using traditional techniques. Surprisingly, this sacred monument, which is a fine example cf modern Alouite style, was designed by a Vietnamese architect living in Paris. Fortunately for posterity, everyone, Muslim and non-Muslim alike, may enter (and take photographs) and gaze down at the white onyx tomb of Mohammed V, splendid on its floor of Portuguese black marble, which is polished so hard that it looks like some unfathomable black lake. In one corner is the slightly smaller tomb of the present king's brother, Prince Moulay Abdallah, who died in 1972. Nearby sits an imam reading the Koran aloud.

Notice the superbly carved dome (in mahogany which resists Rabat's humid climate better than cedarwood), the stucco-work of incredible delicacy and the minutely executed mosaics. The colours and designs of the mosaics are typical of Moroccan art; almost 20,000 pieces of burned and glazed clay were needed to produce 1 sq m, with a total area of over 1000 sq m. Notice too the bronze lamp which was made in Fez. It weighs 1500kg and has some 400 bulbs. The bronze doors were also made by Fez cra.tsmen.

Some people dislike the fact that any modern building (albeit a royal mausoleum) should be erected on the site of Rabat's oldest and most sacred historic monument. Others consider that the two monuments belong together—the one in memory of the Almohades who built Rabat and made Morocco great in the 12C, and the other in memory of the Alouite king, Mohammed V, who regained Morocco's independence and greatness some 800 years later. Behind the mausoleum is the *mosque*, which non-Muslims may not enter, though it is possible to peer through the grille. This building is of ochre coloured stone and forms a quiet contrast with the ornate mausoleum. Adjoining it is a *library* which is sometimes open to visitors. At intervals around the whole complex are royal horse guards splendidly arrayed in white robes. The sand boxes in which their mounts are allowed to stand are a surprisingly gentle touch.

Merenide minaret with storks, Chellah, Rabat

Chellah

If you follow the Bou Regreg estuary a little further upstream (via Place de Sidi Maklouf) you will notice, on your left, up the hillside from the river, some of the old, turretted, red walls of the Merinide period, which end with a magnificent gateway flanked by two octagonal towers. This is **Chellah**. The gate is open, and you leave your car outside the wall and walk in (for a fee of 10 dirhams). At first sight it appears to be just a peaceful, rather untidy garden, full of orange and lemon trees, bougainvillias and prickly pears. But here are also the remains of two civilisations: Roman and Merinide. On the Roman site there are traces of even earlier settlement by the Phoenicians, which probably dates back to the 8C BC.

Here was the busy Roman river port of SALA COLONIA. In the 1C and 2C AD it would have exported oil, cereals, wine, pottery and wool to Rome. Much of the port installation today lies buried in the silt of the river but above it are the remains of a *forum*, with a triumphal arch at one end, and traces of a flagstoned main street (Decumanus Maximus), with an arcaded wall on one side which may have been a row of shops. The arch was built in the style of the Emperor Trajan and is thought to have been 3.35m high and 4.30m wide; it was probably flanked by two smaller side arches. The residential area was higher up the hill, to which the remains of small houses and one or two oil presses testify. Sala Colonia appears to have been built in a series of terraces. It was essentially a working port with little in the way of luxury or entertainment. Only one rather poor mosaic (still in situ below the main street) has been found, and no traces of noble houses or of an amphitheatre. (The only remains of an amphitheatre in Morocco are at Lixus, near Larache; see Rte 1.) There is, however, a round and quite well-preserved *nymphaeum* and a *thermal bath system* with typical Roman hypocaust still in place. The spring that supplied the Roman baths was used later by the Merinides who placed their baths actually on top of the Roman system, damaging much of it in the process.

The port was abandoned in the mid 12C and the site suffered as stone was gradually removed for incorporation into local buildings: indeed the two small white columns to be seen in the great Merinide gate (see below) are undoubtedly Roman. It was further damaged by the Lisbon earthquake of 1755.

Sala Colonia was rediscovered by the French in 1930. Intensive excavations began in 1960, under the auspices of the Ministry of Cultural Affairs, and many of the treasures, including fragments of sculpture, were removed to the Museum of Antiquities in Rue el Brihi, Rabat. It is possible that there is much more to be found lower down beneath the river silt, but excavation appears now to have stopped. The site is seriously overgrown and fenced off. The public is not admitted, though there are good views to be had through the wire fence as you proceed, downwards, through Chellah gardens.

In the 14C a Merinide sultan, Abou Said (1310–31), decided to build a small fortress alongside the Roman site, which he enclosed with massive walls, that still survive today, though severely cracked in places. The *gateway* is truly magnificent and far more intricately decorated than the earlier Almohade gate of the Oudaias. The two great towers either side frame it to perfection. A distinctive feature here is the intricate stalactitic carving which rises out of the octagonal bastions to form bases for the square turreted top sections. He later built within the ramparts a necropolis for the remains of his royal descendants. His son, Abou el Hassan (1331–51), built a mosque and a zaouia to which holy men came and spent their days contemplating the Koran and living off the surrounding land. Today all that remains of the mosque are some arches and the lovely minaret with coloured faïence still intact. The walls and arches of the zaouia survive, showing the main hall with central basin and the tiny cells where the holy men lived. At the end of the hall was the oratory, and it is still possible to recognise the mihrab at the end where the imam would have stood facing Mecca to lead the prayers. Below the mosque and the zaouia are several royal tombs (all aligned to face Mecca); the largest and most centrally placed, and contained in a kind of pavilion, is that of Abou el Hassan himself. A small distance away, outside the pavilion, lies the tombstone of his favourite concubine and mother of Abou Inan, Shams ed Doura (Morning Sun), who was a convert from Christianity. It is covered in verses from the Koran.

The whole area has now been taken over by families of storks and by fig trees which manage to grow through the walls. Below is a rectangular garden, somewhat better tended than the wilderness above and with hordes of butterflies playing amongst the hollyhocks. There is a real sense of remoteness here, with only the storks for company: below stretches the estuary and above is the wall of the pavilion-mausoleum, beautifully decorated on this side.

Also remaining from Merinide times are seven *marabouts*, and below them, on the right, is a deep pool of clear water fed by a spring which was used by the Merinides for their religious ablutions and is believed to date back to Phoenician times (though it was the Romans who built the bath). In those days it was undoubtedly a hot spring. The earthquake is blamed for the fact that it now runs cold. Beside the pool sits an old man with a large dish of hard-boiled eggs. Families of well-nourished cats sit at his feet. Peer into the depths of the water and you may just discern the dark shapes of eels. What does it all mean? Moroccan women believe that the magical quality of the water on their skins will prevent sterility. The eels add to the magic. Buy an egg from the old man and throw the white into the water. A dark, writhing shape will slowly emerge from the black depths and swallow it. Throw the shells in too, for they help keep the water clear. Throw the yolks to the cats. Everybody is well satisfied including the old man who will tell you that the eels come from the Saragossa Sea by way of the estuary below. It is theoretically possible. The eels certainly come and go; for months there may be none at all; then one day they are back.

Modern Rabat

Modern Rabat is an efficient, white and airy city which turns its back to the sea. The old city regained some of its former importance when the later Alouite sultans, particularly Mohammed V, made it their imperial residence, but it was General Lyautey, arriving in 1912 at the beginning of the French Protectorate, who made Rabat the administrative capital and planned and built the broad avenues and luxurious residences that we see today. Being a man of imagination and sensitivity, he respected Islam and the traditions of the country in which he found himself. Consequently nothing was destroyed. White office buildings appeared alongside ancient mosques and gateways, and openings were made through the Almohade walls for modern highways to pass. The best example of this is the triple arch through which you enter the city on the main road from Casablanca. Alongside it is the second of Rabat's Almohade monumental gates—*Bab er Rouah*, meaning 'gate of the winds'. Even more solid than the Oudaias gate, it was part of the original defence system and is more of a gatehouse, with four chambers inside, now sometimes devoted to exhibitions of art.

The focal point of modern Rabat is the *Mechouar*, the royal enclosure, containing the Royal Palace, the Royal Mosque, the Prime Minister's office and many other important buildings. Anyone can drive into the Mechouar and there are two entrances: one is opposite Chellah but a little further up the main road and on the other side of it; the other goes off the Av. Moulay Hassan in the centre of town. If you enter from the Chellah end, the palace will be on your left. You will be told where you may park (usually alongside the Grand Mosque) and a guide will appear to show you round on foot. Obviously no one is allowed inside the palace itself, but a walk in front of the buildings is rewarding and provides a good opportunity to study the splendour of modern Moroccan decorative architecture. It was in fact built in the 18C but has been fully restored by the present king.

This is a 'working palace' and the Royal Cabinet Office stands behind the three arches, to the right of the residential section. (This is one of three royal residences in Rabat, the others being on the beach at Skhirate and at Dar es Salaam, 10km out of town on the Rommani road.) To the right of the Cabinet Office is the Prime Minister's Office; on the left of the palace are the Royal Library, a necropolis of the Alouite dynasty and sundry offices. On the far left is a wonderful door behind which is the Throne Room where foreign ambassadors go to present their credentials to the king on arrival. Notice, incidentally, the shell motifs above the door symbolising Santiago de Compostela and six centuries of Arab occupation of Spain.

Perhaps one of the most striking and colourful aspects of this great open space dotted with palaces and fountains is the Royal Guard. Noble of bearing and clad in traditional scarlet uniforms, they are known by the Moroccans as 'Sudanese' which simply means 'black'—their forebears came from S of the Sahara. Moulay Ismael was the first Alouite sultan to surround himself with 'Sudanese' guards in his capital city of Meknes, in the late 17C, and the custom has survived to this day in Rabat, though the role of the Guard is now purely ceremonial. Four times a year there is a splendid spectacle in the Mechouar when the King emerges from the Royal Mosque dressed all in white and riding a fine grey, flanked by his colourful Guard.

Modern Rabat is crossed by a network of fine wide boulevards, the most important from the visitors' point of view being Av. Mohammed V, and the Rue Allal ben Abdallah which runs parallel to it (N of the royal palace and the Grand Mosque). In these two streets and in the little roads which join them are to be found the most interesting shops, restaurants and cafés. In this general area too is the **Museum of Antiquities** which is well worth a visit, especially if you have already seen some of Morocco's Roman and prehistoric sites. Like all Moroccan museums this one seems not to want to be found: it hides behind a glass door marked '*Service des Antiquités*' in the Rue el Brihi, which is a turning off the Av. Moulay Hassan. Within are many treasures of prehistoric and Roman times, and many of the smaller items and fragments of sculpture found at Sala Colonia, Lixus and Volubilis have been brought here. There is a good collection of Roman jewellery, oil lamps, cooking utensils, bronze figures, gravestones, millstones, bits of central heating pipe, etc., all of which adds up to a fairly complete picture of how the citizens of Mauritania Tingitana lived. The items are well displayed and labelled. You should ask to see the famous *Volubilis bronze dog* (a wonderfully life-like piece) and the sculpted marble heads of *Juba II* and *Cato*, which are sometimes kept in a locked room. These are the real treasures of the collection. In the little garden alongside the museum are fragments of marble statues, columns, altars, etc.

Hotels. Rabat has three 5-star hotels one of which—the *Hilton*—is in the Luxe category. Located in the leafy suburb of Souissi, it has excellent meeting rooms as well as ballrooms and every kind of sports facility, and is much used by visiting delegations and high-level conferences. The other two—*Fara Sofitel* and *Tour Hassan*—are both in the town centre. The former, on Place Sidi Makhlouf and close to the Hassan Tower, has a roof-top swimming pool and a high standard of service to match the somewhat ostentatious decor. The Tour Hassan is older and more traditionally Moorish in style, with its main reception rooms built around a large flower-decked patio; it is 5 minutes' walk from the Museum of Antiquities. All three have expensive but good Moroccan restaurants. A more modest hotel, which is full of character and memories of the French Protectorate years, is the 3-star B *Balima* which has a lively terrace restaurant and stands on Av. Mohammed V.

Beaches. Between May and October Rabat's beaches come to life but it is really necessary to drive a little way out to reach the best ones. The town beach (beneath the Oudaias gardens) tends to be dirty and over-crowded. The most frequented and relatively safe ones lie off the Casablanca road and are described in Rte 3. The most spectacular by far is the *Plage des Nations* about 12km N, off the Tangier road. The view from above is unforgettable—virgin sand and Atlantic rollers as far as you can see; this is not just a beach but a whole coastline. It is a refreshing experience to walk along the sand in the cool season. In the high summer it is dotted with sunbathers and bright umbrellas. But beware: swimming is only for strong swimmers. There are treacherous undercurrents here and all along the Atlantic coast, except in protected bays such as Agadir. Serious swimming becomes more possible, though still fairly dangerous, from the beaches on the Casablanca side.

The *Exotic Gardens* make an unsual EXCURSION. They are between Rabat town and Plage des Nations, and are signposted '*Visitez les jardins exotiques*' on the Tangier road (open from 09.00 to 18.30 every day, admission 10 dirhams). An enterprising Frenchman after striking water here decided to produce an area of lakes, tropical plants in profusion, palm trees and bamboos. There are paths, wooden huts on stilts above the water, and swinging bridges at tree-branch level. There is much of botanical interest and the gardens have been laid out with imagination and taste. Every space is miraculously filled to overflow with lush green growth—a satisfying contrast with the bare dry landscape facing the Tangier road.

SALÉ is Rabat's sister town and is accessible by modern bridge over the Bou Regreg river (2km).

History. The history of Salé is inextricably mixed up with that of Rabat: it was founded by the inhabitants of Sala Colonia (now Chellah) who in 1154 abandoned their original home and moved across the river to what they considered to be a better site; by the 13C, with the arrival of the Almohade dynasty, Salé had become a thriving port and a place of greater economic importance than Rabat.

Salé's prosperity in medieval times was based on the export of goods from all over the country, including skins, fabrics, carpets and spices, and ships bearing English, Italian and Flemish merchants came into the port to receive the goods. The Merinide dynasty showed little interest in either Rabat or Salé and this provided pirates with the opportunity to plague the area. They menaced the Spanish and French coasts, sometimes reaching as far as England, until well into the 19C. (Known as the 'Sallée Rovers', stories of their exploits have appeared in many adventure books since.)

The town was further enriched (like Rabat) by the arrival of hundreds of Muslims fleeing from Andalucia in the 14th and 15C, and much of Salé's medina was built at this time.

With the rebirth of Rabat at the time of the French Protectorate, Salé sank into relative obscurity, and is now a peaceful and modest town, a maze of winding streets and picturesque houses (General Lyautey did not build his wide boulevards here).

The Almohade ramparts are pierced by several gates, the oldest of which is **Bab Mrisa**. Its name means 'harbour' and it spans a now silted-up canal along which merchant ships used to pass from the Bou Regreg estuary right into the centre of town. Essentially Almohade in the simplicity of its design, it is thought to have been built by the first Merinides in the late 13C. Incredibly high, to allow tall ships to pass, it stands to the left of the road which crosses the bridge from Rabat, a few metres to the S of the much later *Bab Fez*.

Bab Fez leads straight into the busy and colourful souks: Souk el Ghezel (wool market); Souk el Kbir (a large square with covered market in the centre); and the workshops of leather-workers making babouches, and carpenters making table-tops from cedarwood. There are spice markets, second-hand clothes markets and whole sections selling nothing but kaftans. It is all deliciously mixed up and often cheaper than equivalent merchandise in Rabat.

From the souks it is a short walk W along the inside of the town ramparts to the koubba of Salé's patron saint—Sidi Abdallah ben Hassoun (16C)—which stands by the road protected inside a building but visible through the windows. The origins of his sainthood are unclear, but he is thought to have protected sailors from pirates: when the annual moussem takes place, on the eve of Mouloud (the Prophet's birthday), local people dress up as sailors and pirates and process through the streets carrying huge multi-coloured wax candles which are preserved from one year to the next and can be seen next to the koubba. Further on, by the sea, is the very old cemetery which contains the hallowed white koubba of the 14C Andalucian saint, Sidi Benachir. The koubba is still visited by pilgrims and supplicants at certain times of the year. Surrounding it are the remains of what are thought to have been pilgrims' lodging houses.

Across the road from the cemetery is a very beautiful **medersa**, founded in 1341 by the Merinide sultan, Abou Hassan (whose tomb lies in the Chellah necropolis) and recently restored. It has a small pillared courtyard with some strikingly delicate off-white stucco-work, and dark painted cedarwood ceilings. A guide will take you up the staircase to the terrace, off which lie the tiny cells which served as students' rooms. There is a fine view of the whole of Salé. The buildings are predominantly blue and white, and Andalucian in style (compare Chaouen in the Rif which was also built by Andalucian refugees; see Rte 5).

Opposite the medersa is the **Great Mosque**, which is one of the earliest in Morocco and was founded by the Almohades in the 13C but has many later additions, including the minaret. Sadly the non-Muslim can do no more than admire the outside.

Salé is rightly proud of its pottery, which is less ornate and lighter in design than that of Fez, Meknes or Safi. Many potteries are to be found by the roadside between Rabat and Salé near the river, and anyone is welcome to wander in and see what is on display.

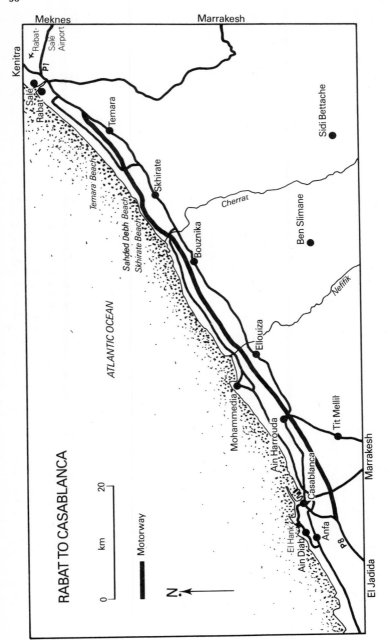

RABAT TO CASABLANCA

3   Rabat to Casablanca

Total distance 93km. **Rabat**—16km *Temara*—10km *Skhirate*—39km
Mohammedia—28km **Casablanca**.

Railway: frequent inter-city service, takes one hour.

There is a choice of three routes to cover the 93km between Rabat and
Casablanca: you can go all the way by the original P1 road which leaves
Rabat by way of *Bab Rouah*; or you can take the coast road which turns
right off the P1 on the outskirts of town and rejoins the main road
occasionally thereafter. The third and most recently constructed route
is to turn right after 16km on to the new motorway.

For those who want to cover this flat and rather uninteresting stretch of
countryside quickly the motorway is the obvious answer. A more leisurely
alternative is the old coastal road which offers fine sea views and gives
access to the many beaches. It passes first through Rabat's least attractive
quarter where poor quality housing grows unchecked and tall blank walls
hide a shameful area of shanty town. The first beach is that of *Temara* (16km
from Rabat)—very crowded by day and humming by night with bars and
discos and all the activity which Rabat is accused of lacking. It has two
hotels and a campsite. *Sehd ed Debh* (formerly Ech Chiana), c 10km further
on, is smaller, but also now rapidly filling up with a variety of urban delights;
and *Skhirate* (almost next door) is a beautiful beach, well equipped with
all facilities, including a good hotel (*Amfitrite*) and some first-class fish
restaurants. It probably owes its distinctly up-market atmosphere to the fact
that the King has his summer palace here (site of the notorious attempted
coup by army officers in the summer of 1971 during his birthday celebrations). There are smaller and no less attractive beaches all along the coast,
offering at the very least a row of changing cabins. You can fish, either from
a boat or simply by standing on rocky promontories which often jut far out
into the sea. The most simple fishing techniques seem to produce results
because quite small boys will be standing on the roadside offering their
catch of loup de mer, crabs and other delicacies for sale.

The biggest and most famous beach is at **Mohammedia** (55,000 inhab.)
which is connected to Casablanca by all three roads (c 28km). Its 5km of
sand are supposed to be second to none in the northern half of Morocco
and conditions for sailing and fishing are some of the best on the Atlantic
coast. Mohammedia is also famous for its 18-hole golf course which once
ranked as the best in North Africa but is now generally considered as
second to the Royal Golf Course at Rabat. There is also a race course, a
thriving casino, a yacht club, and a 5-star hotel: the *Meridien-Miramar*
(there is also a 4-star A hotel: the *Samir*). The town has several important
industries including a large oil refinery with its own port specially constructed to receive shipments of crude oil. It is also a fishing port.
International playground and industrial complex co-exist quite happily,
neither seeming to encroach on the other's space.

If you stay on the P1 road all the way from Rabat you will pass through the town of
Temara (2km inland from Temara beach) with its crenellated *kasbah* now being used
as a stud farm. The only town of any size on the road is *Bouznika* (41km from Rabat).
After this the road passes through a forested region and descends to cross the river
Nefifik. On the left a short tourist circuit has been marked out through the forest, which
makes a welcome escape from what is usually a heavily charged road. There is a right
fork at *Ellouiza* (63km) which leads to Mohammedia (see above).

It is worth noting that at *Ain Harrouda* (just after Ellouiza) there is a left-hand turn signposted *Tit Mellil*, which is in fact the quickest route to Marrakesh avoiding the rather badly signposted route through the back streets of Casablanca.

CASABLANCA (3,500,000 inhab.) is Morocco's largest and fastest-growing city. It is the economic capital of Morocco, with well over half the country's industry on its outskirts, and it has the busiest port. Rich, efficient, and streamlined, with a main street of impressive skyscrapers which could belong anywhere in the world, it is the town which most closely relates Morocco to the 20C. It is not exciting or exotic, or even typically Moroccan, and yet the tourists stream in, attracted no doubt by the well-stocked shops, by the reputation for a lively night-life, and perhaps by the name itself which to many spells adventure and romance.

Life is sophisticated in Casablanca and rather expensive. Do not expect to find much of historical or aesthetic interest here, or a medina which can compare with that of Fez, Marrakesh, or even Rabat. It is the centre of banking and commerce. It has been growing rapidly, in a rather disorganised way, for about the last 30 years, and now buildings of the most modern design stand beside quarters which in their new settings look out of date and decidedly tatty. Avenues of palms display stately residences and, not too far away, high walls hide who knows what squalor. Hotels tend to spring up wherever there is any empty space.

Information. Moroccan National Tourist Office: 55 Rue Omar Slaoui. Syndicat d'Initiative: 98 Blvd Mohammed V.

Post Office. Av. de l'Armée.

Transport. Air terminal: 23 Rue Leon l'Africain. International airport Mohammed V; 28km SW of the city. Railway station: Gare du Port (in the harbour); Gare du Voyageurs, Blvd Ba Hmad (E of the city). There are frequent inter-city trains between Rabat and Casablanca (one hour); and services to Tangier, Meknes, Fez, Oujda and Marrakesh. Bus station: 23 Rue Leon l'Africain. Buses to all destinations.

Hotels. (Full list from Tourist Office.) One 5-star luxe, five 5-star, six 4-star A, eight 4-star B, six 3-star A, two 3-star B, seven 2-star A, four 2-star B, eight 1-star A, one 1-star B.

History. The origins of Casablanca are in *Anfa*, now a very desirable suburb to the W of the city, where the rich and famous have their villas. Anfa was already a significant Berber settlement when the Arabs arrived in 683. The Phoenicians had settled here previously, and it is likely that the beginnings of Anfa are prehistoric.

During the reconquest of the Iberian Peninsula by the Catholics in the 13C and 14C, when the Moorish invaders of Spain returned to Africa, Anfa became a haven for pirates intent on attacking and plundering the heavily-laden Spanish and Portuguese vessels.

At the beginning of the 16C the Portuguese attacked the town several times and finally drove out the pirates. They occupied the town and renamed it Casa Branca (white house). They stayed just over 200 years, until the Lisbon earthquake of 1755 damaged it so severely that they abandoned it. The Alouite sultan Mohammed ben Abdallah (1757–90) arrived soon after, repaired the town, repopulated it, and named it Dar el Beida (Arabic for white house). It was then that the various mosques and most of the houses of the medina were built. The town became Casa Blanca when the Spaniards obtained special port privileges soon after.

This distinctly un-Moroccan and un-Islamic city was transformed into a modern metropolis by the French Resident-General, General Lyautey, at the beginning of the 20C. Today it is known by the international set quite simply as *Casa*.

The **Port**, as picturesque as anything Casa is likely to offer, is fascinating to explore: its great jetties reaching out to welcome ships, which come in from all over the world, and embracing some 117 hectares of still water, give credence to its claim to be the first port of Africa. It is most directly reached by staying on the coast road from Mohammedia. This route does however have the disadvantage of bringing you through a morass of heavy industry and chemical factories all belching fumes into the thickly polluted air.

The **Old Medina** is a few minutes' walk away, and, if you want to make sure of not getting lost, you can walk down either the palm-lined Blvd el Hansali or the Blvd Tahar el Aloui (which follows the medina wall and ends up at the Place Mohammed V), making frequent entries through gaps in the wall as you go. It is not as lively as the medinas of Fez and Marrakesh but it does provide a striking contrast with the ultra modern city close by and to which it is joined by the impressive PLACE MOHAMMED V. In this square stand glossy skyscrapers and some of Casa's classiest hotels; it is the business centre from which radiate the main thoroughfares of the city, lined with exclusive shops and expensive restaurants.

Blvd Mohammed V is a broad and dignified thoroughfare, lined with neo-classical façades which would look equally at home in Paris. A little way down from the Place, is the *Central Market*, which is colourful and surprisingly clean and orderly. The main entrance is lined on both sides with flower stalls, offering a glorious array of roses and birds-of-paradise, etc. Inside the market are vegetable, fruit, fish, meat and grocery stalls where the author would be quite happy to shop every day. A nice touch is the minced meat meticulously laid out in straight lines, all ready to be made into kefta (a type of spicy meatball). The fish department makes any European fishmonger seem dull by comparison; the live turtles caught our eye: '*Pour le jardin,*' said the lady hurriedly, hearing our English voices, '*pas pour manger*'. I was not convinced.

Not far from Place Mohammed V, along Av. Hassan II leading S, is the even more prestigious PLACE DES NATIONS UNIES. Spacious, and graced with a huge fountain which becomes multi-coloured at night, it is something of a magnet for tourists and Casablancais alike, with its water, pigeons, music and general excitement. Standing back, quite modestly, in one tree-filled corner is the French Consulate, in front of which is the fine bronze equestrian statue of General Lyautey. Dominating the square are the Law Courts, and the Town Hall, with its tall thin tower up which one may climb for a splendid view.

Visible from the square, down a side street on the opposite side from the Town Hall, is the old Catholic *Cathedral of Sacre Coeur*, built by the French in 1930. It is remarkable not only for its modern unconventional design but also for its prominence (as a place originally of Catholic worship) in the very centre of Morocco's economic capital. It is now used as a school. South of the Cathedral is the pleasant wooded square known as *Parc de la ligne Arabe* which extends as far as Blvd Mohammed Zerktouni. A short distance eastwards along this road stands a second Catholic church—that of *Notre Dame des Lourdes*, containing tapestries illustrating the appearance of Our Lady in Lourdes. It was completed in 1956.

Continue eastwards along Blvd M. Zertouni and turn right at the first

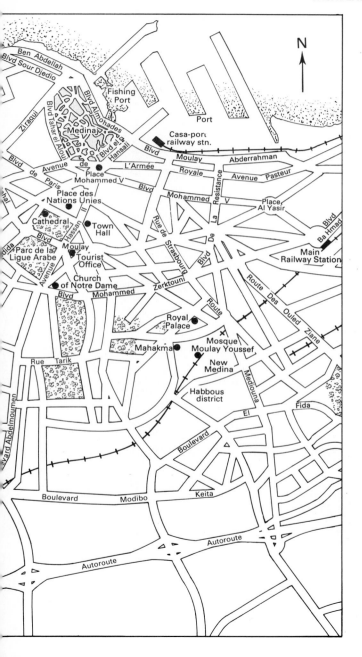

King Hassan's new mosque, Casablanca

roundabout into Rue Hadj Amar Riffi for the **New Medina**—a modern civic centre born of the need to house the thousands of families who came in from the countryside during the 1920s to find work in one of the many new factories. This 'city within a city' is a notable example of the progress

Morocco has made in the field of social amenities and in going some way towards solving the problem of increasing urban population.

On the edge of the new conglomerate is the *Royal Palace* where the King stays whenever he visits Casablanca. It is not open to visitors. Nevertheless, people drive up the avenue of carefully manicured palm trees to take photographs of the walls and of the officials guarding them.

Next to the new medina is the *Habbous district*, once a separate town but now engulfed by its prosperous neighbour. It does however retain much of its authenticity and colour: the stalls displaying kaftans and jewellery alongside the charming *Mosque Moulay Youssef* are well worth visiting. Here too is the Mosque Mohammed V (1938) and the *Mahakma* (law court), which can and should be entered for it is a very fine example of modern Moroccan architecture conceived in the form of an ancient palace.

To the W of Casablanca city is the seaside resort of *Ain Diab*, and rising up behind it is the elegant residential area of *Anfa*, with its fine villas and 9-hole golf course (Royal Anfa Golf Club). Ain Diab is really just a string of exclusive clubs, with swimming pools, and names like *Tahiti, le Miami* and *le Sun-Beach*, each endeavouring to outdo its neighbour in tropical luxury. Behind them are the thunderous rollers of the Atlantic, a really magnificent sight at any time of year and a formidable and dangerous challenge to even the strongest swimmer. The area is well served with good hotels and many delightful fish restaurants: the more modestly-priced ones stand back from the shore and serve delicious freshly-caught *merlan* or *lot*; the best (and arguably the best restaurant in Morocco) is *A Ma Bretagne* which stands on a promontory a little beyond the others. Their *Mousse de St. Pierre, sauce homardine* is memorable. It is worth noting that Ain Diab, facing straight out to the Atlantic as it does, appears to escape the slightly humid atmosphere of Casablanca city (and Rabat) and enjoys an altogether more bracing climate. This probably accounts, at least in part, for its significant expansion along the coast.

Ain Diab is connected with central Casablanca by a splendid corniche road (Blvd de la Corniche) which is served by frequent buses. At the time of writing, this road was blocked by the construction site of King Hassan's new mosque and it is necessary to turn leftwards into town in order to emerge further down the coast. It is intended that the mosque will be the tallest religious building in the world (the minaret is already 175 metres high); it will hold 20,000 people inside and 80,000 more in the surrounding esplanade. A laser beam will shine out from the top of the minaret and extend 30 miles in the direction of Mecca. It is said that every citizen in the land has voluntarily contributed to the cost according to his means, and that hundreds of craftsmen from all over Morocco are carrying out the traditional work of zellige, stucco and wood carving. No-one is allowed to approach the site without authority so we can only stand back and await the completion of this extravagant project with curiosity and wonder—and a degree of concern at the contrast between it and the decidedly impoverished housing which surrounds it (and, indeed, much of Casablanca).

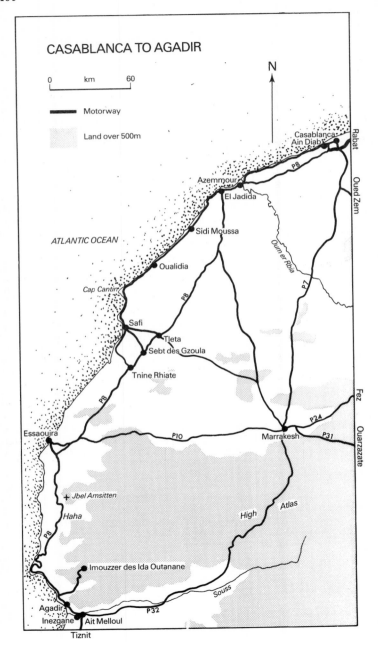

CASABLANCA TO AGADIR

N

0   km   60

━━━ Motorway

░░░ Land over 500m

ATLANTIC OCEAN

Casablanca·
Ain Diab
Rabat
Oued Zem
P8
Azemmour
El Jadida
Sidi Moussa
Oualidia
Oum er Rbia
P7
Cap Cantin
Safi
P8
Tleta
Sebt des Gzoula
Tnine Rhiate
Fez
Ouarzazate
P8
P10
P24
Marrakesh
P31
Essaouira
Jbel Amsitten
Haha
High
Atlas
Imouzzer des Ida Outanane
Souss
Agadir
P32
Inezgane
Ait Melloul
Tiznit
P8

4 Casablanca to Agadir

Total distance 557km. **Casablanca**—P8. 80km **Azemmour**—16km
El Jadida—142km **Safi**—147km **Essaouira**—172km **Agadir**.

The coast from Casablanca as far as Agadir is rocky and inhospitable. The
deserted sandy beaches, though tempting, are dangerous for bathing
unless they are in a bay. With the exception of the important port of Safi
and the once important ports of Azemmour, El Jadida and Essaouira, the
coastal strip is little inhabited. The main road runs inland, so if you want a
view of the sea you must turn westwards along one of the many tracks, or
take the coastal road (where there is one) which is usually deserted except
for the odd slow-moving donkey cart.

The towns along this route are protected by magnificent ramparts. They
were built at the end of the 15C by the Portuguese who, with great skill
and courage, braved the rocks and installed their colonies all the way down
the coast. They did not evacuate their strongholds until late in the 16C, and
in some places later, when forced out by the Moroccans. There is no doubt
that the Portuguese ramparts add greatly to the charm of these towns: they
are heavy and dark red-brown in colour: the Moorish houses are small and
light by comparison and usually white.

Leave Casablanca (see Rte 3) by way of Ain Diab for the coast road; or take
Blvd Brahim Roudani (in the direction of the airport) and turn right for the
faster main road as far as 80km Azemmour.

Azemmour (22,000 inhab.; Tourist Office: 141 Av. Mohammed V) is a
cluster of white, flat-roofed houses along the banks of the river Oum er
Rbia. Kasbahs and minarets rise up to give a vertical note to the line of flat
roofs and the whole is guarded by sentinel ramparts. Time seems to have
stopped here and the importance of Azemmour lies in the past—going back
to its foundation by the Carthaginians in the 4C BC. Up to the end of the
19C it was an important fishing port and a centre for shoemakers, weavers
and blacksmiths. Now, however, little of these industries survives and
Azemmour has been put in the shade by the bigger and more modern El
Jadida, 16km away. But it is still a holy town for both Arabs and Jews, and
many pilgrims come to pray at the tombs of an Islamic saint (who died here
in 1183) and a grand Rabbi who was said to have performed miracles. It is
worth spending an hour or two wandering through the narrow by-ways of
the medina but the rather neglected ruins of the old mellah and kasbah are
less interesting.

The main road turns left as soon as it reaches the medina walls; it is worth
stopping here for a fascinating and energetic walk around the top of the
ramparts which extend two thirds of the way round the medina, after which
you continue at ground level. (It takes about one hour.)

You climb up alongside the main entrance flanked by a Portuguese tower
with distinctive triangular windows out of which boiling oil would have
been poured to deter invaders. You will see a mosque which started life as
a Portuguese church, and the ruined fortress of *Dar el Baroud* (House of
Powder) with its fine Gothic window, its turrets and its subterranean
passage leading out to the sea which was a Portuguese escape route.

The view from the walls down into cramped little courtyards of clean
white houses is a fascinating one. This is a small and very friendly medina
(as you will see when you walk back from the end of the wall), worth

stopping for if only because most visitors pass by in their haste to get to El Jadida and Safi. As you leave, notice the synagogue with mellah behind it—empty (so the guide said) since 1955.

1.5km S of Azemmour is the lovely sheltered beach of *Haouzia*, much appreciated by local townspeople and now earmarked by the tourist authorities for development which will include an 18-hole golf course and a hotel with apartments.

The P8 road continues 16km to **El Jadida** (120,000 inhab.), beautifully situated in the arms of a bay. The Moroccans christened this town, whose name means 'the new one', when they recovered it from the Portuguese (who had called it Mazagan) in the middle of the 18C. Azemmour is the Berber word for 'old city', so called because it had already been wrested from the invaders some 200 years earlier. El Jadida therefore bears traces of a more profound Portuguese penetration.

It is possible to drive into the old Portuguese quarter to see in particular the impressive *underground cistern*—an immense square hall supported by 25 columns and lit only by a circular opening in the roof. The Portuguese built it originally as an arsenal but transformed it in the mid 16C to a cistern and a mark on the wall records the then water level. Now there is just enough water on the floor (carefully controlled) to show a stunning reflection of the arcaded roof. The cistern is open every day from 8.30 to 18.30 and the best time to come is at 14.00 hours when the sun is directly over the illumination hole. It was discovered, quite by chance, in 1916. Nearby is the 16C Church of the Assumption known as *le Catedral* and used today as an exhibition hall.

The Portuguese built on a lavish scale and much of the town wall (around which there was a moat) and four out of the five great bastions survive. Two of these—*le Saint-Esprit* and *l'Ange*—overlook the harbour which was once of major importance but is now too shallow for more than the sardine fishing fleet. Walk out to *Porte de la Mer*, the old sea gate, or up to the top of l'Ange, for fine views.

Today, once again, El Jadida is an economic success story with an agricultural hinterland and a healthy textile industry which has caused the population to rise from 90,000 to 120,000 over the last 5 years. The once decidedly shabby town centre is being spruced up quite noticeably and squares and streets (such as Place el Hansali) are animated and full of cafés. There are also several good hotels, ranging from the very adequate one-star *Hotel de Provence* (near the centre but with the sea at the end of the road) to the fabulous *Palais Andalous*, a converted pasha's house in Andalucian style with 28 rooms around a traditional courtyard (for all its splendour, a double room at time of writing costs the equivalent of £20).

The town is also blessed with long stretches of sandy beaches and a temperate climate with near constant sunshine and a good deal of wind, which keeps temperatures down even in high summer. A superb beach is at *Sidi Bouzid*, a short drive down the coast road, which is currently being turned into a holiday village with chalets, a campsite and a restaurant. The advantages of Morocco's west coast between Casablanca and Agadir are really only just being discovered by the world at large, and a controlled effort is being made by the tourist authorities to offer adequate accommodation, sports facilities and entertainment which will fit in with the environment rather than destroy it.

8km along the coast road (S1301) is the village of *Moulay Abdallah* with its impressive white zaouia surrounded by a crop of marabouts, and a fine Almohade minaret with a different design on each side (like the Hassan

Tower in Rabat). The zaouia was founded by the son of a holy man, Ismael Angher, who arrived from Medina in Arabia with his two brothers during the reign of the Almoravides (11C). Later, the Almohades came and built a ribat, parts of whose defensive wall still survive by the shore. The area immediately around the zaouia is still a holy place, visited by pilgrims every August when there is a large moussem. Casual, non-Muslim, visitors simply wanting to take a look are not welcome.

On the landward side of the village there is a second, older, minaret; it is Almoravide, much simpler and smaller and narrower than the one by the sea: it stands alone and unappreciated amidst ramshackle houses and is accessible by driving round the walls and turning left through an opening (when facing away from the sea).

5km further SW is the village of *Jorf Lasfar*, formerly Cap Blanc and now transformed into an ultra-modern phosphate port with chemical works and a holiday village for the work force just along the coast. After this the road rejoins the main coastal road (S121) which will take you all the way to Safi (142km from El Jadida) through a prosperous market gardening region (tomatoes, peppers, carrots, etc). About half-way along the route is the small town of *Oualidia* which overlooks a natural lagoon. It is named after a Saadian sultan, El Oualid, who built a kasbah here in 1634 to defend what he saw as a good natural harbour, one wall of which survives by the road. Today Oualidia is famous for its oysters which are relatively cheap, always fresh, and available all the year round.

There is a sizeable oyster industry here: the first oyster farm was started in 1952 in the lagoon of Sidi Moussa (further N toward El Jadida) but in 1956 it moved to Oualidia because the original lagoon was becoming buried by sand. Conditions at Oualidia's lagoon have proved to be excellent, with constantly changing waters, thanks to the high Atlantic tides, and complete freedom from pollution. The oysters are of the large Portuguese variety but there are also some smaller 'Japanese' ones, and there are now three large farms in operation.

Oualidia's two rocky promontories also provide perfect conditions for swimming, water-skiing and fishing, and there are three hotels with fish restaurants: *L'Hippocampe*, *La Lagune* and *A l'Aignée Gourmande*. The coastal road continues past the Ghorane caves (*Grottes de Ghorane*) and rounds Cap Cantin for a particularly lovely 34km stretch before reaching Safi.

The main road is about 30 minutes faster (though slightly longer) and very dull. To reach Safi turn right on to the P12 at *Tleta* (131km).

Safi (160,000 inhab.) is a historic town dating back to the Almohades (12C) who created an important cultural and religious centre. Some historians give it an older pedigree and claim that it was the point at which the first Arab conqueror, Oqba ben Nafi, reached the sea in 683. The Portuguese devastated the old town in the 15C and built the by now familiar ramparts to protect their conquest. After they left, the Saadians brought new prosperity to Safi by exporting sugar from Marrakesh. The Alouite dynasty continued the rehabilitation process, rebuilding religious institutions and restoring the ancient medina.

Today Safi's economic importance is threefold. Much of Morocco's phosphate (mined in the Khouribga area SE of Casablanca) is processed and exported from here, although the recent creation of Jorf Lasfar has somewhat diminished Safi's pre-eminence; secondly, it is one of the busiest sardine ports in the world with a huge fishing fleet and a canning industry to match; thirdly, it produces pottery which is sold all over Morocco and in many parts of Europe. Some of it, to Western eyes, is over-ornate, but much of it is delightful and it is certainly relatively cheap. A visit to the potters' colony behind the medina is a must.

Park between the 16C Portuguese fortress known as *Dar el Bahar*, or *Château de la Mer*, and the town walls (in a small square with a marabout in the centre) and walk through the very small medina along its main street (*Rue du Socco*). As you reach the walls on the other side you will see the distinctive beehive kilns on the hill in front of you ('*la colline des potiers*').

The potters (over 850 of them) work in co-operatives, using traditional methods to work the clay which is washed downhill by a stream. They welcome the opportunity to take visitors round and explain the whole process: the kneading of raw clay, as if it were dough, to get rid of stones and impurities; the skilled fashioning of pots on wheels worked with the feet underground; the laying out of the articles to dry in the sun for a day; the first firing (at 750°), the painting on of the design with fine horsehair brushes; the glaze (coming from France); the second firing (at 950°).

Pots in every imaginable shape and size, as well as tiles (green for the mosques) are produced in seemingly endless quantities by this very cheerful band of men and boys, often working in family groups, using methods which have changed little over the centuries. A good selection is laid out for inspection and sale in one street at the bottom of the hill (on the left as you come down).

For a panoramic view of the whole smoky process, walk up to the terrace at the top of the hill. Here too is a view of the *Kechla*, an 18C kasbah with green-tiled roof and shabby white exterior which is now used as the offices of the local Mahkzen.

As you walk back through the medina, look out for the Great Mosque (17C Saadian with imposing minaret) and the scant remains—the choir, in fact—of a Portuguese cathedral which is behind the mosque in Rue Cadi-Ayed, off the Rue du Socco.

Not surprisingly there is a good selection of fish eateries in Safi, with the more basic cafés often selling the most delicious grilled sardines. For a more upmarket menu, and a table in a delightful shady patio, go to the *Calypso* Restaurant on the main square beside Château de la Mer.

There are three roads out of Safi, all of which eventually join up with the P8 going S towards Essaouira. One is the road to Marrakesh, the P12 mentioned above which joins the P8 at *Tleta de Sidi Bouguedra* (26km). Another is the slightly more southerly route signposted to *Sebt-des-Gzoula* (20km). The third is a coastal route which takes you through Safi's industrial zone, past the fish canneries and the chemical works, turns left c 15km before the small seaside resort of Souira-Kedima, and rejoins the main road at Tnine-Rhiate. Without doubt the last of these three routes is the most rewarding.

The latter part of the road between Safi and Essaouira is wild and mountainous for you are crossing the outer arm of the High Atlas on its way out to sea. This is wind-swept, olive tree and mimosa country, and the air is scented with aromatic herbs. The final plunge down into Essaouira is triumphal as the road spirals through the dunes to the tiny sparkling white town at the foot of the cliff.

Essaouira (28,000 inhab.; Tourist Office: Place Moulay el Hassan) was called *Mogador* by the Portuguese when they invaded it in the 16C. Later it became Essaouira, deriving from the Arabic Al Swaira, which means 'fortress surrounded by ramparts'. The French rechristened it Mogador during the Protectorate, and now, once more, it is Essaouira. The medina, with its white houses with blue doors, and its narrow, winding streets, is glimpsed through ornately decorated arches. It is one of the cleanest and brightest medinas in Morocco. It is small and will take only an hour to explore. None of this is surprising for it is not old at all but was built in the second half of the 18C by the Alouite sultan Mohammed ben Abdallah, with the aid of a French architect. It was intended to be a commercial town and rapidly filled up with European and Jewish merchants. It became extremely prosperous until the French came in 1912 and made Casablanca the centre of commerce and finance. Essaouira then began to decline economically and is only now beginning to find its rightful place on the tourist maps.

The main street of the medina is Avenue d'Istiqlal (which means independence), and everywhere you look there are men making and selling tables, chests, cigarette boxes, etc., of sandalwood (called *thuya*) encrusted with tiny pieces of mother-of-pearl and ebony. This delicate marquetry work is Essaouira's speciality; it turns up in souks all over the country but is certainly cheaper here. The locally-made silver and gold jewellery is also worth examining and leather-work is another local speciality. The central market in an arcaded square just off Istiqlal is a joy with all kinds of fish and vegetables interspersed with locally made basketware and bright blue barrels full of olives. The women add a strange enchantment as they dart to and fro, enveloped from head to foot in white haiks with only the narrowest of slits left for the eyes.

The fishing harbour—*Porte de la Marine*—is a veritable hive of activity with hundreds of boats bobbing up and down in the shelter of two massive Portuguese bastions and a massive sea wall crowned with heavy iron and bronze cannons. A lot of ship building goes on here and the jagged orange-painted wooden hulls, in various stages of construction, make a colourful addition to the scene. Nets are mended and catches unloaded, sorted and packed with the gulls wheeling excitedly above. Early evening is a particularly lively time.

Out to sea are two rocky islands known as *les Iles Purpuraires*. The name is significant for it is here that the Berber king, Juba II of Mauritania, is believed to have set up an important purple dye-works. The larger of the two islands is now crowned with a large building, formerly a prison.

Essaouira's beaches are long and sandy and safe, although slightly more exposed than those of Agadir. The sun shines all the year round and there is a constant wind keeping the temperature down which is particularly welcome for the people of Marrakesh who come here to escape the midsummer heat.

There is a large modern hotel on the front with a perfect sea view—the *Hotel des Iles*—only 2 minutes' walk from the medina. Other less pretentious hotels cluster around the Place Moulay Hassan which joins the medina to the harbour. The Restaurant *Chalet de la Plage* (opposite Hotel des Iles) does a good 4-course meal for just over £4; the somewhat dingy decor is compensated for by the charm of the elderly waiter and the beaming face of the cook who watches through the hatch.

There is a fast road going E from Essaouira to Marrakesh (171km).

The road to Agadir (172km) takes you first past some gigantic sand dunes, which have had to be stabilised by careful planting in order to to prevent them encroaching upon the town of Essaouira, then through hills spotted with argan and thuya trees.

The argan (*Argania spinosa*) is a scrubby, feathery tree which grows only in this part of Morocco, and here in great profusion. It is appreciated most of all by the goats which climb right up into it with astonishing agility and devour its leaves and fruit. Bright little goat boys, knowing that tourists will want to stop and photograph this sight, stand well to the fore, quick to ask for a dirham or else push the goats down out of the trees.

The tree is very useful to humans as well as to the goats: the kernels, left behind by the goats after they have eaten the fruits, are crushed to make a kind of red oil which is used domestically throughout the region. The thuya produces the wood that is used to make the beautiful marquetry work so prevalent in the Essaouira medina (see above).

This is wild and featureless country though there is still the occasional outlying spur of the High Atlas to conquer, particularly that forming *Cap Rhir* which juts a long way out into the ocean and forms one arm of the Bay of Agadir. The road skirts it and then turns SE. This last part of the journey, winding down to the wide bay, is unforgettable. Agadir lies at the mouth of the river Souss, and its hinterland, watered by this river, is one of the most fertile areas in Morocco, producing abundant early vegetables and fruit and a most delicious strain of tiny pink-tinged banana not found anywhere else.

12km north of the city there is a left-hand turn signposted *Imouzzer-des-Ida-outanane*. It is the road itself rather than the destination which is significant for it follows a green and luxuriant valley alive with cascading waterfalls, which appear in startling contrast to the arid lands behind and to the south. For those who want to go all the way (50km), Imouzzer is a white hilltop village known particularly for its delicious aromatic honey, and its honey festival each July. It has a modest hotel—*Auberge des Cascades*—with fabulous mountain views.

The origins of **AGADIR** (90,000 inhab.) before it was occupied by the Portuguese at the end of the 15C are little known. They called it *Santa Cruz de Ghir* and transformed it into a fortress. In 1540 the Saadians attacked it in force and, after a siege, drove out the invaders. The town prospered and became an important outlet for Saharan produce. It came briefly into the limelight in 1911 when the Germans sent a gunboat—the 'Panther'—into the bay and shot off a few rounds. This act signified a protest against French and British plans to divide up the whole of North Africa between them; it had the desired effect and Germany was placated by being ceded territory in the French Congo.

After Independence (1956) hotels began to be built and the future looked bright. Then, in a mere 15 seconds in February 1960, Agadir was almost completely destroyed by an earthquake; 15,000 people died. The town has been reconstructed slightly to the right of the worst hit area, and the buildings (besides being anti-seismic) are on the whole colourful and architecturally exciting. But the new town, which has been scientifically planned, lacks a heart; one misses the throbbing beat of the medina, so much a part of other Moroccan towns, and there are still empty spaces to be filled. For a complete picture of the town and its harbour, you should drive up the steep road to the *Kasbah* (overlooking the harbour), now no more than a few ruined walls on top of a hill. This, the centre of the disaster, has been left as a kind of earthquake memorial.

Agadir's greatest asset, which the earthquake could not touch, is the extent of its beaches—stretches of fine golden sand protected by the arms of the *Baie de Ghir* and offering some of the safest bathing in Morocco. Sailing, water-skiing, skin-diving, fishing, are also possible here. With an ideal temperate climate (January minimum temperature: 16°C; July maximum temperature: 27°C), Agadir is one of Morocco's favourite tourist resorts, much used for package holidays, and it is still growing.

Information. Moroccan National Tourist Office: Place Prince Heritier Sidi Mohammed (tel. 228-94). Syndicat d'Initiative: Av. Mohammed V (tel. 226-95).

Post Office. Av. du Prince Moulay Abdallah.

Transport. Airport: 4km S of the town on the Inezgane road. Flights to Europe, Marrakesh, Casablanca, Tangier and Laayoune. Bus station: Place Lahcen Tamri (off Blvd Mohammed Sheik Saadi). Buses to Casablanca, Tiznit, Tafraout and Marrakesh.

Hotels. One 5-star, seven 4-star A, seven 3-star A, four 3-star B, five 2-star A, two 2-star B, three 1-star A, four 1-star B. Also eight 'villages de vacances' consisting of chalets around a central amenities block.

Many of the hotels stand clustered together in a relatively small area along the Blvd Mohammed V, which runs parallel with, but some way back from, the shore. The 5-star Sahara is positioned well back and probably the best site of all is taken by the vast holiday complex of *Club Mediterranée*. The 3-star *Oumnia* and *Dunes d'Or* ('*village de vacances*') are close to the sea and many other hotels are in process of construction as the town spreads visibly southwards. All the bigger, more resplendent hotels have been built primarily to cater for large groups, which often means that their service and attention to detail leave much to be desired. There is a large international campsite just off Blvd Mohammed V (at the harbour end).

Competing with the hotels for an uninterrupted view of the sea from the Blvd Mohammed V is the *Royal Palace*, which is set in splendid gardens. Behind the boulevard stretches the new town with its geometrically laid out streets, its residential area and its industrial zone. But restaurants, night-clubs, casinos, shops and banks are all concentrated along the coastal strip, mainly around the two broad parallel boulevards, Mohammed V and Hassan II.

A few fish restaurants are to be found in the port and also in Rue des Oranges, off Hassan II, but there really is a dearth of imaginative eating places and it is obviously assumed that tourist groups will eat in their hotels (which they tend to do). The keen gourmet will perhaps want to make the effort to go out to *La Pergola* at Inezgane, 10km S of Agadir, which serves a range of excellent French food. Inezgane is a pleasant, tranquil town, containing several restaurants and a Golf *Club Mediterranée*.

5 Tangier to Oujda

Total distance 710km. **Tangier**—P38. 53km **Tetouan**—63km **Chaouen**—P39. 100km *Ketama*—114km **Al Hoceima**—175km *Nador*—13km **Melilla**—135km *Saidia*—58km **Oujda**.

There are three ways of getting from Tangier (see Rte 1) to Tetouan. The shortest (53km) and most direct route is the P38 which leaves Place d'Europe in the modern town and then crosses the Jbala plain alongside the river Mharhar, with good views of the tail end of the Rif range. A more leisurely route is followed by leaving Tangier in the easterly direction of Cap Malabata, turning S at the fishing village of *Ksar es Srir* (Little Fortress), which has Portuguese ramparts. The third route is even slower and takes you E along the coast from Tangier as far as *Jbel Moussa*, turning S just behind Ceuta to wind down the Mediterranean coast past the many holiday resorts described in Rte 6.

TETOUAN (170,000 inhab.) is a white hill-side town surrounded by olive groves and gardens. It has a strong Spanish atmosphere, which is not surprising since it has been intimately connected with that country throughout its history, not least during the Protectorate (1912–56) when it was capital of the Spanish Zone. Even today it is sometimes known as 'the daughter of Granada'.

Information. Moroccan National Tourist Office: Blvd Mohammed V.

Post Office. Place Moulay el Mehdi.

Transport. Bus station: Av. du General Orgaz. Buses to Tangier, Ceuta, Chaouen, Meknes, Fez.

Hotels. One 4-star A, two 2-star A, one 2-star B, three 1-star A.

History. The origins of Tetouan lie in prehistory, in the Berber city of TAMUDA which was destroyed by the Romans in 1C AD, probably as part of the campaign to quash the Berber rebellion against direct rule from Rome (cf. Volubilis, Rte 9). The Romans built their own town on the ruins. (The remains of Tamuda are to be found today 5km out of Tetouan off the Chaouen road by the river Martil.)

In the 13C the Merinides founded a new city alongside Tamuda. The kasbah (1286), was a massive fortification intended to protect the important N–S Tangier–Fez route from marauding Rif Berber tribes. This well-protected town prospered for about 100 years until the Spanish king Henry III of Castile crossed the Straits and destroyed it, massacring most of the population and leaving only a ruined site behind him.

The medina and kasbah that survive today were built on the ruins of the Merinide town during the 15th and 16C by Muslims and Jews who had fled Spain and Portugal during this period. Later, the Alouite sultan Moulay Ismael surrounded the medina and kasbah with massive ramparts, much of which still stands. As relations with Spain improved, and not before time in view of Tetouan's geographical proximity to both mainland Spain and the Spanish enclave of Ceuta, trading links were set up and one or two of the Catholic orders were even allowed to establish foundations within the city walls. It seemed natural therefore—Tangier having been declared an international zone—that Spain should choose Tetouan as capital of the Protectorate in 1912, and it was the Spanish who built the modern city on the W side of the wall.

However the Spaniards did not have an easy time, for just to the S was the great range of the Rif which harboured some of the most fierce Berber tribes in the whole of North Africa, led at that time by the legendary Abd el Krim. He was imprisoned by the Spaniards for a relatively minor matter, managed to escape, and, fired with desire for revenge, gathered up a huge army of rebellious mountain Berbers who stood up to the Spaniards in what became known as 'the Rif War', which lasted 14 years. Massive defeats were inflicted on the Spaniards who were almost driven back into the sea in a battle near *Al Hoceima* (1921), and who lost their mountain stronghold of Chaouen. For a time Abd el Krim was in complete control and declared himself President of an independent Rif Republic, but following his decision to strike southwards towards Ouezzane and Fez (where he planned to have himself declared sultan of all Morocco) the Spanish and French formed a somewhat uneasy alliance to get rid of this common enemy. Together they managed to defeat him and he was sent into exile in 1926. With the loss of their leader Berber resistance dissolved and the Rif war came to an end.

There followed a period of peace within the Spanish Zone which was maintained even throughout the Civil War.

At the centre of Tetouan, between the medina and the modern city, is PLACE HASSAN II. It is an impressive square filled with flowers and fountains and overlooked by the Royal Palace, built by Moulay Ismael in the 17C and restored in the 1930s for use by Mohammed V. It is not, unfortunately, open to visitors. The Spanish Consulate dominates the square, a grand building which was once the residence of the Spanish Governor.

The **Medina**, which you enter from the Place by way of the Bab Rouah, is quite small and full of interest. Its charm lies in the preponderance of tiny squares, vine-trellissed streets, and very small mosques (22 in all), many of which have brilliant-white minarets. Throughout the medina are the souks, among them: *Souk el Fouki* selling both cloth and clothes; *Souk el Hout*, which must be one of the liveliest fish markets anywhere in Morocco (for although Tetouan is not on the coast it benefits from the rich waters of the river Martil estuary); *Souk el Houdz*, a Berber market where the women sell the red-and-white striped material from which they make their distinctive skirts (*foutas*); and *Ghersa el Kbira*, which is a fruit and vegetable market by day, and in the evening a sales-point for second-hand clothes. There is also a small tanning works (fairly easy to find if only because of the sickly smell), where skins of camel, goat and calf are scraped, cleaned, soaked and dyed in great open-air vats, and then laid out to dry in the sun. There is also a surprising proliferation of barbers, their Sweeny Todd-like chairs gleaming in shadowy rooms awaiting the next victim, and dentists, who announce their trade to passers-by with glass cases full of grinning dentures. This is a very varied medina, and one which seems content, for the moment, to resist the commercial pressures that have affected, for example, Tangier.

There are two museums in Tetouan. *La Musée d'Art Folklorique* is in an old palace right up against the ramparts, near to the beautiful Queen's Gate (*Bab el Okla*). It exhibits artisanat of the region, including some interesting wedding costumes. The *Musée Archeologique* is situated on Place el Jala near Place Hassan II; it shows artefacts from Lixus (see Rte 1) and Tamuda (the original Berber/Roman site on the road to Chaouen) and also some prehistoric megaliths from the one-time Spanish zone of the western Sahara. Equally interesting is the school of Traditional Arts and Crafts (*Ecole d'arts et de métiers*), which is also near Bab el Okla (but actually just outside the ramparts). Occupying another old palace, this active school is run by the government to teach young people some of the traditional crafts which might otherwise die out. In term-time the visitor may enter the various workshops and see the processes of carpet-making, cedarwood carving and painting (for ceilings), and the delicate art of inlaying olive-wood with silver and fragments of sea-shells to make elegant cabinets and desks. During school holidays it is still worth going in to see the finished articles, even if the 40 or 50 students are not there.

The *Kasbah* lies to the N of the medina and can be reached either by car from outside the ramparts or on foot (a steep climb) from within the medina, going up Rue Tala (near Souk el Fouki). However, the fortress, built by the Muslim refugees from Spain c 1600, is now occupied by the Moroccan army and is not open to visitors. The approach, by car or on foot, is through an uninspiring part of town and can be an anti-climax after the undoubted charm of the medina.

The road from Tetouan to Al Hoceima (276km) is one of the loveliest in Morocco for it takes you into the very heart of the Rif mountains and then along the top of the ridge. The first section, as far as 63km **Chaouen** (16,000 inhab.), climbs gently southwards over cistus-studded hillsides, with enticing glimpses of the high Rif peaks in the distance. The name Chaouen (or Chefchaouen as it is sometimes called) literally means 'the peaks' (or 'see the peaks'), and the reason for this becomes apparent as you approach the town which clings to the side of the mountain with the Rif, rugged and untamed, all around it. Like Tetouan, Chaouen was also built by Muslims and Jews fleeing from Christian persecution in southern Spain in the late 15C, and it too has a distinctive Andalucian atmosphere. But unlike Tetouan, and largely because of its impregnable mountain situation, Chaouen has remained closed to the outside world for centuries. Even the Spaniards failed to enter it until the final assault on Abd el Krim, the Berber leader, in 1926. When they did finally succeed in storming the town they discovered, to their amazement, some of the skills last seen in 15C Cordoba, and long forgotten.

Information. Syndicat d'Initiative: Place Mohammed V.

Post office. Ave Hassan II.

Transport. Bus station: in the market place W of town (just outside the walls). Buses to Tetouan, Al Hoceima, Melilla, Ouezzane, Fez, Meknes.

Hotels. One 4-star A, one 3-star A, one 2-star A, two 1-star A, one 1-star B.

A short stay in this enchanting place is recommended. The two principal hotels, the *Asmaa* and the *Parador*, are very different form each other in both atmosphere and location. The luxurious *Asmaa* is easy to find: it stands—a huge, white, unlovely building—on top of one of the hills that dominate the town and so has a superb view, but it is totally disassociated from the life of Chaouen. The more modest *Parador Chaouen* stands in the main Dar el Makhzen Square, with the medina (which comprises most of the town) and the kasbah only two minutes' walk away. A room at the front of this hotel affords a view over the red-tiled roofs which range up the hill in glorious disorder and are clustered around a very old brick minaret crowned with a white turret. In the square below are the orderly rows of stalls of various merchants, shoemakers, potters and sellers of mysteries. A room at the back of the hotel looks out over the lower slopes of the mountains, with a rushing stream far below and the white ruins of a one-time Catholic church above.

It is pleasant to walk beside the stream; the abundance of water in Chaouen makes possible a great deal of profitable activity, including at least one very old water-mill still in use for grinding local cereals into flour. There are also several olive oil presses, unchanged in design for hundreds of years and still being used.

A walk through the *Medina* (entered by the path exactly opposite the Parador Hotel) is a memorable experience, though somewhat less tranquil than before since Chaouen has been discovered by tourism which has caused attitudes to change and become more commercial. As everything is on a slope, the walk is quite strenuous. The medina has four sections—'Moroccan', Andalucian, Berber, and Jewish—an historic distinction probably dating back to when Berbers (and certainly the Rif Berbers) were not considered to be Moroccan. Originally each section would be locked up at night behind great wooden doors. Some of these doors still remain (permanently open now), and the one giving access to the Jewish quarter has been well preserved. Only the Andalucian section is markedly different from the rest, with the typical Ajimez paired windows, so prevalent in southern Spain, with their delicate wrought-iron grilles. In fact all of the medina is strongly Andalucian in atmosphere; many of the tiled roofs are outlined in white, and there is only the occasional minaret or rounded marabout dome to remind that you are in Morocco.

The women from the Andalucian section dress quite differently from the rest, enveloping themselves almost completely in white robes. The Berber women wear the traditional red-and-white striped shawls and skirts, and straw hats and gaiters; the latter designed to protect their legs from mountain thorn bushes. The walls, and also sometimes the steps of the houses are painted bluish-white, which is said by the locals to keep away mosquitoes. It also produces an effect of coolness. The whole town is immensely picturesque and colourful.

Every Monday and Thursday morning the medina bursts into life when Berbers come in from nearby mountain villages to sell their wares. But there is a lot of quiet hard work going on all the time, much of it based on wool as sheep-rearing is an important part of the Rif economy. You will see wool being spun everywhere, often by quite small children, and groups of men working in large rooms that open on to the street weaving lengths of cloth for djellabahs on traditional hand looms; it is usually the older men who sew the woven lengths of cloth into garments. In other rooms women will be knotting carpets (traditionally women's work, as weaving and sewing appear to be men's). They will probably not mind if you watch them work, but they may well dislike having their photographs taken.

There are many Koranic schools in this ultra-traditional town and the muted chanting of children's voices from behind thick walls is one of the more characteristic sounds of the medina. By law all children between the ages of five and seven should attend such a school where they will acquire an early grounding in the essential wisdom of the Koran before going on to primary school. There are also a number of *hammams* in Chaouen, often identifiable by piles of firewood in the street outside; the men usually bathe in the morning, and women in the afternoon; some hammans also have family rooms. There is even a square called *Uta al Hammam* (place of the bath) right in the centre, an animated spot surrounded by cafés and preserving a 15C bath which still functions (but only for men). Close by, on the S side, is the *Great Mosque* with fine octagonal minaret. It was built in the 15C by Cherif Ali bin Rachid, founder of Chaouen and head of the Emirate of Chaouen and Tetouan, a minor dynasty related to the Wattasides who ruled somewhat disastrously from Fez until ousted by the Saadians in the mid 16C.

Dominating the Place el Makhzen is the great aggressive bulk of the *Kasbah fortress*. It was built in the 17C by the Alouite sultan Moulay Ismael, to keep the Berbers in order; later, in the early years of the Spanish Protectorate, it became the headquarters of the Berber leader Abd el Krim, and was the last stronghold of his resistance; finally, in 1926, it became his prison when the Spanish at last succeeded in storming it. Within the curtain walls remains the house of Abd el Krim (now a museum), a dungeon and a large garden, where there are traces of further building.

The *museum* has some interesting exhibits, including some unique examples of *cajas de boda*—hand-carved and painted wooden carriages in which brides were carried to their weddings. There are two sorts of carriage: one type was pulled by a donkey, and the other carried by men, and both are so incredibly small that you wonder how the bride in her wedding regalia could possibly sit inside. There is also a collection of musical instruments, Berber and Andalucian, and a very fine heavy wooden door said to have survived from the original building of the kasbah. The *dungeon*, still dark and miserable, has chains with metal collars and leg irons still in place to remind one of past barbarities. The gardens outside provide a cheerful contrast and beneath them is an underground chamber which is today filled with water and cannot be entered but which was once connected with the outer walls and beyond by a maze of passages.

The road leaves Chaouen in a southerly direction and at 8km Derdara it forks left for Al Hoceima (right for Fez; see Rte 10). Just before reaching Derdara it is worth stopping for a splendid view back over Chaouen. The road (P39) follows the backbone of the Rif range, which forms a shallow crescent between Tetouan and Al Hoceima. An admirable feat of engineering, the P39 was built soon after Independence and effectively ended the centuries of isolation to which the Rif people had been subjected, cut off by the inhospitable coastline to the N and the 'Taza Gap' to the south. The sheer scale of the mountain scenery along the route is striking, and you will notice that wherever the ground is almost level it has been minutely cultivated; life is very hard here and the population is sparse.

The road begins to climb towards Bab Taza and then reaches the BAB BERRED PASS (1240m) after some breathtaking serpentine bends. *Ketama* (1600m), exactly 100km E of Chaouen, lies at the heart of a forest of cedars and pines and is rapidly becoming a very popular place for holidays. The air is clear and fresh, and the countryside, dominated by the cedar-crowned *Jbel Tidighine* (2448m) to the SW, is alive with cascading waterfalls and translucent streams. There is a comfortable hotel (the 4-star *Tidighine*) which offers a swimming pool, tennis, riding and many other facilities, including shooting, fishing and climbing. Winter sports facilities have also been developed as the snowfall is reliable (more so than at Oukaimeden near Marrakesh); and Ketama sees itself as Morocco's third skiing centre (Mischliffen, near Ifrane, being the second). The northern slopes of the Tidighine mountain are well covered in winter, and the starting point for most of the runs is the picturesque village of *Asilah* whence the summit can be reached on foot.

From Ketama there is a spectacular road (also built just after Independence) which crosses the Rif and goes on to Fez (156km). It is known as the *'Route de l'Unité'*.

After Ketama the P39 follows the valley of the river Ouringa and climbs up to the BAB TIZICHEN PASS, from which point a track winds steeply down to *La Pointe des Pêcheurs*, a little fishing settlement on the coast 60km to the north.

30km E of Ketama is the sleepy village of *Targuist*, surrounded by olive groves and oak trees, and just beyond it *Beni Hadifa*, a village which bursts into life on Mondays when it has its market.

Some 65km E of Targuist, the road suddenly dips and descends very steeply to **Al Hoceima**, which stands on the W bank of a huge natural bay backed by steep cliffs. After hours of hard driving over the dry and dusty Rif road this place looks something like paradise. It could so easily have been spoilt, but the Moroccans have controlled all development and the result is a harmonious complex with all amenities, and in a breathtakingly beautiful setting. There are three large and two small hotels, and a variety of well-appointed holiday chalets. Shopping can be done in the old village of Al Hoceima where there is an abundance of tempting seafood. Bathing is safe here and the sun can be very hot; conditions are perfect for sailing, water-skiing, and scuba-diving. Anyone looking for the perfect seaside holiday would find it hard to fault this place (which has its own airport with regular flights from Paris in the summer). On one of three small islands facing the village is an old Spanish fortress-prison—*Peñon de Alhuceimas* a grim reminder that life here was not always so pleasure-bent.

There is little to tempt you E of Al Hoceima. The road climbs inland, following the river Nekor up to the ridge, and then zigzags down in a series of sharp turns, described on the map as 'the toboggan', to the village of *Talamagait*. After 156km it forks left to Nador and Melilla (and right to Berkane and Oujda). *Nador* is a dull little town, and its development as a port has been somewhat hampered by the fact that the sea in front of it—the *Mar Chica*—is enclosed by a sand spit which no amount of dredging will clear. It has a beach and a 3-star hotel but its importance is economic rather than touristic and it acts as an outlet for iron and steel from the Jerarda district to the S. It also has a cement-works and a sugar refinery.

13km N of Nador—half-way along the peninsula—is the Spanish enclave of **Melilla** (90,000 inhab.) whose name comes from an Arabic word meaning 'the white one'. However, the Phoenicians who founded it as a trading post called it RUSSADIR. The Romans occupied Russadir for a time and then in 927 it was captured by Abderrahman III of Cordoba, and governed from there until the fall of the Caliphate in the early 11C. In 1492 the Muslim king Boabdil landed in Melilla after being thrown out of Granada by Ferdinand and Isabella of Spain. Four years later it was captured by a Spanish raiding party and handed over to the Catholic monarchs, and it has remained Spanish ever since, despite efforts by several Moroccan sultans to recapture it.

The usual Customs formalities are necessary to enter Melilla and the main reason for going there would be to visit the Municipal Museum housed in the *Bastion de Concepción* which is part of the 16C ramparts. The contents of the museum reflect the various civilisations that have left their mark, going right back to prehistory and it is open every day except Monday and Friday.

A walk around the ramparts is pleasant enough, noticing particularly the splendid *Gate of Santiago* which displays the coat of arms of the Emperor Charles V; inside is a military barracks which is closed to visitors.

Apart from that there is little to see. The new town with its typical leafy *Plaza de España* is not remarkable. The population has decreased significantly in recent years as Melilla's strategic importance has obviously diminished and it is now little more than a stopping point for ferries and flights between the Spanish mainland and Morocco.

It is possible to reach the tip of the peninsula without going through Melilla by taking the track to *Cap des Trois Fourches*, which is met just before the Customs post. The tip of the Cap gives some wonderful sea views, and it is not part of the enclave.

Return southwards for 24km and there is a turning left for Berkane and Oujda in the far E of the country. The road here is flat and uneventful; about half-way to Berkane it crosses the *Oued Moulouya*, Morocco's longest river (450km), which is controlled for irrigation purposes about 50km upstream by the *Mechra Klila dam*, completed in 1967, one of Morocco's proudest achievements.

20km beyond the river is a turning right to Taforalt and the Beni Snassen mountains, which offers a short and worthwhile DIVERSION along the precipitous *Zegzel Gorge* and comes eventually back on to the main road.

Berkane is a modern agricultural town serving the immensely fertile Beni

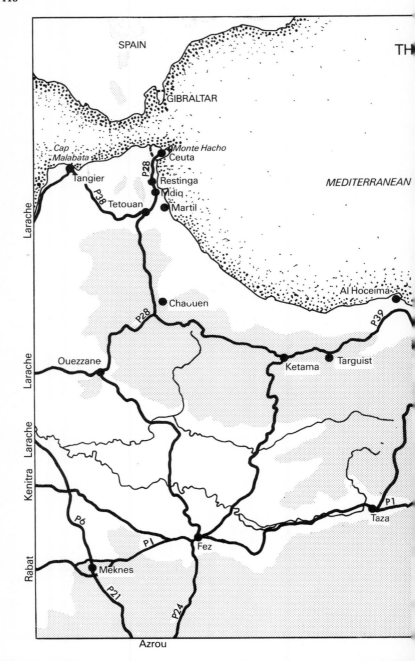

SPAIN

GIBRALTAR

TH

Cap Malabata

Monte Hacho
Ceuta

Restinga

Tangier

P28

Mdiq

MEDITERRANEAN

P38

Tetouan

Martil

Larache

Chaouen

P28

Al Hoceima

P39

Ouezzane

Larache

Ketama

Targuist

Larache

Kenitra

Larache

P1

Taza

P6

P1

Fez

Rabat

Meknes

P21

P24

Azrou

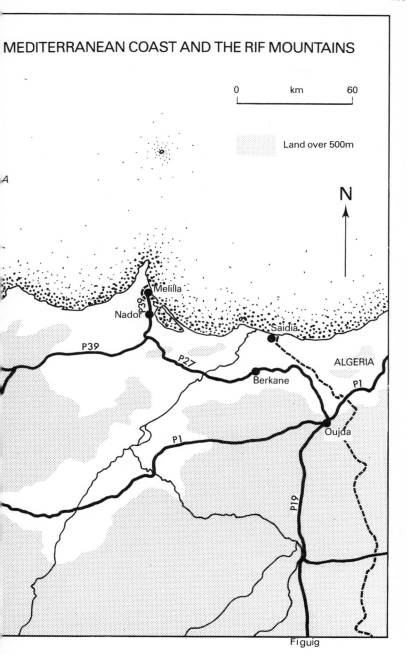

MEDITERRANEAN COAST AND THE RIF MOUNTAINS

0   km   60

Land over 500m

N

A

Melilla

Nador

P39

Saïdia

P39

P27

ALGERIA

Berkane

P1

P1

Oujda

P19

Figuig

Snassen region: rich in vines above all, but also fruit and vegetables, almond trees, and orange and lemon groves.

About 20km to the N lies Morocco's most easterly seaside resort: *Saidia*, with 12km of sandy beach and near perfect bathing conditions. However, it serves a large area and gets very crowded in summer. From here there is a direct road to 58km **Oujda** on the border with Algeria. Because of its position Oujda has been much fought over. Founded in the 10C, it was destroyed and rebuilt by the Almoravides in 1070, and then by the Almohades (who built the ramparts) in 1206. In the 13C the Merinides took it and enriched it with mosques, medersas and fountains. Later came the Saadians who used it as a base from which to march on Fez and, finally, the Alouites were here. It was the great Alouite sultan Moulay Ismael who was responsible for much of the building that we see today. After his death in 1727 Oujda passed into the hands of the Turks arriving from Algeria (it was the only part of Morocco ever to do so), and was not regained from them until the early 19C. The French, who started infiltrating from Algeria, took possession of Oujda in 1907—five years before the official start of the Protectorate. It was, therefore, French longer than any other town in Morocco.

Not surprisingly for a town that has passed through the hands of so many civilisations, there is a great variety of architectural styles. The medina still contains much that is Merinide, including the *Great Mosque* (14C); and there is one fine 17C gate, *Bab Sidi Abd el Ouahad* (or Gate of the Heads), so called because enemy heads were hung from it in time of war. The area around the gate has become a centre for story-tellers and players of traditional instruments and is perhaps the most atmospheric spot left in the medina today. There is a wide variety of souks, including *Souk el Ma* where water used to be rationed and sold in time of drought. Directly S of Souk el Ma (which is right in the centre of the medina) are the Merinide *Grand Mosque* and *Medersa*, neither of which is open to non-Muslims. Going S again you can walk through one of the babs in the ramparts to a very pleasant park—*Parc Lalla Meriem*. From here the massive Almohade structure looks particularly impressive and there is a small *Museum* on the right (as you face the walls) which exhibits local crafts and costumes.

Oujda is also a town of wide flower-covered avenues and anonymous box-like buildings. The busiest part of the modern town is that immediately around the railway station and customs sheds, for this is the main point of departure for traffic leaving Morocco for Algeria by rail and road. There is a very adequate 4-star hotel here—the *Terminus*—where you can dine comfortably in pleasant gardens in the warm evening air to the sound of shunting and whistling trains which have just arrived from Algeria. There are two 4-star hotels A, one 4-star B, one 2-star B, two 1-star A and one 1-star B.

7km out of Oujda is the **Oasis** and **Mausoleum of Sidi Yahia**—a saint whom Muslims and Jews identify with John the Baptist. This is a weird and haunted place made beautiful and fertile by an abundance of springs, and shaded by palm trees and ancient baobabs. Amongst the trees is a village of white-domed saints' *koubbas*, and under one of them, you will be told, Sidi Yahia's body reposes. The others belong to lesser saints who had followed him to this peaceful place. There is a holy well which is believed to have been Sidi Yahia's sole water supply when he stayed here, other water sources having sprung up since his death. There is also a sacred grotto—*Ghar el Hourijat* (Cave of the Houris: Houris were maidens promised to good Muslims in Paradise).

From Oujda there is a road W to Fez via Taza (see Rte 14), and another S to Errachidia via Bouarfa (see Rte 22).

6 Tetouan to Ceuta along the coast

Total distance 38km. **Tetouan**—P28. 12km *Martil—Cabo Negro—Mdiq—Restinga-Smir*—18km **Ceuta**.

A pleasant drive of 12km along a right-hand turning off the P28 takes you eastwards from Tetouan (see Rte 5) to *Martil*, a spacious sandy beach overlooked by its little fishing town, which is now almost deserted because of recent expensive seaside developments further up the coast. In Martil the potholes in the roads are getting bigger and the one beach restaurant has an air of neglect. There is a main street, just behind the beach, with one or two shops and an astonishingly good restaurant (*Restaurant Andalucia*) offering a wide assortment of fish dishes. It is said that Martil will also be 'developed', which perhaps explains why, for the moment, it has a somewhat wistful air of abandon.

This beautiful Mediterranean coastline with its miles of golden sand and its coves wedged between rocky promontories relatively safe for bathing is a paradise for holiday-makers. The Moroccans have not been slow to realise this and between Martil and the northernmost point of Ceuta there is now an almost continuous sequence of holiday villages and hotels. On the whole it has been tastefully done and the region is not yet spoilt but it could well become so if too many more hotels are squeezed in.

Immediately N of Martil is *Cabo Negro* (also known as Taifor), with its modern white buildings all facing the sea and all dedicated to pleasing the visitor—hotels, holiday homes, restaurants, night-clubs and casinos. Further N is *Mdiq*, infinitely preferable for the non-extrovert, and still retaining its colourful little fishing port, with a holiday village tucked well back on the hillside. Mdiq has a long-established annual moussem in praise of the sea.

Next comes *Restinga-Smir*, also until recently a modest fishing village but now one of Morocco's most successful tourist centres. Restinga-Smir is a large and well-spaced complex of well-appointed bungalows, chalets and apartments, two luxury hotels, shops, supermarket, swimming pools, tennis-courts and night-clubs. The Restinga bay, with its calm, crystal-clear but cold water, is ideal for water-skiing and underwater fishing, and there are plenty of boats and water-skis for hire, and instructors for those who need them. Inexperienced swimmers can feel quite safe so long as they swim within the buoy-marked area, which is shallow except at high tide and constantly watched by a *maître-nageur*. Sea-fishing is recommended here and the water is rich in tiny squid, langoustes, crabs, etc.

The coast road (P28) continues N a further 18km, past other, smaller, holiday areas, to the Spanish enclave (one of only two left in Morocco) of **Ceuta**, which stands on the isthmus of Africa's most northerly promontory formed by the rock of *Monte Hacho* (180m). To enter Ceuta means crossing a frontier with the usual passport formalities and sometimes long delays. The town is also known as *Sebta*, so named because there are seven points on the Jbel Moussa ridge behind it. The Moroccans first lost the town when the Portuguese captured it in 1415. Prior to that the great Almoravide leader

Youssef ben Tachfine had embarked from here on his numerous Spanish campaigns. In 1580 Portugal and Spain were briefly united under one crown. When they separated 70 years later Ceuta remained under Spanish rule, and has done so ever since, despite several attempts to win it back by various Moroccan sultans.

There is nothing much to see in Ceuta except three very Spanish-looking churches; there is the heavy Baroque *Church of our Lady of Africa*; the *Church of San Francisco* which contains the body of King Sebastian of Portugal who died in the Battle of the Three Kings at Ksar el Kbir in 1578; and the *Cathedral* which was built over a mosque in the 15C and received Baroque additions later on.

Ceuta's chief importance today is as a ferry terminal and the Trans-mediterranée Line has several sailings daily for Algeciras (on the mainland) and Melilla.

A drive out to the rock of Monte Hacho is worthwhile, if only for the views. The fortress on top has recently been converted to a military museum.

A very pretty road turns left off the P28 just before Ceuta and returns inland to Tetouan (see Rte 5), making a round trip of c 80km.

7 Tangier to Fez

Total distance 310km or 355km. **Tangier**—53km **Tetouan**—63km
Chaouen—60km **Ouezzane**—P28. 134km **Fez** via Zegotta Pass. P26.
179km via Fez el Bali.

Follow Rte 5 as far as Chaouen.

The road between Chaouen and 60km Ouezzane offers an easy mountain drive with sweeping bends and glorious views over the pink oleander-covered slopes of the Rif to the river far below. Here and there a herd of goats, usually guarded by an incredibly small child, will provide a speck of movement in an otherwise lonely landscape. The Fez road branches off just before Ouezzane, but a short visit to this remote hill-top town is recommended.

Surrounded by 600,000 olive trees **Ouezzane**, when seen from a distance, is a mass of white houses which spread in a kind of orderly chaos over the side of the hill. It once marked the boundary between 'Bled el Makhzen' (country which was governed) and 'Bled es Siba' (country which was lawless, i.e. the Rif) and, as such, it was a base for influential sheiks who held the balance of power. These sheiks, known as the Ouezzani, claimed to be descended from the founding dynasty of Muslim Morocco—the Idrissides—and became influential spiritual leaders, acquiring a great following. In 1727 one of their number—Moulay Abdallah—established an exclusive brotherhood known as Tabiya, which was powerful and some-times fanatical. He built a mosque (where he was buried) in Ouezzane, and this sanctuary formed a focal point for devout Muslims, and a centre for pilgrims almost as significant as the holy town of Moulay Idriss itself, and it was jealously guarded from outsiders such as Christians and Jews.

The *Mosque of the Tabiya brotherhood* stands close to the central square—*Place de l'Indépendence*—up a small stepped passageway. It has a distinctive octagonal minaret covered with green tiles which was restored in 1968. All around are the remains of pilgrims' lodgings and a derelict Ouezzani palace. Close by is a lively area of souks with carpenters, blacksmiths and weavers hard at work. Painted furniture and heavy woollen rugs are the particular speciality of this town and a good range can be seen in the *Centre Artisanal* facing the Place de L'Indépendence.

Most of the streets of the medina are steep because the town was built on the lower slopes of the Jbel Bou Hellal. It is perfectly possible, though tough going, to walk the extent of the medina and emerge into the olive groves on the other (upper) side where you are rewarded with a fine view back over the town. Tourists seem to be few in these parts and one may wander freely and without hassle. Ouezzane may lack the softening Andalucian touches of its picturesque Rifian neighbour, Chaouen, but its dilapidated streets have a certain raw charm and its people are naturally friendly.

There are two ways to get from Ouezzane to Fez. One is the fairly featureless and relatively straight road (P28) which runs directly southwards across the Cherrarda plain. In places the edges of the road have been eroded away and so your speed will depend on whether or not you are the sort of driver who moves automatically on to the soft shoulder when another car approaches. After crossing the Zegotta Pass the road joins up with the main Sidi Kacem–Fez road just N of Moulay Idriss (see Rte 9).

The P26 from Ouezzane is a more easterly and a more leisurely route 51km along the edge of the Rif foothills, as far as the little village of *Fez el Bali*. 20km further on there is a turning left to 17km *Ourtzarh*, from where a track of 37km leads to a high point in the heart of the Rif known as *Lalla Outka* with some spectacular mountain views. 30km E from Ourtzarh the road joins up with the 'Route de l'Unité' running between the main Rif road and Fez.

Back on the P26 heading towards Fez, the *Jbel Amergou* (681m) appears to the right of the road. It is crowned with the ruins of an 11C Almoravide wall. The road crosses the river Sebou and then climbs in a series of steep curves up the side of the *Zalagh mountain* (906m), but stops short of the top. The descent into Fez (see Rte 10) is magical, with a characteristic view of the white medina nestling in its hollow, and the Middle Atlas mountains in the far distance, beyond the Sais Plain.

THE INTERIOR: THE MIDDLE ATLAS

8   Rabat to Meknes

Total distance 127km. **Rabat**—P1. 56km *Tiflet*—25km *Khemisset*—46km **Meknes**.

Tiflet—20km *Dayet-er-Roumi*—70km *Oulmes*—56km Maaziz—43km **Roummani**.

Khemisset—c 43km *El Kansera*.

Leave Rabat (see Rte 2) by one or other of the two bridges across the Bou Regreg river. The road (P1) passes alongside the cork oak *forest of Mamora* (136,000 hectares), which is a particularly attractive area for walks and picnics, with a carpet of wild flowers in early spring and only the occasional cow or donkey for company. The first town of any size is *Tiflet* (56km), which is notable for its colourful pompommed hats which are made locally and held out for sale on long poles as you pass through. *Khemisset*, 25km further on, is a market town with one wide arcaded street where, in amongst the open-air stalls of indescribable cuts of meat and rather fly-blown vegetables, are to be found locally-made articles of carved wood.

Apart from getting you quickly and uneventfully to Meknes, this road offers some good EXCURSIONS. One of these is to *Dayet-er-Roumi*, a large natural lake in hilly country. On its shore is a good restaurant which provides swimming and fishing facilities in season. The drive to the lake (c 30 minutes) starts just after Tiflet along a road marked to *Oulmes*, and then left at the sign indicating the lake.

From the lake you can either continue along the road which rejoins the main Meknes road at Khemisset, or extend the excursion as far as *Oulmes*, about 70km SE into the Jbel Mouchchene. The mountains are thickly wooded and covered with cistus and other aromatic growth which gives off a wonderful bittersweet smell in spring. This is wild boar country. Oulmes is a watering place and one can scramble down from its modest but clean *Hotel les Thermes* to the point where the water springs from the rocks (Lalla Haya) and becomes a raging torrent. There are no facilities for swimming, but the water is delicious and healthy to drink and is sold in bottles all over the country. This area is highly recommended for its truly magnificent scenery—the soaring wooded heights, the deep ravines and the turbulent rivers pouring over the rocks. There are many tracks which go up into the mountains but their surface condition varies considerably. It is also easy to get lost and villages are fairly few and far between.

From Oulmes you can extend the tour still further by returning to 56km *Maaziz* and then going left to 43km *Rommani*, another charming town in a hilly setting with a good simple restaurant in the centre. Rommani is equidistant from Khemisset and Rabat (to the N)—about 82km.

Another EXCURSION leaves the main Meknes road just after Khemisset along a road signposted 43km *El Kansera*. This is a long artificial lake formed by damming the Oued Beth. The road crosses the dam and then climbs on to a high but fertile plateau which grows vines. Scenically this is a rather tame trip when compared with that to Oulmes. The road, if followed N, eventually joins up with the main Rabat–Tangier road.

MEKNES (550,000 inhab.), 46km from Khemisset, is one of Morocco's four 'Imperial' cities. Situated on the edge of the Middle Atlas mountains, at an altitude of 522m, it enjoys an equable climate and is surrounded by extremely fertile land growing vines, olives, and citrus fruits. It has some small industry on the outskirts centred mainly on fruit and vegetable preserves and wine.

Information. Moroccan National Tourist Office, Place Administrative (tel. 524426); Syndicat d'Initiative, Esplanade de la Foire (tel. 520191).

Post Office. Place Administrative.

Transport. Main railway station: Ave de Gare. Trains to Tangier, Rabat, Casablanca, Fez, Marrakesh, Oujda. Bus station: Ave des Forces Armées Royales. Buses to Rabat, Casablanca, Fez, Errachidia, Erfoud, Ifrane, Volubilis-Moulay Idriss.

Hotels. One 5-star, two 4-star A, two 3-star A, two 3-star B, two 2-star A, three 1-star A, one 1-star B.

History. Meknes was founded in the 10C by a Berber tribe known as the Meknassas. They were succeeded by the Almoravides in the second half of the 11C, and in the 12C by the Almohades, who destroyed most of the monuments of the preceding dynasty. A century later came the Merenides. While Fez was chosen as the capital, the Merinide dynasty did build in Meknes a number of mosques, and, most notably, the Bou Inania Medersa. However, it was not until the 17C that Meknes reached its apogée, under the rule of the Alouite sultan Moulay Ismael, who reigned for 55 years (1672–1727) and is believed to have had 360 wives and some 800 children. He was without doubt one of the most effective of all Moroccan rulers and also one of the cruellest. His first act on being made sultan, was to send 10,000 heads of members of rival tribes whom he had slain in battle to decorate the walls of Fez and Marrakesh, thus making it clear that he would have neither of these troublesome towns for his capital.

Moulay Ismael built on a gargantuan scale. He enclosed his town in 25km of massive walls, pierced by monumental gates. He made sumptuous palaces and gardens watered by great reservoirs, stables for his 12,000 cavalry horses, and countless mosques and mausoleums. Despite his cruelty history has judged Moulay Ismael a wise, indeed a great man, because he united Morocco and earned the respect of the major European powers for so doing. For the first time in centuries all the warring tribes in Morocco were subdued (with the exception of the Rif Berbers whom, arguably, no one has ever succeeded in rounding up, let alone conquering). His philosophy was that people expected to be ruled by the sword and would only relapse into chaos when the yoke of cruelty was lifted. There was no mercy in him, but people are said to have respected his rough justice and it is generally recognised that he created order and stability where before there was widespread disorder. To make all this possible Moulay Ismael created an army of some 30,000 'Sudanese' soldiers, mainly descendants from slaves taken by the Saadians from S of the Sahara. ('Sudanese' in Morocco is used to mean, quite simply, black.) Contingents of these men roamed the country, collecting taxes, putting down any signs of insurrection, and meting out punishment generally. The historian Ahmed el Nasiri (1834–97), in 'Kitab al Istiqsa', wrote that by the end of Ismael's reign it was possible for a Jew or a woman to walk from one end of the country to the other without being molested by unruly tribesmen. One supposes they would need to keep clear of the Sultan's army as well.

Today Moulay Ismael is proclaimed above all as the builder of Imperial Meknes, which he visualised as a copy of the Versailles of his contemporary Louis XIV of France, for whom he had the greatest admiration and with whom he exchanged ambassadors. He is said to have employed some 2500 Christian slaves to build the Imperial city, a number which astonishes until one sees the actual volume and extent of the walls. Stories of extreme cruelty were brought back by Europeans who escaped, some no doubt exaggerated. Whether he really built a bridge across the river using rushes interwoven with the bodies of prisoners can be neither proved nor disproved; and whether he could be exonerated by the fact that most of his murders of infidels were committed on Fridays (and therefore by divine decree) would have been a point for endless discussion between succeeding generations of devout Muslims. What is certain is that Moulay Ismael himself thought that what he did was right. So sure of himself and of the supremacy of his faith was he that he proposed to Louis XIV that he too should become a Muslim; he also asked for the hand of one of his daughters in marriage but was politely refused on both counts. Towards the end of his long reign he actually allowed Catholic missionaries to minister amongst the thousands of Christian prisoners still working in Meknes, a strange irony amongst so much savagery. Perhaps the smooth and civilised life-style of *le roi soleil* did have some effect on the excesses of this larger-than-life tyrant. (There are Franciscan nuns in Meknes to this day, running an orphanage and teaching embroidery.)

The walls of the Imperial city are of overwhelming size, but there are also great open spaces, where nothing has yet been built. Meknes is not as prosperous as it was. Unlike Fez, it has not really kept up with its past. The vestiges of past splendour remain in the form of palaces and noble babs but few people today know what to do with the spaces which are left. Moulay Ismael presumably dreamed of creating even more than he did, for he had unlimited space when he built Meknes. When the Merinides built Fez, in a narrow crack in the hills, there was no space to spare and the effect today is infinitely more striking. The Lisbon earthquake of 1755 caused much damage to the city of Meknes.

Old Meknes, within its 25km of ramparts pierced by monumental gateways, comprises the Imperial city and the original medina with the mellah alongside. Joining all this into a somewhat ill-matched whole is the PLACE EL HEDIM, a large and animated square which has recently been 'sanitised': water sellers, craftsmen and other colourful characters have all been tidied away and replaced by a fruit and vegetable market on one side, and fountains on the other. The square is dominated by the **Bab el Mansour**, named after its architect, a convert from Christianity. It is the most immense and perfectly proportioned of Moulay Ismael's gateways, decorated all over with green and white ceramic and flanked by square bastions, similarly decorated and standing on elegant marble columns brought in from Volubilis. It was completed by Ismael's son Moulay Abdallah in 1732.

The Imperial city

Go through a gate to the left of Bab el Mansour, which is called *Bab Jema en Nouar*. To appreciate the Imperial city fully it is necessary to know that Moulay Ismael conceived it as a mighty fortress with no fewer than four sets of walls, one within the other, and with 24 royal palaces in the centre as well as mosques, barracks, stables and ornamental gardens. It is advisable to drive (or take a taxi) rather than attempt to see everything on foot, and there is ample parking all the way.

Just inside the Bab is a pavilion—*Koubbet-el-Khiyatine*—where foreign ambassadors were invited to come and negotiate with the sultan for the release of their fellow countrymen imprisoned in the dungeons below. These dungeons are now open to the public and the entrance is opposite the door to the Pavilion. A guide will take you down with a flickering candle and assure you that the outer reaches of the maze of tunnels—extending over 7sq km—have been closed since a couple of French trippers went in shortly after Independence, got lost and were never seen again. 40,000 slaves, mostly European Christians but also Turks and Berbers, were incarcerated here at night and brought out during the day to work on the Imperial City. It is an arresting thought, and perhaps a salutary prelude to your tour of the city which they built.

Above ground again, the first significant point of interest, on your left through a triple-arched doorway, is the **mosque** containing Moulay Ismael's tomb. It was restored in 1959 by King Mohammed V and it was he who decreed that non-Muslims should also be given access (except on Fridays). It is the only mosque in Morocco where this is so. You will be asked to remove your shoes before passing through a series of courtyards and arriving at the door of the sumptuously decorated room which contains the tomb, along with three others—one of Moulay Ismael's preferred wife and two of his sons. Behind the tomb, looking slightly incongruous and very European as they stand like sentinels guarding the great horseshoe arch, are two very fine French longcase clocks, still apparently keeping perfect time. These were a gift, in 1700, from Louis XIV, intended to mitigate the Sultan's disappointment at not being allowed to marry a French princess. (Two exactly similar clocks stand in the corners nearest to you but you cannot see these since you are not allowed to go beyond the doorway.) The ante-chamber where you stand is remarkable in its own right. The pillars are of marble, brought from Italy in exchange for sugar on an ounce for ounce basis. The stucco-work is particularly striking. Behind the mosque and accessible through a small gate is the area known as DAR EL KBIRA, once a complex of palaces and evidence of Moulay Ismael's extraordinary energy and ostentation. It was completed by 1677, only to be destroyed 50 years later by his jealous son Moulay Abdallah. It is now a crumbling ruin.

In a building opposite the mosque there is a permanent exhibition of local artisanat, most distinctive being the vases and figurines made of damascene (iron inlaid with silver), a highly skilled local technique which tends to crop up in bazaars all over the country. Craftsmen are happy to demonstrate the delicate work of scratching designs on to the metal surface with a blade, which is followed by an application of silver. Also on show is Berber embroidery and here again demonstration is available if you want it; the fine linen tablecloths and napkins are remarkable for being exactly the same on both sides. Then there is the usual assortment of Berber rugs, djellabahs, jewellery and cedarwood items. This is as good a place to shop as any because of the broad range and the above average quality. Prices, said to be 'fixed', turn out not to be at the moment you start walking away.

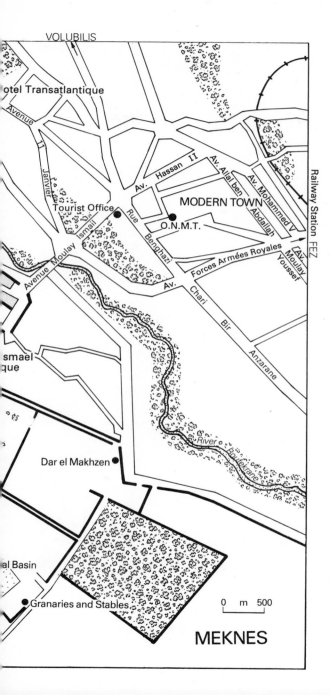

MEKNES

The Stables, Imperial City, Meknes

To the right of the mosque a path leads through the wall into a vast expanse of parkland which was once an ornamental garden for the wives of the Sultan; now it has been converted into an 18-hole golf course (the Royal Golf Club).

Return to the mosque and take the long straight road which runs for c 1km between the impregnable walls and under *Bab el Rih* (Gate of the Winds). This gate is not decorated like the others but incorporates marble columns removed by the Sultan from Volubilis and from the Saadian El Badi Palace in Marrakesh. To the right of the walls is **Dar el Makhzen**, the last of the great imperial palaces, completed at the end of the 18C. In recent years painstaking restoration of the palace has made it possible for the royal family to stay here when visiting Meknes. This unfortunately means that it is closed to public view.

After a right-hand turn the road passes alongside the main entrance to the palace and (on the left) to the botanical gardens, now belonging to the College of Agriculture. It eventually leads to one of the most evocative parts of the whole imperial complex—the ruins of the barracks, granaries and stables, all looking rather similar. It was here that the 30,000 'Sudanese' soldiers of the Royal Guard were housed. To feed them and the royal household grain was stored in 22 granaries known as *Heri-es-Souani*. These vaulted underground chambers, still standing today, remain at a constant temperature of 13°C even in the heat of summer, due to the thickness of their mud and pebble walls. You will see deep cisterns containing chain pumps which horses used to turn to bring water to the surface. In one of the chambers, propped against the wall, is a door, taken from the Ambassadors' Pavilion—*Koubbet-el-Khiyatine*. An image of the sun has been carved on to it, no doubt in honour of Louis XIV, *le roi soleil*. No-one seems to know why the door was removed and brought here.

Above, accessible by steps alongside the entrance, is a pleasant garden with extensive views giving some idea of the immensity of the ruined city. Notice particularly the old and new royal palaces, side by side. There is a small café in the middle of the garden.

Next to the granaries are the stables which once held 12,000 horses. There were 3000 of the powerful square columns, each providing a stand for four horses. The roof between the arches was destroyed by the earthquake, but what is left of the stables is impressive enough, rather like some clumsy barbaric cathedral or mosque. The scale is breathtaking. Nearby is the *Aguedal Basin*, some 4 hectares of water which Moulay Ismael used as a reserve in case of siege but which now waters the royal gardens. Next to the Basin there is a large campsite. In the distance is a white palace known as *Dar el Beida* which was built by Mohammed ben Abdallah at the end of the 18C. It has been restored and turned into a Military Academy. Apart from that there are only a few ruins in sight, which are in a sorry state and cannot be identified, even by the local guides.

At this point either turn back or drive on until you come once more to the Place el Hedim, by way of the old Mellah, once the home of over 3000 Jews, and the very fine **Bab el Khemis**, one of the town gates that bestrides the Rabat road. The original gate was built by the Almohades but it was embellished and refined by Moulay Ismael. Like all babs, it is best seen from the outside (looking in towards the city) from where its green and blue ceramic design is particularly striking against the sunburnt colour of the walls.

The Medina

From the Place el Hedim the medina is on your right and the best entrance is through the opening in the far right corner of the square as you leave Bab el Mansour. The medina pre-dates Moulay Ismael. It is animated and refreshingly intimate after the spacious and somewhat daunting echo of past splendour represented by the Imperial city. Its narrow winding streets, so typical of the medieval cities of Morocco, are often shaded from the sun by rose or vine-covered trellises, and the merchandise in the souks is varied and plentiful: Berber rugs; embroidered goods; copper and silverware; pottery and damascene. Go in to the fondouks, set back from the streets, to see co-operative groups of craftsmen at work.

   In the heart of the medina lies the **Medersa Bou Inania**, built in c 1350 and named after a Merenide sultan. If you just keep going along the road by which you entered the medina, which will soon turn left, you will reach the medersa in a few minutes. Of the same period as its namesake in Fez, but slightly smaller, its lovely central courtyard is softly coloured with the usual perfect balance of mosaic, stucco and cedarwood. The mihrab is particularly striking in highly decorative Andalucian style. From an upper floor of students' rooms there is a close-up view of the minaret of the Great Mosque next door; and also over the ruined *Medersa Filada* which was built some 300 years later by Moulay Ismael, and which in its decoration appears coarse by comparison. There are 14 other, smaller, medersas and mosques awaiting discovery in the maze of little streets. At the far (N) end of the medina, where the road and encircling defensive wall are met, is *Bab Berdaine*—gate of the saddlemakers. This was created by Moulay Ismael as the principal entrance to the medina and it resembles somewhat the central section of Bab el Mansour. Like Bab Khemis, it is best appreciated from outside where it is decorated in green tiles and patterned with flower-like designs picked out in black.

   A little way W of here (outside the walls) is a vast cemetery in the centre of which is the tomb of Ben Aissa (d. 1553) who was founder of a sect of Islamic mystics which was later much encouraged by Moulay Ismael. The cult, known as Aissaoua, was one of the most violent in Morocco with devotees working themselves into a frenzied trance, eating snakes and cutting themselves with knives. Today the moussem still takes place on the eve of Mouloud, but with all the unpleasant extremes expunged.

   You should not leave old Meknes without visiting the **Museum Dar Jamai** (closed on Tuesdays), which is housed in the 19C palace of the Grand Vizir (Prime Minister) of Sultan Moulay el Hassan. It is situated at the medina end of Place el Hedim with its entrance exactly opposite Bab el Mansour. Here you can relax and enjoy the perfect peace of the inner garden, which always seems to be filled with bird song. Although less rich than the Dar Batha in Fez, the museum offers some interesting wrought-ironwork, some beautifully simple Andalucian-style tiles, Meknes pottery (including a soup bowl said to have belonged to Moulay Ismael), Berber jewellery, traditional kaftans and lots of embroidery. The building itself is a joy with fine cedarwood ceilings and there are some upstairs rooms which are furnished in 19C style including a fascinating *salon* with a large central throne for the man of the house and a chair in each corner for his four wives.

Modern Meknes

Built—like modern Fez and modern Rabat—by the French after World War I, modern Meknes is separated from the old city by a deep ravine, at the bottom of which runs the river Boufekrane. It is a thriving town of prosperous-looking white buildings, and it lives on the produce and profits of the surrounding fertile agricultural land.

It has some good shops and 13 classified hotels of which the 5-star *Transatlantique* is the best. It has a traditional and a modern section each with its own swimming pool and stands high above the town with a fine view over the medina.The most worthwhile restaurant is probably *La Hacienda*, 10 minutes' drive out of Meknes on the Fez road, where the food (Spanish, French, Moroccan) is imaginative and reasonably priced. For atmosphere and Moroccan food, go to the Restaurant *Zitouna* in the medina (44 Jamaa Zeitouna).

Horse lovers will wish to visit the Royal Stud (*Haras Royal*) in the S of the new town (well signposted from Ave Mohammed V). There are some 600 superb specimens of which 160 are pure Arab and the rest Berber (mainly kept for fantasias) and half-breeds and one may walk in the gardens and peer into stables at leisure. This is the most important thoroughbred Arab stud in Morocco.

9   Meknes to Fez

A.   Via Volubilis and Moulay Idriss

Total distance 100km. **Meknes**—35km **Volubilis**—3km **Moulay Idriss**—62km **Fez**.

Take the Tangier road out of Meknes (see Rte 8) and after c 15km turn right on to a minor road which curves and climbs steadily up to the Zerhoun plateau. The road is lined with olive trees and agarves. In spring there are wild flowers and the pink feathery blossom of the tamarisk tree. The view over patchwork plains and misty mountains is unique.

Soon, to your left, you will see the distinctive forms of the Roman city of **VOLUBILIS**. Few people are not moved when they first catch sight of the lonely remains of this far-flung Roman outpost glinting in the sun in a setting of serene beauty. From a distance the site is dwarfed by the vast plain on which it stands and is overshadowed by the nearby Zerhoun mountains.

History. Archaeological evidence suggests that there was a settlement here from the Neolithic period. By the time the Romans arrived, in the last century BC, there was undoubtedly already a town of some importance here, built by Berbers who had become relatively prosperous in this fertile and well-watered region under the civilising influence of the Carthaginians.

It was in 25 BC that the Emperor Augustus granted the Berber kingdom of Mauritania to Juba II and added to it the whole of Numidia (now Algeria).

Juba is thought to have been part Berber, part Carthaginian; he may have been a descendant of Hannibal—a very fine bronze head of Hannibal was found at Volubilis in 1944, presumed to have belonged to Juba. Juba was educated in Rome, and in 19 BC married Cleopatra Silene (the daughter of Mark Antony and Cleopatra). He was scholarly and ruled his kingdom wisely. He is said to have written some 50 learned books, and also to have discovered that the milky juice from a kind of spurge that grew freely throughout the Atlas mountains was good for conjunctivitis. He named the plant Euphorbia after his physician Euphorbus. Opinions differ as to whether he actually lived in Tingis or Volubilis: both were by now important cities in the western half of Mauritania.

Juba died in AD 19. He was succeeded by his son Ptolemy, who was murdered by the Emperor Caligula in AD 40, leaving no heir. Four years later the kingdom came under direct rule from Rome and was divided for easier administration into two provinces: Caesariensis (eastern) and Tingitana (western), but not before there had been serious rebellions by Berber tribes determined to avenge the murdered Ptolemy. Under their leader Aedemon, who was a freedman and minister of Ptolemy, the Berbers threw themselves into a fierce and bloody revolt against the encroaching power of imperial Rome. This was finally quashed in AD 47 by Marcus Valerius Severus, a Roman official in Volubilis, with the help of citizens of the town. Having successfully quelled the rebellion he returned immediately to Rome where the Emperor Claudius conferred Roman citizenship and immunity from tribute for ten years on the city of Volubilis for its loyalty. It was probably for this reason that the seat of provincial government was placed firmly in Volubilis and not in Tingis, despite the fact that the province was named after the latter.

From this time on the town of Volubilis grew and prospered. The region became one of the granaries of Rome and also a major producer of olive oil and of copper, which was mined in the hills. At this time there are thought to have been some 15,000 inhabitants. The town also became a base from which to control the uneasy and often rebellious Berber tribes in the nearby hills. Four military outposts were built to protect the town, and one of these, TOCOLOSIDA, was situated where the village of *Ain el Kerma* is today (just off the Sidi Kacem–Rabat road). By 168 the great encircling ramparts of Volubilis were complete, and sections of these still remain. They are thought originally to have extended over 2km and to have had six gates. Most of the great buildings which remain as ruins today—Capitol, Basilica, Triumphal Arch of Caracalla—were constructed at the beginning of the 3C and some historians believe that they replaced earlier buildings that had previously been destroyed, probably in some particularly violent Berber uprising.

By the end of the 3C the Romans were beginning to withdraw, probably in the light of mounting Berber pressure and of more pressing problems elsewhere, and the seat of administration moved N to Tingis. However, Volubilis remained a centre of Roman culture, preserved by its Romanised and increasingly Christian population. Unlike neighbouring Spain, Mauritania Tingitana was never totally overrun by tribes from the N, and Volubilis remained with its Latinised traditions more or less intact until the arrival of the Arabs and their all-embracing and uncompromising Islam at the end of the 7C.

The new culture took over absolutely. By the time Moulay Idriss I arrived in 786 the Romanised Berbers had already converted to Islam and Volubilis had been renamed *Oulili* (after a local flower). It was at this point that the town was abandoned. We know that Moulay Idriss I preferred to live in the neighbouring hills. He was murdered in 791. His son, Moulay Idriss II (804–828), also disdained to live in Oulili and founded Fez as his capital. Neither, fortunately, took it upon themselves to destroy the Roman city, which remained standing, although decaying and empty, throughout the centuries until it was severely damaged by the Lisbon earthquake of 1755. This was very nearly its end, but towards the end of the 19C a party of foreign diplomats travelling from Fez to Tangier via the shrine of Moulay Idriss stumbled on some of its remains. Serious excavations were begun by the French at the beginning of the Protectorate in 1915, and now the Moroccan government continues the work. There is much still to do but enough has already been revealed of this important Roman town to suggest how life was lived by the Roman colonisers and latinised Berbers of that time.

You should allow at least an hour for your walk through the ruins, more if you want to examine closely and to photograph (although many of the statues and small pieces have been removed to museums, particularly that in Rue el Brihi, Rabat). You will be taken first along an original paved road past a series of oil presses. (For want of a better system many of the houses and smaller buildings have been named after the mosaics or statues found therein.) The first major point of interest is the *House of Orpheus* on your left, so called because one of its mosaics is dedicated to Orpheus, the god of music, and shows him with a fascinating collection of animals, such as elephants and lions, which may well have roamed the countryside in those days. This seems to have been an important house. The domestic quarters include a kitchen and three rooms for family bathing: the caldarium, frigidarium and tepidarium. Bathers would enter the hot room first for a hot water bath, then plunge into a cold water bath in the second room, finally emerging to enjoy a leisurely massage and oiling of the skin in the open court or peristyle. The tepidarium, as the name suggests, was something between hot and cold and was probably used only in the winter. There would have been a hypocaust underneath the floor where hot air from a furnace would circulate between the supporting pillars and then be passed up the walls through hollow tiles and bricks to heat the water and the air in the rooms above. One of the rooms has a mosaic depicting dolphins, which were considered by the Romans to bring good luck. The reception area, or living quarters, consists of further rooms arranged around a larger court where there is a charming *mosaic of Amphitrite* in a chariot drawn by a sea-horse and surrounded by other exciting sea creatures. One of these rooms contains the Orpheus mosaic.

Next, on the left, are the old *public baths* restored by the Emperor Gallienus in the 3C AD. Bathing was taken very seriously by the Romans and public baths fulfilled an important social role, enabling people to relax together, eat and drink, talk business and exchange gossip. There is very little left here of a decorative nature to suggest any of this and the baths were probably not very big.

You are now approaching the great administrative centre of Volubilis, comprising the Capitol, Basilica and Forum, whose ruins today make a proud and impressive sight. The *Capitol*, dated by inscription 217, is thought to have been constructed over an earlier building of similar nature. It comprises a rectangular court surrounded by Corinthian columns, with a temple at one end approached by a flight of steps. At the foot of the steps is a sacrificial altar. The temple was dedicated to Jupiter, Juno and Minerva.

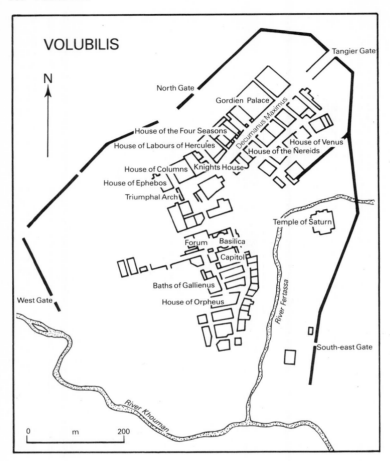

VOLUBILIS

N

Tangier Gate

North Gate

Gordien Palace

Decumanus Maximus

House of the Four Seasons

House of Labours of Hercules

House of Venus

House of the Nereids

House of Columns

Knights House

House of Ephebos

Triumphal Arch

Temple of Saturn

Forum

Basilica

Capitol

Baths of Gallienus

House of Orpheus

River Fertassa

West Gate

South-east Gate

River Khouman

0   m   200

The tall slender columns are particularly fine and some have been well restored.

Adjoining the Capitol is the *Basilica*, or Law Courts, which would have had an apse at both ends and a large rectangular area in between which was probably divided into five aisles. An important and central part of Roman life, this building would have been used not only for dispensing justice but also as a centre for commercial exchange. The blind arcades here have been recently restored.

The *Forum*, nearby, is a large open space which served as a place for public meetings and political speeches—the focal point of city life. Surrounding it would have been the main administrative buildings and temples. It was probably built during the reign of the Emperor Septimius Severus (193–211), and it is his family which is commemorated on stone plinths to the right of the path; also included is the bust of Marcus Valerius

Severus who put down the Berber revolt led by Aedemon (see History above). Other statues which no doubt lined the Forum have been removed to the museum in Rabat.

Next you will pass the remains of the house where the famous *bronze dog* was found (also removed to Rabat). This is quite one of the finest pieces to come out of Volubilis and should be seen if at all possible. Not far away is a house which has amusing mosaics of fishermen and acrobats, including one who rides backwards on a horse. Next comes the **Triumphal Arch** which was the only edifice to survive the earthquake intact. It provided the clue which provoked the initial excavations. It was erected in honour of the Emperor Caracalla in 217, the year of his death, and seems to have had a purely ceremonial function as it does not really lead anywhere—to the W of it is an empty space. Only the E face and the two sides have been lavishly decorated with statues, columns of imported marble, and medallions, including four charming ones representing the seasons. The top section of the arch is now missing and one can only imagine how it would have looked surmounted by the bronze figure of Caracalla himself driving a six-horse chariot.

On the far side of the arch is the *House of Ephebos* (named after a bronze head of Ephebos now in Rabat), and next to it is the *House of Columns* (easily identifiable). Both would have belonged to patrician families. They are large and have traces of splendid mosaics in the public and private rooms, which are grouped, as was the fashion, around three separate courtyards. One particularly charming mosaic shows the three gods, Bacchus, Venus and Cupid; others portray sea-nymphs (a favourite theme) or geometric designs of interlocking circles or squares.

Next comes the *Knight's House*, in a ruinous state apart from the one lovely mosaic of Dionysius discovering the sleeping Ariadne. Next to it (up a little side street) is the *House of the Labours of Hercules*, which contains what is probably the most famous mosaic of all, in excellent condition with the god's well-known exploits easily recognisable in ten out of the 12 squares. The mosaic is in what was probably the banqueting hall and there are stone benches on three sides where guests would have reclined and feasted. These four noble houses occupied a prime site on DECUMANUS MAXIMUS, the main street of Volubilis, where there would have been market stalls and shops behind the shade-giving colonnades which lined both sides as far as the Tingis Gate on the NE town wall. Notice the marks of chariot wheels still visible on some of the paving stones.

The houses further up the street are somewhat smaller but also contain fine mosaics—the most remarkable being that of *The Four Seasons*, each season depicted in its own medallion. Another mosaic shows nymphs bathing. Only one house—that of the *Wild Beasts*—disappoints, for its mosaic has been removed. Next to it, and nearest to the Tingis Gate, is the impressive *Palace of Gordian*, called thus because of an inscription which dates the construction to the reign of Gordian III (238–44). It impresses by its size and its large bath house, and is thought to have been the residence of the Provincial Governor, which seems reasonable in view of its close proximity to the Tingis Gate.

Most of the houses on the S side of Decumanus Maximus are in total ruin and indistinguishable one from another; however, the *House of the Nereids*, opposite the House of the Four Seasons, merits a closer look by virtue of its mosaics. The streets alongside it join Decumanus Maximus with a parallel, lesser street to the south. Standing out amongst the mass of ruins is the *House of Venus*, notable for having been the source of the bronze heads of

Cato and Juba II which are now in Rabat. This was undoubtedly an important house, and owned by someone with superior artistic taste. Its many courtyards and rooms are decorated with mosaics of woodland nymphs and mythological scenes. Facing the entrance, across the central court, is a group of rather worn mosaics, including one that one depicts ducks pulling chariots in a hippodrome. The real treasures are beyond, in what must have been the public rooms, where the mosaics are better preserved. The two most outstanding *mosaics*—thought to be slightly later than the others (possibly early 3C)—are Diana bathing with her nymphs and surprised by Actaeon; and Hylas captured by nymphs.

From here it is possible to rejoin the well-trodden visitors' path and follow the ravine of the river Fertassa back to the SE gate. You will pass by a tumulus and, on the far side of the river, a large rectangular ruin known as the *Temple of Saturn* which is thought to pre-date the advent of the Romans and to have had its name changed by them. The walk back to the gate offers a good opportunity to appreciate the extent of the encircling ramparts (with a little imagination).

If Volubilis is the monument to Roman civilisation, (3km) **MOULAY IDRISS** is the shrine in memory of the beginnings of Islam and of the Sultan Moulay Idriss I (788–791), founder of the first Arab dynasty in Morocco. The view of Moulay Idriss from Volubilis is a striking and provocative one, exuding mystery and a rare other-worldliness, and there is everything to be said for visiting the two sites in this order. You return to the main road from Volubilis and then climb 3km to the foot of the great massif which holds up the little holy city whose houses seem to grow out of the rock.

Moulay Idriss is a city apart. Conscious that the possession of the tomb of the founder of Moroccan Islam is sufficient reason for its existence, it really awakens from its torpor only once a year in August and September when thousands of pilgrims from all over the country come to the moussem to honour their first king, called el Akhbar (the old) to distinguish him from his son (buried in Fez). Indeed Moroccans who cannot afford to go all the way to Mecca are allowed instead to make five pilgrimages to Moulay Idriss (which ranks fifth amongst holy cities in the Arab world) though this will not entitle them to adopt the courtesy title of '*el Hadj*', bestowed only on those pilgrims who have been to Mecca. This is one of the most important moussems in Morocco, attended sometimes by members of the Royal Family. Initially it is a religious festival but it soon becomes a lively affair with fantasias, markets, singing and dancing. The surrounding countryside is dotted with tents, and the feasting and rejoicing continues for many days and nights. The spectacle is one of the most colourful that the visitor to Morocco can see. However, it is essential to remember that it is, above all, a holy festival and should therefore be treated with great respect. There are no hotels in Moulay Idriss and there probably never will be. Tourists are welcome but must never be encouraged to such a degree that the intrinsic apartness of the 'city of the Shrine' is lost.

At any time other than August and September, Moulay Idriss is a peaceful corner. A certain amount of controlled expansion is however now taking place and one cannot but notice the over-large white building alongside the road on entry which turns out to be a new covered market. Cafés are springing up around the squares, artisanat stalls are proliferating and the number of 'student'-guides is certainly increasing.

The Great Mosque and shrine of Moulay Idriss stand in the hollow between the two hills which make up the town. It was rebuilt by Moulay

Ismael in the 17C and is firmly barred to non-Muslims by a wooden barrier. Alongside it stands a modern palace belonging to the present king. The hills are known as *Khiber* and *Tasga*; the latter is still spoken of as *'la ville sainte'* and retains sections which are completely closed to visitors; Khiber, which is the higher of the two, can be freely and extensively explored and its narrow winding streets are a joy.

It is now possible to drive up to the deservedly famous viewpoint on Khiber known as the *Terrace of Sidi Abdallah El Hajjam*, though purists will still prefer to climb the steep path and steps (which start to the left of the main square), if only to enjoy the enchanting views back through alleyways as they ascend; look out too for the cylindrical minaret covered in green and white Koranic script and restored in 1939.

From the terrace you will look down on the hill of Tasga which is a perfect dome—a symphony of white and various gradations of white, through grey to light brown, with the occasional green-tiled roof of a mosque. The general hum of activity rises towards you: cocks crowing; donkeys braying; children crying; but all muted like the colours. There is also a good aerial view of the Great Mosque and of the complex series of courtyards and outbuildings which surround it: behind the white arcades is accommodation for pilgrims; the white dome covers the tomb of Rachid, Moulay Idriss' lifelong companion and friend, and regent after his death until the infant Idriss bin Idriss became king.

Strongly recommended is a drive around the well-signposted *'Circuit de Zerhoun'* (about 10km in all) which takes you to the foot of the Jbel Zerhoun mountains and offers some magnificent views over the Meknes plain. The plain is one of the most richly cultivated areas in the country, with particular emphasis on vines. You can then either take the road N from Volubilis, which takes you past a brand new hotel (4-star A) with stunning views over the Roman site and continues 10km through olive groves to join the main Sidi Kacem–Fez road just before the Zegotta Pass, or you can take the equally beautiful road from Moulay Idriss E for about the same distance and join the same road a little closer to Fez at *Nzala-des-Beni-Amar*. From here it is 35km to the junction with the main P1 road coming from Meknes, and a further 10km to Fez (see Rte 10).

B. From Meknes to Fez direct

Meknes—P1. 60km **Fez**.

Via *Ras el Ma*—66km. Including *Moulay Yacoub*—90km.

The most direct route to Fez from Meknes is to take the main road (P1) which crosses the fertile Sais Plain (60km).

Half-way along this route the S310 goes off right to El Hajeb and the Middle Atlas region (see Rte 11).

Towards the end of the journey you will notice a rough road turning off to the right signposted *Ras el Ma*. It leads, in a few kilometres, to the high point on which, history tells us, Moulay Idriss II stood and decided to build his city. Ras el Ma is Arabic for 'head of the water' and it is here that the river Fez bubbles out of the ground to become, further down, the powerful river that provides the main water supply for the people of Fez.

7km out of Fez there is a turning, left, for the thermal spa of *Moulay Yacoub* (15km) which is thought to have been the Roman AQUAE DACICAE. The waters are rich in sulphur and believed to be particularly beneficial to sufferers of rheumatism, skin conditions, and ear, nose and throat complaints. There are swimming pools, and massage and 'special' treatments are available by appointment (which your hotel or the *Syndicat d'Initiative* in either Fez or Meknes will usually be happy to book for you). Very recently a new source of hot therapeutic water has been discovered along the same road and this is known as *Ain Allah* (the eye of Allah).

10 Fez

A visit to **FEZ** (550,000 inhab.) is a rewarding and memorable experience. It is the oldest of Morocco's four 'Imperial' cities and it dominated the country's religious, cultural and political life for a thousand years—until the French arrived in 1912 and removed the seat of government to Rabat. The medieval city of **Fez el Bali** (old Fez) remains complete and is unspoiled. It is fervently Islamic, deeply traditonal, and closed to the motor car. Its physical collapse over the centuries has been halted by UNESCO who have made it the object of a Cultural Heritage plan and have restored many of its glorious buildings.

Information. Moroccan National Tourist Office: Place de la Resistance (tel. 234-60). Syndicat d'Initiative: Place Mohammed V (tel. 247-69).

Post Office. Corner of Blvd Mohammed V and Ave Hassan II.

Transport. Airport: 11km S on Route d'Immouzer (tel. 247-12) Internal flights to all major cities; also flights to Paris. Airport bus from Place Mohammed V. Railway station: N of Ave des Almohades (New Fez). Trains to Casablanca, Tangier and Oujda. Bus station: Blvd Mohammed V (main terminal); also Place Baghdadi (near Bab Boujeloud). Buses to Rabat, Casablanca, Marrakesh, Meknes, Chaouen, Oujda, Tangier, Azrou and Sefrou. Buses for Oujda also leave from Bab Ftouh.

Hotels. Three 5-star; two 4-star A; one 4-star B; four 3-star A; two 2-star A; three 2-star B; two 1-star A.

History. The traditional story of the foundation of Fez, as it appears in the chronicle 'Raoud el Kartas', by Ibn-Abi-Zar-el-Fasi, the 13C historian from Fez, states that in 808 Idriss II decided that Volubilis, the old Roman capital, was too small and so sent his vizir to search for a new site. The vizir discovered a fertile plain watered by many springs which were the source of a river. He followed the river down into a long flat valley enclosed by ranges of hills and chose this site as the place for the new city. Idriss was well pleased and gave orders for construction to begin. The story states that first he built a walled settlement on the right bank of the river with a mosque—Mosque of the Sheiks (el Sheikh)—and a year later he built an exactly similar walled settlement on the left bank and another mosque—Mosque of the Cherifs (el Chorfa).

This story is sometimes questioned by modern historians who doubt whether Idriss II would have built a second separate town exactly like the first and so close to it in time and space. Levi-Provençal, in his book 'La Fondation de Fes' (1938), quotes the Arab historian Abou-Bekr-er-Razi, who wrote that it was Idriss I who considered Volubilis too small and that it was he who built the first (right bank) town of Fez in 799. Moreover, this story goes, when he began digging the foundations he uncovered a golden pickaxe (or *fas*) and so the place was named the town of the pickaxe or *Madinat Fes*. Nineteen years later when Idriss II succeeded his father he decided that this little settlement (which was essentially Berber in character) was not grand enough and began to build a more dignified capital on the other side of the river which was to become predominantly Arab in character. The second explanation seems more likely to be true.

The etymology of the word Fes is also a subject for speculation. The French historian Henri Gaillard, writing in 1905, listed four legends, one of which is mentioned above. The second concerns a group of Persians, known as Fars, who were present at the moment when the boundary was being marked out and were buried under a sudden rock fall. The place was therefore named to commemorate them. Another relates that when Idriss was asked what should be the name of his new capital he replied it should be called after the first man who passed by that morning: someone duly appeared and answered that his name was Fares, but as he lisped it sounded like Fes. The fourth claims that Idriss was visited by a very old monk who was overjoyed to learn about the plans for a new city because he had read in a holy book that one day a man called Idriss who was descended from the Prophet would build a city called Sef (sic) in this very spot where, he said, there had earlier been a great city.

Moulay Idriss II was a good leader and spent the 24 years of his reign (804–828) strengthening and enlarging his father's kingdom and consolidating the capital. He was assisted by the timely arrival in 818 of some 8000 Arab families who had been expelled from Andalucia by the Christians. Idriss welcomed them and installed them in the right-bank city, which from that moment became known (and still is) as *Fes el Andalous*. These people brought from Spain the skills in mosaic, wood-carving and stucco-work which later made Fez famous. Seven years later 2000 Arab families came to Fez from Kairwan in Tunisia, also seeking a peaceful place to live. They, too, were welcomed and were offered a place on the left bank of the river which thereafter became known as *Fes el Karaouyine*. In '*Raoud el Kartas*' it was said that the inhabitants of el Andalous were 'strong, brave and good at cultivating the soil'; those of el Karaouyine were 'better educated and more given to luxurious living; the men were handsome but the women were less pretty than those of *el Andalous*'.

In 828 Idriss II died and his tomb became the principal shrine of the city that he had created. He left many sons who subsequently divided the kingdom between them: usually a recipe for disaster but in this case, at least at first, Fez remained the most advanced and prosperous town in Morocco. In 859, during the reign of Idriss II's grandson, Yahia, the two great mosques of Karaouyine and Andalous were founded (on the sites of the original el Sheikh and el Chorfa which had become much too small). In keeping with Islamic law the two mosques soon became centres of culture as well as prayer. Since Islamic learning centred around the Koran, which was read aloud in mosques, what more natural than that they should become not only places of prayer but also of religious and scientific knowledge. Under the Idrissides, houses, shops, public baths (thanks to the glorious abundance of water) and flour mills were built on both banks of the river. Merchants from far and wide poured in to buy and sell in the prosperous markets, and fondouks were built to accommodate them. (Fondouks were two-storey lodging houses with bedrooms above and space for pack animals and merchandise below.)

The Berbers. This peaceful period of self-assured progress was shattered in the second half of the 10C by the Zenata Berber tribe of Meknassas who came from the S and made sudden and repeated attacks on the totally unprepared Fassis. A period of unprecedented violence followed, during which the two halves of the city found themselves fighting one another. To make matters worse the attackers were soon joined by another tribe of Zenatas, and the two leaders, who were brothers, installed themselves one on each side of the river, which exacerbated the feud. Their arrival coincided with (or perhaps caused) a period of intense famine. Such was the desperate hunger of the occupying Berbers that whenever they saw smoke rising from a Fassi's home they forced entry and grabbed whatever food was being prepared. The people soon grew wary and began to dig caves in which to hide their food.

The Almoravides. This situation continued until the arrival of the Almoravides in the 11C. The leader of this group of fanatically religious Sanhaja Berbers was Youssef ben Tachfine. He had already founded Marrakesh as his capital in 1062, but he knew that Fez, traditional capital of Morocco, must be forced into submission before he would be able to declare himself Sultan of the whole country. The people of Fez, already exhausted by hunger and in-fighting, could offer little serious resistance. Nevertheless, there were many battles and the remaining Zenatas either fled or were massacred.

The unpleasant preliminaries over and rightful power established, Youssef ben Tachfine proceeded to embellish and enlarge Fez to such an extent that the quality of life for the Fassis surpassed anything else in Morocco at that time. He made use of resident Andalucian talent—and probably imported more—to erect all kinds of public buildings, including mosques, baths, fountains, markets, and fondouks, to accommodate the increasing flow of merchants. The river was ingeniously harnessed so that by 1069 every house had running water available to it. There is one outstanding act which forms a milestone in the history of Fez: he joined the two halves of the city together by demolishing the wall which had divided the two adouar—el Karaouyine and el Andalous—and by building a bridge across the river. He was the first to see that in order to achieve real progress, the two quarrelling factions must unite. In fact the two welded together only very slowly, and some would say never completely.

The Almohades. Peace reigned for over 70 years until the next dynasty of religious fanatics, the Almohades, arrived c 1154. The people of Fez barricaded themselves inside the city. The Almohade leader Abd el Mumene built a dam across the river with wood and rubbish, so that on its release tons of water hurtled down, taking with it city walls, houses and people. Having captured Fez, Abd el Mumene had much of the delicate Almoravide carving in the mosques plastered over, declaring that it was too ornate. He also demolished the Almoravides' town walls, saying 'only justice and the sword shall be our ramparts'. His successors were to regret this impetuous act and started building new walls and babs. One of the best preserved today is *Bab el Mahrouk* (Gate of the Burned One), so called because a rebel leader was suspended from its arch and burned. It was built so high that a soldier could enter on horseback without having to lower his standard. The city is still enclosed by what is left of the massive Almohade walls. Fez el Bali (Old Fez) is no bigger today than it was in Almohade times and herein lies the secret of its unique harmony and authenticity.

Although the Almohades also chose Marrakesh as their capital, Fez became even more prosperous under their positive and educated guidance and was soon the centre of a vast Islamic empire comprising much of Spain and almost the whole of North Africa. Cultural and spiritual life flourished and the Karaouyine became a regular meeting place for learned men, scientists and doctors from all over the Empire. The 'Raoud el Kartas' recounts that at this moment of supreme greatness, at the beginning of the 13C, there were 785 mosques, 80 fountains, 93 public baths, 9082 shops, 372 flour mills, 135 bread ovens, 467 fondouks, 89,236 houses, and 125,000 permanent inhabitants, with hundreds more people passing through, all of which must have made Fez easily the biggest town in the Moorish empire at that time. Such was the intensity of cultural activity in the city that most of the smaller mosques became places of learning with their own libraries and professorial chairs—all under the aegis of the Karaouyine. In the Arab world it became the dearest wish of anybody with power and influence to send his son to be educated in Fez.

The Merinides. The city continued to prosper under subsequent dynasties, with only the occasional outbreak of inter-tribal violence. During the late 13C the Merinide sultan Youssef returned from successful conquests in Spain to find the city closed to him. On regaining entry he executed six of the rebellious Fassis and fixed their heads to the ramparts. His son, Yacoub II (1286–1307), forgave this infidelity and made Fez his capital.

The Merinides had arrived in vast numbers and the old city could expand no further. A new town was built outside the Almohade walls, close but not too close to the old town and dominating it from higher ground. Called *Fez Jdid* (New Fez), it was essentially a garrison town and one is still struck by the military character of its ramparts. The army was permanently stationed here, mainly for the purpose of continuing the campaign against Spain, but also to be on hand should there be any further revolt by the people of Fez el Bali. A royal palace and mosque were built and many fine houses for high-ranking Merinides. The new city did not compete with its neighbour for spiritual or educational superiority but it did provide administration and protection. It also provided somewhere for the increasing Jewish population to live. Hitherto, Jews had been scattered throughout the old city in isolated groups, officially tolerated by the Muslims but not welcomed, often misused and frequently made scapegoats. The Merinides built a Jewish quarter, which was protected by high walls pierced by only one gateway. Today the remains of the Mellah are recognisable by the unusually high walls, and houses with tiny windows.

Yacoub II was one of the first Berber sultans to show any signs of philanthropy. He actually sought to improve conditions for the people, especially the blind, the sick, and above all the poor students who could not afford lodgings within the city. The Merinides are best remembered in Fez for their medersas—buildings comprising two storeys of small rooms, some of them bedrooms and others classrooms, around a central courtyard. Here the students found board and lodging for little or no money. Some medersas even had their own mosques, or at least an oratory where students could retire to say their prayers. Although the little rooms were simple inside, the carved decoration and mosaics around the courtyards were made with a degree of expertise formerly reserved only for mosques. Medersas were not just students' lodgings, they were monuments to Islam. All were grouped around one or other of the two big mosques—the Karaouyine and the Andalous—and only one was built in Fez Jdid, which is proof that the Merinides were content for the older town to remain the spiritual centre.

The Merinides built very few mosques in Fez el Bali because it already had so many. They did, however, manage to squeeze in more houses, more fountains and more palaces; all more exquisite than anything put up by the sober Almohades. These palaces, created by master craftsmen from Spain, were fairylands of marble, carved cedarwood, stucco, and fine mosaics. Today one must visit the Alhambra in Granada to see a typical example of the flamboyant palatial style of the Merinides. No such palaces survive today in Fez, though many of the medersas are still well preserved and remain a faithful reflection of the Merinides' penchant for elegance and grace.

The Saadians. With the death of the last Merinide ruler in 1465 there followed a series of weak rulers of the related El Wattas tribe. Chaos ensued throughout the country as Christian invaders arrived unchecked from the N and rebellious Berber tribes rose up to try and take control of the interior. Religious leaders prayed for a strong leader and in 1541 the Saadians arrived from the Draa valley under Mohammed. He drove the El Wattas out of Fez but found the people hostile and scornful of his uncouth ways. He humiliated them by banishing their leaders to the desert and then made Taroudant in the S his capital. The defeated Fassis lived a quiet and fearful existence until 1576 when Abd el Malik, a grandson of Mohammed esh-Sheik, swept into the city and, with the help of Turkish troops from neighbouring Algiers, made Fez the Saadian capital. Once enthroned he quickly paid off the troops and sent them back lest they should decide to stay, although for some weeks prayers were said in the name of the Turkish caliph.

An English ambassador visited Fez for the first time in 1577, appointed by Queen Elizabeth I to 'the king of Maruecos and Fesse'. Abd el Malik tried hard to negotiate a political alliance with England against the Spaniards but failed. A trade agreement did follow however, by which English cloth was exchanged for sugar, dates and almonds. Once secure in Fez the Saadians settled down to continue the process of embellishment which their predecessors had left unfinished. This was done in the same Spanish-Muslim style and their only innovation was the use of Italian marble, which they imported in large quantities together with the skilled artisans to work it. They paid for the marble, weight for weight, in locally grown sugar. By this time (the late 16C) the Saadians had shed their rough manners and were even adopting some of the refinements of the Fassi way of life: dressing in silks, eating at intervals during the day instead of all at once like desert nomads, and holding discussions with scholars. Abd el Malik was succeeded by Ahmed in 1578. He was nicknamed *'Edh Dhahabi'* (the golden one), and was only interested in plundering gold and slaves from Timbucktoo. He put the people of Fez to work minting gold coins, but he preferred to live in Marrakesh, where he spent most of the new-found wealth. At his death in 1603 his three sons battled for the throne, and a period of civil war followed during which Fez was sacked repeatedly. Fez el Bali and Fez Jdid were ranged against each other, family fought family, and even the call to prayer from the minarets was suspended.

The Alouites. In despair the people of Fez invited another race of Shareefs (descendants of the Prophet) to take control. These were the Alouites, who came from the Tafilalet region (having arrived from Arabia three centuries earlier), and who still reign today. The first sultan, Moulay Rachid, was welcomed to Fez in 1666, where he restored order, lent money to the ruined merchants and brought back strict observance of Islam. But he was a cruel tyrant and his successor, Moulay Ismael (1672–1727), even more so. Ismael chose Meknes as his capital. He mistrusted the Fassis and appointed a number of governors to rule Fez in his absence, and they were so fearful for their own heads that they punished the slightest misdemeanour with death. Many eminent Fassis left the town and the population dwindled for the first time in its history. When Moulay Ismael died, aged 81, he was succeeded by a series of quarrelling and incapable sons and grandsons. Real power now lay in the hands of the infamous Black Guard which the old Sultan had built up for his own protection, mainly from descendants of slaves. They owed loyalty to no one and could make or break sultans at will. This they did and Fez was severely affected, with one seige lasting 27 months.

Not till 1757 did an Alouite sultan emerge who was able to bring the over-extended Black Guard under control. This was Mohammed III, and he gradually repaired Fez to something approaching its former glory. But the two years of his son Yazid's (1790–92) reign were by contrast most destructive. He was nicknamed by his contemporaries 'the Bloodthirsty', and his ruling principle was that a sultan should keep a continuous stream of blood flowing from the palace gates to the city walls, so that the people would live in fear and obedience. This he managed to do until he was removed by his jealous brothers. He was followed by a string of uninspiring monarchs who did nothing to improve the sterile condition into which Fez and the whole country was sinking. The reign of Moulay el Hassan between 1873 and 1894 was comparatively peaceful. At first the people of Fez el Bali shut their gates to the new sultan, and he, not daring to use firearms for fear of damaging the holy shrine of Moulay Idriss, had to wait outside until one of his men had penetrated the walls and persuaded the Fassis to lay down their arms and open the gates. Subsequently he joined Fez el Bali and Fez Jdid together by constructing a palace (the Bou Jeloud Palace) between them with an entrance at each end; and by constructing an avenue joining Bab el Mahrouk with the Royal Palace in Fez Jdid. He died in 1894, worn out in the end by his struggle to quell the country's increasingly ungovernable tribes. His sons, Abd el Aziz and Moulay Hafid, were no more successful and in 1912 Fez was occupied by the French and a treaty was signed relieving Hafid (1908–12) of his power to govern and declaring the greater part of the country a French Protectorate.

The French. General Lyautey, the first French Resident-General, showed extraordinary sensitivity in building new cities (including modern Fez) alongside the old, leaving medinas and monuments intact and not destroying (or even undermining) centuries of tradition.

Fez remains the proud centre of Islamic Morocco, able to retain its dignity and traditions the more for having handed over the burden of government administration to the new capital, Rabat.

There are three cities: Fez el Bali (the medina) founded in the early 9C; Fez Jdid, founded alongside it in the 13C; and modern Fez, built by the French at the far end of Fez Jdid at the beginning of this century.

Fez el Bali

A visit to the **Medina** is an unforgettable experience, and you should allow
at least a day, or preferably two separate half days; an in-depth visit will
require three or four days. An initial drive (15km) around the '*Route de Fez*'
is strongly recommended. It follows the rim of the basin in which the medina
is tightly wedged and so provides very good views—best times are early in
the morning or at sundown. The route is well signposted and you can join
it at almost any point. If you are approaching from Modern Fez, leave by
Ave Hassan II and Blvd Moulay Youssef; turn left where the ramparts begin
and follow them round, turning right and right again where the road is
joined by another coming from Meknes. Continue along the ramparts and
you will pass the early 14C Merinide gate—*Bab Segma*—with its single
remaining octagonal tower; on the left is the *Makina*, an old royal ordnance
factory which is now a carpet factory; on the right is the *Cherrarda Kasbah*,
which was built in the late 17C by the first Alouite sultan, Moulay Rachid,
as a vantage point over the city (it now contains an annexe to the university
and a hospital); and also *Bordj Nord*, a 16C fort built by Christian slaves
and now containing a museum of weapons. Just beyond is the 5-star *Grand
Hotel des Merinides* (with panoramic terrace at the back). Very little is
known about the nearby *Merinide Tombs* (late 15C), except that they
constitute one of two Merinide necropli, the other, earlier, one being at
Chellah in Rabat. All that remains are a few crumbling ruins with a place
for stopping the car (or taxi) to take advantage of what is probably the best
view of the medina. Far below you will see a conglomeration of buildings
in shades of brown, grey and white, interspersed by the colourful minarets
and green-tiled roofs of the mosques.

The road zigzags down to reach *Bab Guissa* and then on to Bab Jamai
(through which is the *Hotel Palais Jamai*, originally a vizir's palace, built
just inside the walls) and continues to wind round, leaving the roads from
Ouezzane and Taza on the left, to the the S side of the city. It passes *Bab
Ftouh* (giving access to the Quartier Andalous) and eventually arrrives at
Bordj Sud (equivalent to the look-out fortress you saw on the N side). From
here there is another fine view of the city. Continue past the ramparts, *Bab
Jdid* and *Bab el Hadid*, to return to the Ville Moderne.

No cars are allowed in the medina (the streets are too narrow). Donkeys
are the only form of transport here and the cry of *'Balak, Balak!'* (Attention,
Attention!) is frequently heard and really means 'please stand aside as I
need to get past you with my donkey'. It is just as well to act quickly or you
can find yourself pinned against the wall by a pannier full of table legs, or
iron pots, etc. Everyone seems to be busy making, selling or carrying
something. The skills of the craftsmen are those of Andalucia, brought back
to Morocco by victorious sultans in the 13C and 14C, and by Muslim
Andalucians in the 15C when they were expelled by the Christians. Their
way of life has changed very little over the centuries. They have their proud
traditions and their unique skills, their strong sense of family loyalty and
their deep Islamic faith. It is perhaps an irony that the ebullient artisanat
economy is now sustained by the tourist trade, either through personal
purchase or export. It is to be hoped that the delicate balance will remain
and that this enchanting city will be able to retain its quintessential
character despite all the flattering attention from outside.

The medina comprises 187 *quartiers* and in each of these there are, by
law, a mosque, a koranic school, a bakery (bread oven to which families

Bab bou Jeloud, Fez el Bali

bring their own dough to be baked on the spot), a water fountain and a hamman ('turkish' bath). There are five medersas, 14 city gates and over 300 mosques. To see even a fraction of this unique medieval city it is necessary to plan with some care.

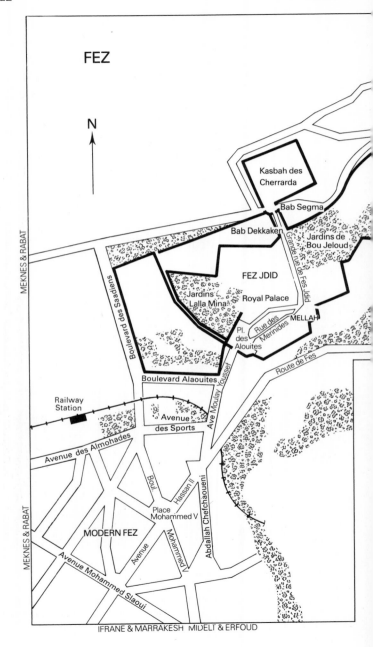

FEZ

N

Kasbah des
Cherrarda

Bab Segma

Bab Dekkaken

Jardins de
Bou Jeloud

FEZ JDID

Jardins
Lalla Mina

Royal Palace

MELLAH

Pl.
des
Alouites

Rue des Merinides

Grande rue de Fes Jdid

Boulevard des Saadiens

MEKNES & RABAT

Boulevard Alaouites

Route de Fes

Ave Moulay Youssef

Railway
Station

Avenue
des Sports

Avenue des Almohades

Bd

Hassan II

Place
Mohammed V

MODERN FEZ

Avenue

Mohammed V

Abdallah Chefchaoueni

MEKNES & RABAT

Avenue Mohammed Slaoui

IFRANE & MARRAKESH MIDELT & ERFOUD

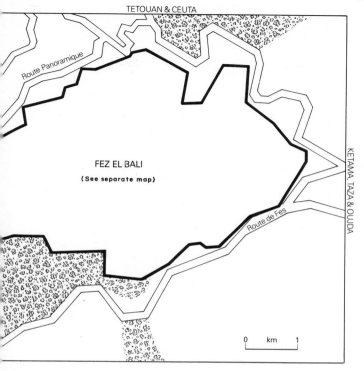

Would that it were possible simply to wander in, guidebook in hand, and be left alone. (Even if it were possible, you would undoubtedly get lost the first time.) The reality is that people will flock to help you and it is best to appoint your guide from the start, and he will then fend off the others. It is important to make clear to your guide what you want to see, otherwise you run the risk of being whisked at speed through the maze of narrow alleyways from one carpet or kaftan co-operative to another, for the obvious reason that any purchase you make will activate a rake-off for your guide.

A logical place to start is the *Bab Bou Jeloud* (at the Fez Jdid end) and there is a parking area outside it. This is one of the newest city gates (1913), built in the traditional style and covered in ceramic tiles, blue outside and green inside. The view through it gives a foretaste of what is to come: the green minaret on the left is that of the 14C Bou Inania Medersa, and the grey minaret on the right is that of the 11C Sidi Lazaz mosque. Go through the Bab and plunge into the noise and excitement of the GRAND TALA (*Tala Kebira*), which bends round to the right and then goes left of the two minarets. It is one of the main streets and will take you right into the centre of the medina. The smell is of oranges, mint and spices of all kinds. Much of the way you are protected from the sun by a rough covering of reeds over the street. You will pass first the fruit and vegetable section—always of high quality and clean. Notice the cords hanging from the roofs of the stalls by which the vendors swing themselves in and out over the piles of produce; there is often no other way.

You will soon come to an impressive entrance (on your right) which is the **Bou Inania Medersa**. This was built as a lodging house for students of the Karaouyine by the Merinide sultan Abou Inan in 1355. Generally considered to be the finest of all Moroccan medersas, this beautifully restored example of Islamic architecture at its best should not be missed. You go through a small entrance-hall, with its own splendid stalactitic dome, into the glory of the building which is the court. The walls are quite breathtaking; it seems that not a centimetre has been left undecorated, and yet because the colours are so muted and the proportions so near perfect the overall effect is not confusing. The whole is framed from above by a layer of finely carved cedarwood, while below is a terrace of delicate stucco. The stuccowork, like fine threads of lace, outlines the simple openings of the tiny cell-like students' rooms. (It is worth climbing one of the flights of stairs, which go up from the entrance hall to the terrace, for an exceptional view of the court and nearby buildings.) Below the stucco on three sides of the court is a horizontal band of black Kufic script painted on wood. The columns beneath it are covered with minutely worked zelliges, which form the only point of colour, other than browns and creams, in the whole complex structure. Between the columns are elegant wooden grilles, and behind these are the rooms which would have served as lecture halls.

In the centre of the court is the small ablutions fountain, fed by waters from the river Fez, a spot of perfect peace in its natural surround of plain flagstones, presenting an acceptable contrast to the contrived perfection around it. At the far end of the court, opposite the finely proportioned door through which you entered, is the oratory, with its delicately sculpted mihrab, where the imam stands facing Mecca to lead the prayers. This part of the medersa is still in use and, depending on the good nature of your guide, it may or may not be possible to peer in. The green-tiled minaret is one of the most elegant in Fez.

Leaving the medersa you will notice a curious phenomenon high on the wall opposite: a row of 13 wooden blocks with simple brass bowls projecting below 13 windows—seven of the original brass bowls remain. This was once a *Magana* (or water-clock), created c 1317 by a local craftsman. It was discovered in about 1355 by Sultan Abou Inan, who erected it opposite the medersa, which was being completed at that time. The clock was undoubtedly intended to draw the attention of passers-by to the medersa and also to ring out the hours of prayer. There is much speculation as to how it worked, the most likely explanation being that there were two water-tanks hidden inside the house behind the wall; water flowed at a controlled rate between them, and the falling level in one or the rising level in the other activated a series of levers which caused a weight to fall through a window into one of the brass bowls. Next-door to the clock, and also part of the Bou Inania complex, are the original 'Turkish-style' latrines; even they are built around a central court and have a carved plaster ceiling.

As you go deeper into the medina, it is important to keep looking up at the countless minarets which are one of its special charms. Notice particularly that of the 14C *Ech Cherabliyin Mosque* (the slipper-makers' mosque) on the right, as you descend the Grand Tala. Its decoration is said to have been modelled on that of the Almohade Koutoubia in Marrakesh, and is still in its original form. You will pass the leather souks where they make pouffes and book covers tooled with gold; and the brass souks where there is a man who says his father designed the seven gates of the Royal Palace in Fez Jdid and who will gladly chisel for you an intricate pattern on a sheet of brass which will turn into a tray before your eyes. You will eventually reach (although not necessarily in this order) the zaouia and mausoleum of Moulay Idriss, Place Nejjarine, the Attarine souk and medersa, the Karaouyine mosque, and the Place Seffarine with its medersa; all of this before getting to the river which divides the city into its two halves—Fes el Karaouyine and Fes el Andalous (originally two quite separate walled towns; see History above).

The *Zaouia of Moulay Idriss II* was built by the Idrissides in the 9C but later fell into disuse and decay during the rule of the Almoravide and Almohade dynasties. It was rebuilt in the 13C by the Merinides who rekindled the cult of the Idrissides and of Moulay Idriss in particular. It was the succeeding dynasty of Wattasides who rediscovered Moulay Idriss' tomb, and from that moment it became the most revered sanctuary in Morocco: the object of pilgrimages and source of comfort to rich and poor alike. Until quite recently the zaouia also held the documents of allegiance from all the tribes to each new sultan. It is still a place to gather in time of trouble and, even to this day, it retains the right of 'horm' (holy asylum) and the streets leading to it are barred by wooden beams which mark the boundary of the horm area. Significantly, Sultan Moulay el Hassan, who found himself shut out from the city in 1873, forbore the use of gunpowder for fear of damaging this place (see History above).

The four doors are often open, so it is possible, discreetly, to peer in and look at the magnificently carved wooden ceiling (Merinide), and at the tomb in white marble, with people sitting cross-legged in front praying and lightly touching it. Old men sit and chant verses from the Koran. It is unwise to try to photograph it. Notice, as you approach, the copper plaque on the outside with a hole into the wall where people can place their hands for a moment of comfort and blessing (baraka).

All around the zaouia there is an area of specialised souks: nearest the building are the candle-makers; next are the jewellery-makers and goldsmiths. The *Kissaria* (covered market), was built to replace one that burned down in 1954. Traditionally a kissaria is a place where imported goods are sold. This one seems to be filled with fabrics—it is a treasure house of silks, brocades and woollen materials (much of which appears to have been made locally) and the guides refer to it as 'the fabric souk'. Nearby are the carpenters' workshops of the *Souk Nejjarine*, which give off a heady aroma of cedarwood. Here men sit on the ground and hold table legs between their toes whilst they use both hands to plane the wood, or carve intricate patterns on table tops. There is a huge demand in Morocco for this highly specialised work.

You are now in the PLACE NEJJARINE, with its 17C fountain, beautifully decorated with mosaic tiles and carved and painted wood, and its fondouk (early 18C), with a magnificent entrance under an imposing porch roof.

The *Attarine souk*, on the NE corner of the square, is the centre for herbs and spices and is said to be the busiest souk in Fez. The more everyday spices like coriander and turmeric are piled in great heaps on open display, whilst the rarer varieties are kept in small jars in murky interiors; the rarest and most expensive of all is musk. Recommended are the ready-made

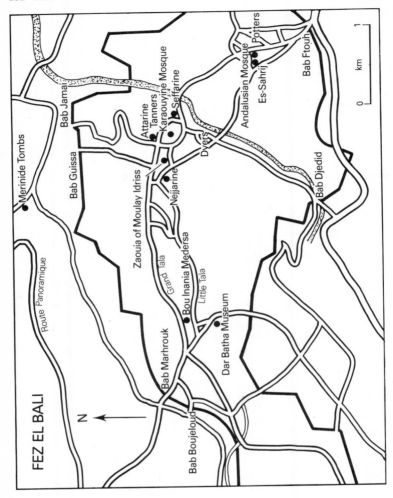

mixtures of five or seven spices which will transform an everyday chicken casserole into a feast. Notice the strange twists of dried grasses on sale to Berber women who use them for cleaning their teeth. Close by is the *Henna souk* presenting every kind of beauty aid including henna paste and leaves, kohl and phials of exotic perfume. And if all else fails, there are lizard skins and terrapin shells for magic potions and aphrodisiacs.

At the end of the souk is the bronze door which leads into the *Attarine Medersa* (1325). It has the same ground-plan as the Bou Inania medersa but it is considerably smaller. It also has the same sequence of wall decoration: zelliges, stucco, and carved wood. In the courtyard square tile-covered piers support an arcade with particularly finely carved capitals.

The floor is also tiled—unlike that of Bou Inania—and the whole effect is one of an infinite variety of geometrical patterns comprised of squares and circles and 10-point stars, each design a point of visual repose in its exquisite symmetry. The oratory is by comparison very simple. It is no longer in use and so may legitimately be entered. The entire building has recently been well-restored and its first-floor terrace affords an excellent view into the courtyard of the Karaouyine.

The **KARAOUYINE** is the biggest mosque in North Africa, with space inside for some 20,000 people who enter through 14 separate doors. It was founded in 859 by Fatima el Fihri, a young girl originally from Kairwan, who sponsored the building of the first mosque as a tribute to Allah in memory of her father, a wealthy merchant. It is said that she consulted local wise men as to the siting and planning of the mosque in relation to Mecca and that she had the original building made out of materials extracted from the chosen site so as to avoid the introduction of any impure substance. It started as a simple rectangle measuring 32m by 36m. It was raised to the status of cathedral mosque in 933, and in 956 given a new minaret which still survives and is simple to the point of austerity. Both the Almoravides and the Merinides enlarged the mosque, and by the end of the 13C it had reached its present dimensions.

In keeping with Islamic law it became very early on a centre of culture as well as prayer—a university as well as a mosque. Learned men lectured students who crowded round them in circles squatting on the floor—the most interesting teacher collecting the biggest circle. The lectures could take place only between the times allocated for prayer. Teaching centred on the Koran, but at an early stage subjects such as law, geography, astrology and arithmetic were introduced. It is believed that Arabic numerals and the zero may have been developed here. Many famous scholars, including the historian Ibn Khaldoun, studied here. Much of the learning was by rote (as it still is in the Koranic schools) and it is doubtful whether many students actually learned how to apply the knowledge they had so painfully absorbed. They might have attended classes for ten years or more before gradually starting to teach themselves, either in the mosque or in the neighbouring medersas. Today the students have moved out to more comfortable premises in the modern town, both to live and to work, and the Karaouyine has reverted to its original sole function as mosque.

It is ironic that such a vast place, so central to the life of Fez throughout the ages, is actually quite difficult to find. It is so hemmed in by lesser buildings, alleyways and stalls, all tightly packed against its very ordinary walls, that the unguided visitor can quite easily pass by without noticing it. It does not tower above the city in the style of a Christian cathedral. The only hope for a non-Muslim to see anything at all is to be fortunate enough to find one of the doors open.

The Almohade interior of 16 aisles is simple: the arcades of identical horseshoe-shaped arches and undecorated columns give a great sense of space. Far more ornate is the open courtyard built by the Saadians in the 16C. It has a black-and-white tiled floor, and at each end a pavilion with carved stucco arches over slender columns and a green-tiled roof. On one side of the courtyard is the main archway through which the King himself passes: an elaborate textbook of Muslim architecture covered with fine stucco-work, mosaics and, at the top, the stalactitic plaster carving for which the Saadians were renowned (cf. the workmanship with that of the Saadian tombs in Marrakesh). The courtyard strongly resembles the Court-yard of Lions in the Alhambra at Granada.

Tanners at work in Fez

Walking round the outside of the Karaouyine, in a clockwise direction from the Attarine, you pass the rather dilapidated but once elegant *Mesbahiya medersa* (1346). It has a floor of Italian marble and a very splendid marble basin which was brought over from Andalucia by the Saadians. It also has finely carved wooden decoration above the door. The rest of the woodwork has been taken to the Dar Batha Museum. Next you will pass the Tetouani fondouk, once a hostelry for merchants from Tetouan and now a carpet shop.

You will also see the *Karaouyine Library*, housed in a simple building separate from the mosque. Believed to go back to the foundation of the mosque in the 9C, it received in the 14C a unique collection of Korans and other Islamic works returned from Andalucia as part of a peace treaty by the King of Castile. Sadly, many of these have been lost over the years, but there still remain enough rare volumes—including an original copy of Ibn Khaldoun's 'History'—to make this one of the most prized collections in the Muslim world. In the late 1950s, King Mohammed V added a spacious reading room for students of the University. (It is closed to the public.)

In front of the library is the pretty PLACE SEFFARINE (Brassfounders' Square). All around there is furious activity and noise, for men are hammering huge cauldrons into shape. There are treasures in every conceivable metal here—copper urns, silver trays and family-sized pots for making cous-cous. Here too is the *Seffarine Medersa*. Built in 1280, by the Merinide sultan Youssef, it is the oldest of the Fez medersas. The entrance (through a heavy studded door) is hidden down a narrow lane which leads out of the left-hand corner of the square. In need of some restoration, its 30 students' rooms are tucked away behind a fine, arched balcony above the court. It was built in the style of a traditional Fassi house.

By now you are approaching the river Fez, the waters of which are used by the dyers and tanners. The latter have established themselves near a bridge just below Seffarine, and merit a visit—you will be offered a sprig of mint to counter the sickly smell of the tanners' materials.

The round dried-earth pits are filled with different coloured liquids, some for treating the skins and some for dyeing them. The skins (sheep, camel, kid and cow) are first washed, then scraped, then soaked for two or three days to soften them; then laid out to dry; then dyed and dried again. Only vegetable dyes are used: indigo, poppyflower, mint and saffron. The methods have not changed in thousands of years. The scantily clad and highly skilled tanners hop nimbly from vat to vat, nursing the skins through the various processes.

A little way up the river are the dyers, using the same vegetable dyes to colour wool for carpets and cloth, and the streets are hung with the drying skeins.

Cross the river to visit **Fes el Andalous**—the Andalucian quarter. There are two bridges—*El Aouad* and *Bein el Moudoun*—both dating originally from the 11C and still in use. One can see that even now the Andalous and Karaouyine quarters are only thinly joined.

Fes el Andalous is quieter, more spaced out, rural even, but certainly not without points of interest. To reach *la Mosquée Andalous* (sister mosque to the Karaouyine) take either of the two bridges and continue steadily up the hill; Rue Sidi Youssef is the more direct route. Founded in 860 by Miriam—sister of Fatima responsible for the Karaouyine—the mosque began as an oratory and achieved status as a mosque after the Almohades enlarged it in 1200, at which point it began also to fulfil an educational function like the Karaouyine. Most beautiful is the N portal (with a stepped street leading up to it), which dates from the Almohade period. It has been restored quite recently. The magnificent horseshoe arch is set off to perfection by the dark stucco-work around it, the verses from the Koran painted in black above, and the important carved cedarwood section above that. This is the highest gateway in Fez and from its top the ulemas watch for the thin crescent of

Es Sahrij medersa, Fez

the Ramadan moon. To the left of the portal is a Merinide fountain for ablutions. Although one is subject to the usual frustration of not being able to look inside there is (at present) a large crack in the S door.

The Merinides built two medersas in the immediate vicinity: *Es Seb-baiyne* and *Es Sahrij*. The former, meaning 'seven' was so-named because it was here that students were taught how to chant the Koran in seven different approved styles. The latter is particularly worth seeing. It has extremely rich zellige decorations and fine wood carving, in the simple Almohade patterns. It was built c 1320. Es Sahrij is also remarkable for its large rectangular pool which creates an unusual optical effect: it appears to be deepest at whichever end you stand. This is a trick of the refracted light and the guides enjoy asking you what you can see and are highly amused when you peer in expecting to see a fish or perhaps some writing on the bottom. This medersa is currently undergoing restoration and it is not possible to go upstairs to see the students' rooms.

To your left, as you continue up the hill, are the workshops and kilns of the potters. Jars, vases, plates, bowls, everything from the most homely of shapes to the most delicate refinements of form and colour can be found here, or be seen in the process of formation. The pottery, with its distinctive blue markings, is greatly valued throughout the country. These craftsmen are also masters of the art of cutting mosaics (a skill that was certainly brought in from Andalucia) and it was from here that they were taken to Rabat to work on the modern Mausoleum of Mohammed V, and to Casablanca to decorate the new royal mosque.

Bab Ftouh is a little further up the hill (leaving the potters on your left), and close by it is the gleaming white *koubba* of the 12C saint Sidi Harazem, adopted by the students as their patron, and the subject of a colourful moussem every spring.

Cross back over the river and turn up the hill to the right towards Bab Jamai and the renowned *Palais Jamai Hotel*, which will provide welcome refreshment (at a price). It is the only luxury hotel within the medina walls. The original part of the this hotel was a palace, built at the end of the 19C by Si Mohammed Ben Arib el Jamai, Grand Vizir to Sultan Moulay Hassan. The rooms, with modern comforts added, are traditionally decorated with all the lavish detail and colour that will by now be familiar to you, and there is a faint smell of cedarwood over all.

For tired feet, it is but a short taxi ride from the Hotel back to Bab Bou Jeloud. Otherwise, return on foot by way of the PETIT TALA (Tala Seghira) which starts just above Place Nejjarine and offers a slightly different sequence of artisanat and also a view of the sculptured roof of the Bou Inania Medersa from behind. It will eventually rejoin the Grand Tala and take you back to Bab Bou Jeloud.

You will probably allow yourself, at some point, to be persuaded into a co-operative. Co-operatives are often housed in former palaces and usually display a very wide range of merchandise, about which the 'front man' will be glad to impart a limitless flow of information. Do not take too seriously the claim that 'here prices are fixed'; it is surprising how fast they become unfixed once you walk towards the door. These highly organised places generally start with higher prices than the smaller independent merchants and you may wish to search more widely.

Some of the larger palaces have been turned into restaurants where traditional Moroccan food is served in a suitably authentic setting. This is probably the best way of tasting such delicacies as *pastilla*, which are usually only made in large quantities. Many of these places are also open in the evenings (when there might also be a floor show), but you may need to book in advance, which you can do from your hotel. The price often includes transport to and from your hotel and a guide to get you there from the nearest bab.

Fez el Bali is not just shops and workshops. People also live here and many of the unpromising walls without windows which line the side streets hide beautiful and rich interiors. Houses are built on a square around a central patio, often with gardens and fountains, and all the windows look inwards.

Fez Jdid

FEZ JDID, or new Fez, was built by the Merinides in the 13C. Unlike former dynasties they were not motivated by religious fervour but rather by the desire for power and property, and a love of ostentatious wealth. Fez Jdid was built to house the Merinide sultans in splendour and also as a centre of administration. It therefore has a very different character. Inside the long stretches of wall are palaces, and military and administrative buildings, but very little private housing, private enterprise or mosques. There is a great deal of space with enormous squares and courtyards lacking animation.

Fez Jdid has not really found a role for itself. Some of its royal splendours are on show to the public—but only from the outside—and it has become essentially a museum town as all the administration has been transferred to the modern city.

To enter from the N end (nearest Bab Bou Jeloud) pass first through the very solid 14C *Bab Dekkaken*, which was the main entrance to the city until 1971, and you come into a small walled square known as the *Petit Mechouar*. Go through an archway on the right and you will enter the relatively tranquil *Quarter of Moulay Abdallah* where you will find the 13C *Grand Mosque* with koubba alongside which marks the tombs of the Merinide Sultan Abou Inan. A little further on is the 18C *Mosque of Moulay Abdallah*, recognisable by its charming slender minaret; it has become a mausoleum for Alouite sultans including Moulay Youssef, the grandfather of the present king.

Back in the Petit Mechouar, drive down the Grande Rue de Fez Jdid and through 14C *Bab Semmarine*, which leads into the mellah. Continue down the Rue des Merinides (formerly Rue du Mellah) which is lined with high-walled houses with large wooden balconies with commercial premises at ground level. There are very few Jews here now, but originally the mellah was constructed by the Merinides to rehouse those who were living in the precinct of the Karaouyine in order to make space for medersas. No doubt the Merinides also realised that if the Fassi Jews were kept all in one place and close to the central administration (Makhzen) their commercial activities could be overseen. Jews were offered protection within the mellah in exchange for their absolute loyalty to the sultan and they were discouraged from ever leaving the precinct right up to the French Protectorate (1912) by being forbidden to wear shoes outside it. The use of the word *mellah* (meaning salt) in this context originated in Fez and is thought to refer to the task allotted by the early Fassis to the Jews in their community of salting the heads of vanquished enemies before they were set up on the babs as trophies.

Rue des Merinides will lead you into the *Palais Royal* (Dar el Makhzen) by way of PLACE DES ALOUITES, which is a very exotic place. It is a huge court with many palaces, pavilions and audience halls built over 700 years by the various dynasties (for no sultan would have wished to live in anything built by his predecessors), and includes the present royal palace, built in 1880 and recently restored. This has seven gateways, three on each side of an important central portal. The doors are superbly worked in brass and surrounded by green and blue ceramic mosaics. An essential and colourful, but slightly anachronistic, part of this whole 'Arabian Nights' scene is the Royal Guard, dressed in traditional costume. It is unfortunate that one cannot actually enter any of these palaces.

It is not certain whether Fez Jdid or Fez el Bali should lay claim to the **Dar Batha Museum**, since the palace it occupies was built by Sultan Moulay el Hassan in 1873 for the purpose of joining the two cities together and has a gate at each end. It is certainly one of the more rewarding museums (open every day except Tuesday) and should not be missed. It is a two-minute walk from Bab Bou Jeloud: facing the Bab and looking in towards the medina, walk down the street going off to the right—Ed Douah—and the palace is on your right. It was built in the form of a square around a central patio with a fountain in the middle. There are at least eight rooms full of exhibits, which one visits in the company of a guide, usually a very old man, who although informative (he will attempt three or four languages) will usually be incapable of answering questions.

Notice the hand-painted doors and ceilings, they are all different. The museum is particularly noted for its collection of arms—rifles, pistols, spears and daggers, finely ornamented in silver and gold and often encrusted with precious stones. The Koran forbids the wearing of jewellery by men, but to make up for this tolerates unlimited luxury in their weapons. You will also see 11C brass sextants made in Marrakesh, brass-studded leather bridal chests, Berber carpets from the Middle Atlas, a fascinating collection of marriage costumes from different regions, an original 12C door taken from the Karaouyine, complete with its very fine knocker, and a collection of *mouches arabies* (carved wooden screens used in mosques to divide women from men and made in such a way that the women can see through but not be seen).

The gardens attached to the palace are small and consist mainly of carefully planted trees. The *Bou Jeloud Gardens* are a short distance away in the direction of Fez Jdid (on the other side of Ave de l'UNESCO). They are lush, cool, and full of fountains and cypresses.

Modern Fez

La Ville Moderne was built by the French at the beginning of the Protectorate and is an entirely separate city c 1.5km from Fez Jdid. It is crossed by some fine boulevards, and has many excellent shops, hotels and restaurants, a railway station and a Centre Artisanal on Blvd Allal ben Abhallah.

11 Fez to Marrakesh: the Middle Atlas

Total distance 563km. **Fez**—P24. 36km **Imouzzer-du-Kandar**—25km **Ifrane**—17km **Azrou**—82km *Khenifra*—99km *Kasba Tadla*—30km *Beni Mellal*—55km *Bine el Ouidane*—28km *Azilal*—40km **Cascades d'Ouzoud**—44km **Demnate**—107km **Marrakesh**.

Alternatively, a faster route from Beni Mellal (total distance 493km) via 119km *el-Kelaa-des-Srarhna* 85km Marrakesh

About an hour's drive from either Fez or Meknes brings you up into the Middle Atlas, a region of folded mountains and high, windswept plateaux; of majestic cedar forests, and lakes and streams full of trout or coarse fish; an area of warm, dry summers and very cold snowy winters. This is Berber country and sheep and goat-rearing is the main occupation of these tough but friendly people. Rugged-faced, tall, thin men, and sometimes quite small boys, muffled up in thick brown djellabahs, even in summer, can be seen tending flocks high up in the rocky valleys. Many of them are semi-nomadic: they do have homes but they also think nothing of following their flocks in search of fresh pasture and spending months in their black weatherproof tents.

This is a most rewarding region to tour. There is a good network of mountain roads (sometimes blocked by snow in winter) giving access to an unbelievable variety of scenery within quite short distances. There are a few modest but well-run hotel-restaurants, many of them started by the French during the Protectorate.

Leave Fez (see Rte 10) on the P24, which is a continuation of Ave Mohammed V which runs through the centre of the new town. After 36km you reach **Imouzzer du Kandar**, an attractive little town on the edge of the plateau, much visited by the people of Fez during summer. It lies at 1350m and the air is fresh and cool in summer compared with the heat of the plain; in winter it can be very cold indeed with temperatures down to minus 18°C.

It is a very open town with two nicely landscaped artificial lakes in the centre and one or two good buildings such as the *Mahakma* (courthouse). At the southern end of the town are prehistoric troglodyte caves, until quite recently inhabited by members of the Berber Ait Seghouchen tribe. There are several hotels and restaurants, notably *Les Truites* with 17 rooms and excellent cuisine. There is a campsite on the edge of town.

There are many natural lakes in the area—indeed one is struck by the abundance of water everywhere—for this is the great watershed of the country. To the S and E are stony deserts and dry river beds; but here and immediately to the N is verdant land. A few kilometres S of Imouzzer is a left-hand turning to *Dayet Aoua*, starting point for the delightful '*Circuit des Lacs*'. Aoua is the largest of the lakes (150 hectares); it has a road going right round it and a hotel-restaurant, *le Chalet du Lac*, with facilities for swimming and daily permits for fishermen. The lake is stocked with pike, perch, black bass, carp, roach, etc., but tends to get over-fished. Serious fishermen will go to the smaller lakes further away from the hotel, such as Ifrah or Hachlaf, which complete the circuit and lead you to Ifrane. The lakeland circuit adds about 25km to the direct route from Imouzzer to Ifrane by the P24, but is good for picnics and walks in the spring through flower-filled meadows. In summer the tranquillity is often tempered by the sound of children's voices from a nearby *colonie de vacances*.

Continue along the main road (P24) S and upwards over a dry, stony plateau and you will reach **Ifrane**, a fairy-tale town unlike any other in Morocco. It was built by the French at the time of their greatest expansion as a kind of permanent holiday village and is now expanding fast. It is a conglomeration of white-walled villas with steep red roofs and gables. It has wide tree-lined roads and ornamental gardens, and it is dominated by a rather grim-looking mansion, distinctly Scottish baronial in style. This is one of the King's palaces and Ifrane is one of his favourite places for relaxation.

Ifrane offers the visitor a remote tranquillity and fresh, dry mountain air. It is sited in a hollow at 1650m, and is bounded on all sides by forests of cedar and of cork oak. The cedar woods are wonderful to walk and picnic in. They offer welcome shade in summer, and in the winter they are covered with snow.

Below Ifrane runs the River Tizguit, a delicate stream with tiny waterfalls bordered on either side by meadows and copses, weeping willows, oaks and many other trees. This is a paradise of wild flowers in the spring, and it is pleasant to leave for a while the exotic bougainvillias and hibiscus below to see violets and primroses growing here. In the autumn there are mushrooms, including the highly prized morelle. This enchanting spot is known as *Les Cascades des Vierges* and the minor road to El Hajeb passes right through it.

Ifrane, and indeed other Middle Atlas towns, has a particular attraction for storks. Every respectable villa has its storks' nest which is returned to every spring. The clacking of their beaks in mutual appreciation is one of the most characteristic sounds of Ifrane.

There is a good campsite with all modern facilities, a large municipal swimming pool and even a brand new stadium. Otherwise, there is the large and insensitively placed *Hotel Mischliffen* overlooking the town, which comes to life during the royal visits when the king's suite takes it over, and is very expensive; and there are one or two modest establishments in the centre, with evocative names like *Perce Neige* (snowdrop) and *Les Tilleuls* (the Lime Trees); the former is cheap and unwelcoming; the latter is, at time of writing closed for reconstruction. Restaurants keep up the floral tradition and *La Rose* offers a basic but friendly meal in the centre of town.

From Ifrane you should certainly do the 20-minute drive up to *Mischliffen* (take the Boulemane road and turn right after 9km). You drive through dark, mysterious forests up over the pass of TIZI N'TRETTEN (1934m alt.) and then turn left and plunge down into the volcanic, cedar-topped crater which is Mischliffen. In summer this view is magnificent. In winter it is one of the busiest skiing stations in the Middle Atlas with hot food and drinks available at the *Ski Club Ifrane*.

There are only two ski-lifts (of the T-bar type) and only the one big bowl to ski in and around but this satisfies people from Meknes and Fez in search of easy family skiing. There is more skiing a little further along the road at *Jbel Hebri*, with a wide piste, a ski-lift and an auberge at the top. Skiing is perhaps slightly steeper here but the facilities are fairly poor. These stations do have the advantage of being easily accessible by road and equipment can be hired from the *Café Chamonix* in Ifrane.

From here you can either continue along the road and turn right at the T-junction for Azrou, or return to Ifrane and approach Azrou (17km) by the main road. 14km along the main road from Ifrane is a turning to *le Cedre Gouraud* which leads to a gigantic cedar 10m in circumference and named after a French Resident-General. Its neighbours are almost as majestic and this whole section of forest is worth stopping for.

Azrou (1200m alt.) is as Moroccan in appearance as Ifrane is French. The main road between the two towns has one of the loveliest panoramas in Morocco: across range after range of mountains in varying shades of blue, blurring eventually into infinite nothingness. The view is best from the point where the road plunges down from the oak forests below Ifrane to the plateau of Azrou.

Clever little Berber boys, knowing that all motorists will stop here, have organised a thriving amethyst industry. There are amethysts to be found in the surrounding rocks and some of what they offer for sale may be genuine but most is not. They will not mind if you lick your fingers and rub to see if the purple paint comes off. They will also, probably, try to sell you wild peonies, wild asparagus (rather bitter), mushrooms (good and quite safe) and wild strawberries (very good).

Azrou lies in a wide, flat valley, dwarfed by its backcloth of mountain slopes, up which perches the original Berber village, home of the Beni Mguild tribe, and consisting of rows of beaten-earth houses with flat white roofs. The modern town below has the usual market behind its main street (especially lively on Tuesdays) and a *centre d'artisanat* which is worth visiting. This is located exactly opposite the rock (*azrou*) which gives the town its name and exhibits a wide range of carved cedarwood objects, metal work, Berber rugs and the sequinned cushion covers which are typical of the region. The hotel-restaurant situation is poor.

From Azrou there are two ways of getting to Khenifra 82km to the south. There is the direct route along the main road via the village of *Mrirt*; or the much more rewarding mountain road which goes E via *Ain Leuh* and the monkey forests. For the latter route take the Midelt road out of Azrou and then turn right after 2km up a steep road which winds its way through oak forests, laden in winter with holly and mistletoe. Through openings in the forest on your right you catch glimpses of misty mountain landscapes. Ain Leuh is another typical Berber village, consisting of flat-roofed houses and a waterfall.

Just before reaching Ain Leuh you will have noticed a track (left) signposted Aguelmane Azigza and Khenifra. Take this (at your discretion if the weather is bad, for the going can be rough) and you approach the remote heart of the Middle Atlas. Tracks go off in all directions through the forest, up and down and round the mountains. This is the region of '*la chasse*', for there is plenty of wild boar in the forest; and also hare and partridge on the outskirts. It is also a trout fisherman's paradise, as the region is crossed and re-crossed by the rich headwaters of the great *Oum er Rbia* river which eventually finds its way out to the Atlantic at Azemmour. *Aguelmane Azigza* is a large lake well-stocked with coarse fish. This is also an area of monkeys. Great families of them live unmolested in these forests. They are in fact the original ancestors of those which inhabit Gibraltar today. So few cars come up this way that they are not afraid and one often sees them crossing the track or even playing by it in great family groups.

It must be stressed that the tracks here are rough and deteriorate the deeper you penetrate. Unless your vehicle is fairly high off the ground, the boulders and high ridges can be a danger. There are also boggy patches which take a long time to dry out. On the other hand, this isolated and mysterious forest land is beautiful and rewarding to explore. As every track looks the same you can easily lose your way. If you do get lost, and the day is drawing to a close, keep going W towards the setting sun and you will eventually emerge at or near the small town of Khenifra.

Khenifra lies on the banks of the Oum er Rbia and is the home of the Zaiane Berbers, once a very important tribe and renowned for their outstanding horsemanship. The small medina is busy, with good souks. There is a fine *Kasbah* alongside the humpbacked bridge. From Khenifra a road has recently been constructed to the spa town of (102km) Oulmes (see

Rte 8). (This is probably the quickest way of reaching Rabat, should you wish to do so after your Middle Atlas tour.)

There are one or two DIVERSIONS to be made if time permits. About 17km out of Khenifra, on the P24 is a left-hand turning to *El Kbab*—a small village specialising in a variety of handicrafts. About 22km before Kasba Tadla a road goes off left to 9km *El Ksiba* whose pleasant hotel-restaurant is located in a woodland setting much favoured by the local monkeys who swing excitedly from branch to branch screaming at the visitors. Further along this road towards Arhbala, at 46km *Tiz-n-Isly*, you can take the wild and beautiful track S which makes a slow but spectacular drive up the high plateau of Imilchil and Dyet Tislit. This track is often blocked by snow in winter but at any other time of year should not cause problems. At Imilchil a track goes E along the crest of the Jbel Ayachi range all the way to Midelt (see Rte 12).

The P24 from Khenifra to *Kasba Tadla* crosses the rich agricultural Tadla plain and more or less follows the Oum er Rbia river. *Kasba Tadla* (99km from Khenifra) was one of Moulay Ismael's outposts. He built the kasbah (17C) here in order to control the wild Tadla Berbers and discourage them from coming any nearer to his citadel at Meknes. The kasbah consists of two walled sections each with its own mosque. There is a lively Monday market in the square which contains a mosque with a white minaret. Moulay Ismael was also responsible for building the noble 10-arched bridge across the river. It is worth crossing for a good view of the town from the top of the hill on the other side.

30km further S is *Beni Mellal*, which has another of Moulay Ismael's fortresses but is really memorable only for its delightful setting amidst olive groves against a backcloth of gentle hills. Recommended for lunch is the hotel-restaurant *Ouzoud*, situated on the outskirts of the town, its peaceful gardens stretching out towards the hills. There is a change in atmosphere here: '*Le grand sud*' and Marrakesh lie ahead, and Beni Mellal is as much a 'gateway to the south' as Midelt is at the E end of the Jbel Ayachi range.

Take the P24 out of Beni Mellal and after 6km turn left towards the lake and dam, signposted *Bine el Ouidane* (the name means 'between the rivers'). The lake is good for fishing and a licence can be obtained from the hotel, *Auberge du Lac*, charmingly sited on the shore and offering good food. The dam is very impressive; it is said to retain 1500 million cubic metres of water, used to irrigate a huge surrounding area. From the lake continue 28km along the S508 to the village of *Azilal*. This is a spectacular road, worth every inch of the steep climb. At Azilal the road turns west. Continue c 22km to a right-hand turning signposted **les Cascades d' Ouzoud**. This is a famous beauty spot—an immense waterfall which tumbles over the vertical side of a deep canyon. Rare climbing plants and strange eroded rock forms give the setting a unique beauty. On the roadside there is a small café overlooking the falls and there are marked trails which lead down to the pool below the falls and along the valley.

Return to the S508 and continue 44km to *Demnate*. This is an interesting small hillside town, surrounded by ancient ramparts and with a very colourful souk on Sundays, when the streets are filled with stalls brimming over with the lush produce of this fertile area. Whilst there it is worth taking the track (6km) up to IMI-N-IFNI which is a natural bridge formed by the eroding effect of the river. There is an air of mystery here. The place is haunted by crows and has its own annual moussem, usually around the Islamic festival of Aid el Kbir.

From Demnate it is 59km back to the main road (P24) and then 55km to Marrakesh (see Rte 15). Or, you can continue the detour by turning left

36km after Demnate and taking a slightly longer route, alongside Lake Ait Aadel and the Moulay Youssef dam, rejoining the main road about 12km out of Marrakesh.

An ALTERNATIVE fast route is to continue on the P24 from *Beni Mellal* to Marrakesh (204km; total distance from Fez, 493km). It is a rather uninteresting journey across desert country, passing through the unremarkable towns of El Kelaa des Srarhna and Tamelet.

12   Meknes to Midelt

Total distance 195km. **Meknes**—P21. 31km *El Hajeb*—38km *Azrou*—33km *Timhadite*—93km **Midelt**.

Leave Meknes (see Rte 8) by the P21 which follows the Boufekrane river and after 31km reaches the sleepy town of *El Hajeb* perched on the edge of the plateau. There is nothing worth stopping for here except the view back over the Meknes plain with its crops of cereals, oranges and, above all, vines. At El Hajeb the road divides, the left-hand fork going up to *Ifrane* (see Rte 11) and the right-hand one going to 38km *Azrou* via the Berber village of *Ito*, from where there is an extraordinary view to the right over a strange lunar wasteland of small hillocks which form the basin of the river Tigrigra.

The road from Azrou (see Rte 11) to Midelt follows the valley of the river Gigou which winds through lush green meadows. It is much fished for trout. After passing through the unremarkable town of *Timhadite* the road rises to the COL DU ZAD (Pass of Zad; 2178m alt.). On either side in the distance are the misty pink shapes of some of the highest peaks in the Middle Atlas. Just before reaching the pass, you will notice a turning on your left signposted *Aguelmane Sidi Ali*. A kilometre down this turning is a very large, deep lake which is rich in pike, perch and other coarse varieties, but sadly closed for fishing since December 1990. This is a region full of streams and as such is a favourite summer pasture for Berber herds. Two of Morocco's principal rivers rise near here: the Sebou and the Oum er Rbia.

Once over the Col du Zad the landscape changes. Behind you are the cedar forests and in front stretches a bare, arid, sandy plateau. There is another range of mountains in the distance, rising far more abruptly than the Middle Atlas, a thin cordillera, black and forbidding in summer, snow covered in winter. This is the *Jbel Ayachi* range and at the foot of it is *Midelt*, which is, as its name implies, right in the middle of Morocco, and it embodies the characteristics of many regions. It is cold and windswept in winter and very hot, dusty and dry in summer. It is distinguished only by its position at the foot of the impressive Jbel Ayachi range.

Midelt lies at the start of one of the main routes through the High Atlas to the desert—carved by the Ziz river and followed by the road (see Rte 21). It is a convenient place to stop on the way to or from the S, and there is a rather depressing three-star hotel—the *Ayachi*—where the dining room extends into a caidal tent.

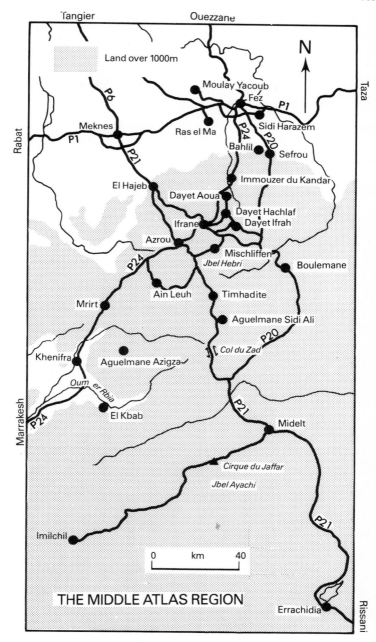

THE MIDDLE ATLAS REGION

13   Fez to Imilchil

Total distance 332km. **Fez**—P20. 24km *Bahlil*—4km **Sefrou**—182km
Midelt—26km **Cirque du Jaffar**—96km **Imilchil**.

The P20 from Fez (see Rte 10) which leaves from Place de l'Atlas in the new
town, crosses the Sais plain and then climbs slowly up on to the high
plateau. After c 24km you reach, on the right-hand side, the strange Berber
village of *Bahlil*, which literally clings to the rocks. It is difficult to see where
the rocks end and the houses start, for they appear to be one and the same
thing. A charming legend attaches to this very ancient village: when
Moulay Idriss (founder of Fez) rode there one day, hoping to convert the
inhabitants to Islam, his horse suddenly became exhausted and nearly
collapsed. The young king fell to his knees and prayed for water,
whereupon a spring gushed forth from the ground where his horse stood.
Doubting Berber onlookers were now convinced that the Islamic god was
a very powerful one and converted forthwith to the faith. The spring was
named *Ait Reta* and is said to flow still from a spot between the bridge and
the great mosque.

Another 4km will bring you to **Sefrou**, best known for its cherry festival
in June. The history of Sefrou is said to go back to the end of the 7C (before
the arrival of the Arabs), when the agricultural Sefrioui tribe built themselves fortified ksours as protection against the many fierce nomadic tribes
who roamed the countryside. Traces of these beaten-earth fortresses still
remain along the Aggai river. Later, Moulay Idriss used Sefrou as a base
while Fez was being built. Later still, the town achieved notoriety as a
stopping place for gold-laden caravans on the way from the desert to Fez.
It became a significant trading centre. Many Jews came to live there, as is
evidenced today by the colourful mellah with its very narrow streets and
taller than average houses. There is also a lively medina which is full today,
as then, of local crafts, including jewellery, pottery and metalwork. Waterfalls and 18C ramparts complete the picture of this interesting little town
which is set amidst cherry trees at the foot of the Middle Atlas.

The road from Sefrou through Boulemane to Midelt climbs steadily across
a wild and featureless mountain landscape, consisting mainly of cork oak
forests. Even *Boulemane*, the only sizeable town on the way, is unremarkable. But this is the quickest way to get from Fez down to the Tifilalet region
of Erfoud and beyond (see Rte 21). It is also worth noting that at approximately 30km before Midelt there is a right-hand turn which follows the
valley of the Oued Moulouya to join the other great road to the S: the P24
to Marrakesh.

Midelt (see Rte 12) is the starting point for one of the most spectacular
drives in Morocco—along the spine of the Jbel Ayachi past the amazing
Cirque du Jaffar. This is a noble circle of peaks (about 26km from Midelt),
and the skilfully engineered track takes you up to a pass 3700m high, from
which you gaze down into this vast amphitheatre. The track is very steep
in places and should not be attempted after heavy rain or in snowy
conditions. Luckily the steepest parts are not precipitous.

The track continues along the ridge for many kilometres, with views over
range upon range of peaks. Driving conditions do not get any easier,
however, and progress is slow because one is constantly having to stop to
remove quite sizeable boulders from the track. Many people are content to
see the Cirque du Jaffar and then return to Midelt. Brave spirits drive all

the way through to 96km **Imilchil**, at the other end of the Jbel Ayachi range. But do not do so without making sure that the track *is* open; even then you should be prepared for the possible disappointment of having to turn back. The drive can easily take all day.

Imilchil, high and solitary in the mountains, is certainly worth visiting, particularly in September when it has a large moussem and *fête des fiançailles*—a kind of marriage fair held in all seriousness by the Ait Haddidou Berber tribe. On this occasion the bare plateau is covered with tents of all shapes and sizes. The merchants are there to buy and sell, the singers and dancers have come to entertain. The young girls of the tribe are dressed from head to foot in striped woollen djellabahs with pointed hoods around which are draped necklaces and silver ornaments. Their faces are not covered. Their high cheekbones are reddened with henna and their eyes are smudged with khoul. The young men wear white djellabahs and carry their best silver daggers. Contracts of marriage are discussed between families, complicated dowries are arranged and festive dances begin. The dancing gets more and more compulsive as the festival progresses. Men and women, huddled together, shoulder to shoulder, move up and down as one human mass to the irresistible rhythms of the drums and the wailing voices of the poets and singers.

Amongst all these celebrations wander the bemused tourists, not so numerous yet as to spoil the authenticity of the occasion. Accommodation consists of tents and mass-produced cous-cous and brochettes. There are no hotels. The occasion is unforgettable, and, to many people, worth a small degree of discomfort.

The setting for all this colourful tradition and festivity is magnificent: Imilchil lies on a vast tableland, broken by the uneven line of distant purple mountains. It is fit only for sheep and goat raising. It is very hot in summer and cold and snow-covered in winter. There are several lakes and rivers in the vicinity which offer some of the best trout fishing in Morocco; but they are often dificult of access. Imilchil consists of little more than a few red-earth kasbahs surrounded by a small area of well-watered green fields, which contrast strikingly with the dry-as-dust landscape beyond.

There are three ALTERNATIVE ROUTES to Imilchil besides the one already described: the even more difficult journey via Ait Hani (see Rte 20); the long but much easier track from Rich (see Rte 21); and the short but mountainous track from El Ksiba (see Rte 11).

14 Fez to Oujda

Total distance 344km. **Fez**—P1. c 11km *Sidi Harazem*—109km **Taza**—65km *Guercif*—50km *Taourirt*—50km *El Aioun*—59km **Oujda**.

The P1 to the E of Morocco leaves Fez (see Rte 10) from the far side of the medina (near Bab Ftouh). After 11km there is a right hand turn to the thermal spa of *Sidi Harazem*. Going back to ancient times this was once just an oasis of palm trees watered by natural hot springs with a saint's tomb in the middle. Now it has been turned into a modern bathing establishment and the waters are of proven benefit both externally and internally. It is possible to take a medicinal bath and there is a pleasant 4-star hotel-restaurant on site. Most people, however, settle for drinking the bottled water, widely available (and without any mineral taste) all over Morocco.

The journey as far as 109km Taza is picturesque and mountainous. After c 55km the road passes through the natural corridor between the great Rif and Middle Atlas ranges, known as THE TAZA GAP. It leads towards Algeria and is the route by which the invading Arabs first arrived from the E in the 7C. Countless armies have since made use of it, and it was certainly used by the Almoravides when they invaded and conquered Algeria in the 11C.

As the road rises to a height of c 560m just before Taza you can observe and judge for yourself the validity of the theory that here lies the original frontier between Europe and Africa. Some scientists claim that the Rif range is an extension of the Spanish Sierra Nevada and that the Straits of Gibraltar and the Mediterranean were formed by a chance sinking of the land. It is certainly true that the Rif to your left is grey-white and the Middle Atlas on your right is red and altogether different in shape and texture.

A recommended DETOUR is along a spectacular mountain road which loops S for about 80km at *Sidi Abdallah des Rhiata* and then rejoins the main road at Taza. It runs first through the dark schist ravine of the Oued Zireg, then climbs steeply and turns E to loop around the S slopes of *Jbel Tazzeka* (1979m). This region is now a National Park. There is a steep and precipitous track going off to the left which climbs for 7km up to the summit of the mountain. This is not a track for wet weather; nor is it suitable for the faint-hearted. The view from the top (shared by a TV aerial) is predictably fine over endless cedar forests and mountains in all directions.

The route continues E and passes (c 10km) the *Friouata Caves* (a signpost on the left points simply to Gouffres). These are worth visiting, though not without a torch or a guide as there is no lighting provided. They form a great network of caverns and are believed to be the deepest in Africa. The entrance to the caves is over 30m wide. On the opposite side of the road, a little further along, are more caves—*Les Grottes du Chiker*. These are also impressive, especially the one called '*Ifri ou Atto*'. Next comes the *Dayet Chiker*—a large depression which sometimes fills with water to make a lake. Now the road begins to descend quite steeply, passing the lovely waterfalls known as *Les Cascades de Ras el Ma* (Ras el Ma is Arabic for 'head of the water'). Here too the amount of water depends very much on the time of year and at the end of the dry season the falls can be reduced to a trickle.

After 12km, passing through a narrow valley lined with cherry orchards, you reach the town of **Taza** (37,000 inhab.), which is today an under-rated and rather neglected place. It is in fact one of Morocco's oldest towns, founded, like Meknes, in the 10C by the Meknassa tribe on a site undoubtedly inhabited since prehistoric times, as evidenced by the quantity of fossils and bones found there. It was also, in its day, of major strategic importance to every invading dynasty coming from the E and making for Fez, and it bears the mark of all of them, particularly the Almohades who built the defensive outer walls in the 12C.

Like so many of Morocco's historic cities, Taza is split into two parts: medina and modern town, the latter built alongside the medina by the French during the Protectorate (and in this case a discreet 3km away). The *Medina*, which is at the W end and stands on the edge of the plateau, has one or two interesting features. If you walk down the main street (known as Mechouar), you will see the best of the souks, which are Berber in character and refreshingly free of tourist-orientated ware, and several Merinide medersas, the best amongst them being the *Bou Abou el Hassan medersa*, which is worth entering. At the end of this street is the **Great Mosque**, built by the Almohade ruler Abd el Mumene (founder of Rabat) in the 12C. It is certainly one of the oldest mosques in the country, but the non-Muslim may do no more than peer in. Nearby is the lovely Almohade *Bab er Rouah* (Gate of the Winds), which was originally the only entrance to the town but now, like its namesake in Rabat, leads nowhere in particular.

At the other end of the Mechouar is the Andalucian *mosque* with its unusual 13C minaret. Behind it, and rather difficult to find, is the house of the Pretender to the Alouite throne, Bou Hamara, who actually had himself crowned Sultan of Morocco at Taza in 1902, believing, and managing to convince others, that he was a saint and descended from the Prophet. He had a habit of riding a donkey (his name means 'Father of the She-Ass') to visit his followers and of performing 'miracles' in front of them. He is particularly remembered for his 'conversations with the dead': he would bury a servant in a shallow grave allowing him a straw to breathe and talk through; having held audible conversations with the unfortunate man, Bou Hamara would then stamp on the straw so that by the time amazed onlookers got around to uncovering the body, it was indeed truly dead. Fortunately this colourful character met his just deserts when Moulay Hafid came to the throne in 1908 and accorded him a suitably dramatic end, drawing him through the town in a cage on the back of a camel, and then feeding him to the lions.

Taza has now dwindled in importance and the Ville Nouvelle, at a lower level than the medina, offers little of interest to the visitor. Such hotels as there are are not remarkable.

From Taza there is a scenic but difficult road N which crosses the Rif and after c 100km joins up with the P39 Mediterranean road between Al Hoceima and Nador (see Rte 5).

E from Taza the road presses on over the sparsely populated plain through Guercif, Taourirt and El Aioun, till it finally (after 165km) reaches Oujda on the Algerian border. Along this route rows of eucalyptus trees have been planted to fix the sand. Nothing else grows here and the journey along the red, dusty and featureless road seems endless.

At *Msoun*, 28km from Taza, the monotony is broken by a fine kasbah built by Moulay Ismael in the 17C, evidence that at one time this empty land was a battlefield—a meeting place of hordes of men from E and S.

Guercif, 65km E of Taza, is a dull market town situated at the confluence of the Moulouya and Melloulou rivers. *Taourirt*, 50km beyond, stands at a crossing place of ancient caravan trails and owes its fortifications to the Merinide dynasty.

A road goes S from Taourirt to the little town of *Debdou* (53km), where the countryside is much greener. The road rises to a plateau (the Gaada de Debdou), with splendid views, and then disappears into the desert wilderness. Debdou is not on the way to anywhere but it makes a pleasant diversion.

50km E of Taourirt is *El Aioun* (The Springs) with a kasbah built by Moulay Ismael. It was captured in 1904 by Bou Hamara, the 'Pretender' from Taza. From El Aioun a road goes N to the Beni Snassen mountains and Berkane; see Rte 5 for this and also for a description of Oujda which lies 59km to the E of El Aioun.

THE SOUTH: THE HIGH ATLAS, THE ANTI ATLAS AND THE DESERT

15 Casablanca to Marrakesh

Total distance 241km. **Casablanca**—18km *Mediouna*—54km *Settat*—70km *Skhour des Rehamna*—29km *Benguerir*—45km *Sidi-Bou Othmane*—25km **Marrakesh**.

Marrakesh, capital of *le grand Sud*, lies N of the Atlas Mountains and is therefore very easily accessible from the N half of the country. The fast, straight road across the plain from Casablanca is scenically dull and there is no reason for not covering it as quickly as possible.

Leave Casablanca (see Rte 3) from Place Mohammed V along the Rue de Strasbourg, which later becomes Route de Mediouna. At *Mediouna* (18km S of the centre of Casablanca) a minor road from Tit Mellil is joined, which is part of the direct route from Rabat to Marrakesh.

The only sizeable town of the whole journey is *Settat* which lies in the middle of a fertile agricultural region. 70km further on is *Skhour des Rehamna* and from here the road goes straight across the plain, which rapidly becomes more of a desert. There is just one small range of hills to cross after 74km *Sidi Bou Othmane*. During the last hour of the journey the shapes of the High Atlas peaks appear on the horizon. The highest mountains are permanently snow-capped and the colours, especially when the sun is low, belie description. Winston Churchill used to spend many hours painting this view. As you get nearer to Marrakesh (25km from Sidi Bou Othmane) the palm trees begin to grow more thickly and the picturesque houses made out of pink beaten earth and straw, often with delicately finished wrought-iron grilles inserted in the rough walls over the windows, appear in greater numbers. Just before reaching the city you come to the famous *palmeraie*—a vast forest of palm trees and the only one N of the Atlas.

MARRAKESH (690,000 inhab.) is the jewel of Morocco's tourist industry, combining as it does a perfect climate, a wealth of ancient monuments, and a unique setting of palm trees against the snow-capped mountains of the High Atlas. Alas, the jewel is in some danger of becoming tarnished by the sheer number of well-heeled tourists who arrive by coach and unwittingly destroy the magic of the place by their very presence, and that of the swarm of hustling 'guides' who attend them. The Tourist Board claims there are 10,000 beds in and around Marrakesh. And it shows. The discerning visitor will take in the principal sights early in the morning or lateish in the afternoon. Marrakesh is well served by all categories of hotels, and is a natural starting point for a journey to the south, either by one of two spectacular roads across the mountains or by a faster route W of the mountains through Agadir.

Information. Moroccan National Tourist Office: Ave Mohammed V (Place abd el Moumene ben ali). Tel. 30258.

Post Office. Place du 16 novembre.

Transport. Airport: 5km SW of the city, signposted off Ave de la Menara. Flights to Paris and London via Casablanca; also to Agadir, Ouarzazate and Tangier. Railway

station: Ave Hassan II. Trains to Casablanca, Meknes, Fez, Oujda, Tangier and Rabat.
Bus station: just outside Bab Doukkala. Buses to all destinations.

Hotels. One 5-star L, five 5-star, fourteen 4-star A, two 4-star B, eight 3-star A, five 3-star B, four 2-star A, three 2-star B, two 1-star A, two 1-star B. One holiday village.

History. Marrakesh, founded in 1062, was twice the capital of Morocco: first under its creators the Almoravides and then the Almohades; secondly under the Saadians in the 16C. The Almoravides originated within the nomadic Sanhaja Berber tribes of the desert and were engaged at the end of the 10C in conquering and converting to Islam the black countries S of the Sahara. Their campaigns were inspired by an overpowering lust for the gold that was flowing into Morocco from the region of the river Niger; they were determined to find its source (but they never did). However, in 1050, one of the Almoravide princes went to Mecca on a holy pilgrimage and returned convinced of the need to reform not only himself but also his fellow men and particularly his greedy kinsmen. Many joined him and soon a large band of pious and fanatic Berbers began to roam the south of Morocco forcing everyone in their path to submit and repent of their lustful ways, in particular the drinking of wine and the taking of more than four wives. Their version of orthodox Islam spread all over the south; even the iniquitous capital of Sijilmassa, which had been the reception point of most of the gold caravans from the desert and consequently a renowned centre for loose living, was mercilessly cleaned up and its dens of vice razed to the ground.

Out of all this fierce puritanism a leader emerged, one of Morocco's truly great leaders—Youssef ben Tachfine. He was the personification of all the virtues claimed by his people: he was renowned for his wisdom, his sense of justice, his courage, and, above all, his simplicity. He was, apparently, a modest man who clothed himself in rough woollen garments, ate only camel meat and drank only camel's milk. He was slight in build and had a brown skin with little hair on his face. His eyes were black and his voice was soft. Even when he became the ruler of a vast empire, he retained a deep-felt consideration for the humblest of his subjects.

In 1062, after leading his men over the Atlas mountains, Youssef decided that the plain to the N, which was warm and protected by the mountains from the cruel Saharan winds, was a good place to pitch camp. He built a mosque and a kasbah and Marrakesh was founded. A serious problem was shortage of water, so the enterprising leader had wells dug and conduits built underground linking one with another. The few skimpy palm trees became the lush palmeraie we see today, and the efficient system of channels is still in use to water the many ornamental gardens. The camp gradually became more permanent (a totally new concept for formerly nomadic Berbers), with buildings made of the distinctive red earth, and Youssef ben Tachfine set about the task of pacifying the whole country. This was not difficult: once Fez had fallen all other resistance collapsed.

In 1085 Youssef was called away to Andalucia where Christian armies had managed to win back the old Visigothic capital of Toledo. The Christians were defeated and he returned to Marrakesh victorious and hugely enriched in both reputation and material wealth. He went back to Spain in 1090 and this time firmly annexed the provinces of Granada and Malaga to the Almoravide empire. During this time his son Ali consolidated and continued the building of the city and erected the first enclosing ramparts, few of which still remain. Inside the walls, mosques, palaces and gateways were being created with the help of craftsmen from Andalucia. This was the beginning of the blending of two cultures: the rough vigour of the desert Berbers with the advanced refinement of Andalucia. Gradually Marrakesh became a centre for men of learning, for artists and makers of fine textiles and leather work. In 1106 Youssef ben Tachfine died at an age of over a hundred years. Predictably perhaps, Ali (1107–44), who had received much of his education in Andalucia and had never experienced tough desert life, was less vigorous and purposeful than his father; and his successors even less so. The influence of the easy-going and luxury-loving Andalucian court was beginning to take hold of Almoravide society. The drinking of alcohol crept in and women began to walk unveiled in the streets. Serious moral decline set in and the time was ripe for another tribe of zealous reforming Berbers to take over.

The Almohades arrived from their stronghold at Tin Mal in the High Atlas and made their first attack, which failed, on Marrakesh in 1130. They were inspired by Ibn Tumart (died 1133), a remarkable man whom many thought to be a *mahdi* (messiah). He had an unshakeable belief in the unity of God and a profound understanding of the Koran, which he caused to be taught for the first time in the Berber language. He was already very old but he had prepared a young, intelligent and deeply religious Berber to take over the leadership from him. This was Abd el Mumene (1133–63), the son of a potter. He launched a successful attack on Marrakesh in 1147. The remaining, by now decadent Almoravides were put to death and their monuments destroyed. The rest of the country put up little resistance and the Almohades went on to conquer Algeria and more of southern Spain. It was Abd el Mumene's grandson, Yacoub (1184–90; known as 'el Mansour': the conqueror), who was responsible for much of the great architecture in Marrakesh, including the ramparts. For a time he transferred his capital to Seville so as to be on hand if Christian armies should threaten again. This was a period of peace and prosperity in Marrakesh. The gardens of Menara and Agdal, with their emphasis on ornamental fountains, date from this period. But the most significant legacy is the Koutoubia mosque, started by his forefathers but completed by Yacoub in 1190 on the spot where, 100 years earlier, the Almoravides had built their mosque. During his reign the court became a fashionable centre of learning for much of the Western world.

However, Yacoub's son Mohammed (1199–1213), was a mere 17 years old when he succeeded his father and morally incapable of carrying on the example of dynamic and single-minded rule set by his ancestors. He had to face a major revival of Christian vigour in southern Spain almost as soon as he began to reign, and in 1212 his army was defeated at *Las Navas de Tolosa* in Andalucia: a terrible battle which proved to be a turning point in the whole Christian reconquest of Spain. From that moment on the fortunes of the Almohades, both at home and abroad, declined and Mohammed's successor (Youssef al Mostansir, 1213–23) was even less capable of stopping the decline.

The Merinides arrived in 1262. They showed little interest in Marrakesh, which lost its capital status to Fez and fell into decay until the arrival of the Saadians 300 years later. The Saadians had originally come from Arabia in the 12C and had settled down peacefully in south Morocco around Zagora. However, with the decline of the Merinides and with all the assurance that their undisputed descent from the the prophet Mohammed gave them, they surged N in the early 16C, quickly despatched the incompetent Merinide rulers and then turned their attention from Fez (which they found too sophisticated) back to crumbling Marrakesh. Fabulously wealthy after many successful forays across the Sahara in search of gold, they spared no expense or effort in making it once more a glorious city. Just two Saadian monuments survive, and one of those is in ruins, namely the Badi Palace which was destroyed by the infamous Moulay Ismael of the succeeding Alouite dynasty. The other is the palace built to house the tombs of the Saadian princes, so superb in craftsmanship that even the vengeful Alouite sultans could not bring themselves to pull it down, though they did build a wall round it to hide it from view.

Never again was Marrakesh to find itself the centre of so much lavish attention as it gradually lost its status, first to Meknes, then to Fez and ultimately to Rabat. However, succeeding sultans occasionally caused great buildings to be erected, most notably Moulay el Hassan, who was crowned here in 1873 and built the Bahia Palace and the Palace of Dar Si Said (now a museum).

Modern Marrakesh, known as *Gueliz*, was built alongside the W walls of the old town by the French, soon after they arrived in 1912. But because of the hold exerted by the Pasha of Marrakesh, Thami el Glaoui, over this whole region French influence in Marrakesh was limited; they decided not to cross this feudal aristocrat, and wisely so as it turned out since it was he who delivered the Sultan, Mohammed V, into their hands in 1953.

The first thing which strikes you on entering Marrakesh is that everything is pink: the ancient castellated ramparts around the old town, the buildings within, and the modern buildings in the new quarter are all in varying shades of the same colour. The **Koutoubia Mosque** in the centre, dominating the whole town with its 77m-high minaret, is also pink. It was begun by the first Almohade sultan, Abd el Mumene, in 1158, and completed by his grandson, Yacoub el Mansour, in 1190. It is one of the largest in Africa and accommodates over 20,000 people. The word '*Koutoubia*' derives from '*Kutubiyin*' (booksellers) and this relates to the bookshops established all around the mosque in its early years when it undoubtedly combined the functions of library, university and koranic school with that of mosque (as did the Karaouyine in Fez). Today's mosque is the second to have been built by the Almohades (on the site of the original one built 100 years earlier by the founder of Marrakesh, Youssef ben Tachfine); their first attempt having been pulled down almost immediately because the orientation towards Mecca had been incorrectly calculated. Traces of this earlier building can be detected along one of the outside walls. The exterior is simple to the point of ordinariness. Inside, its purity of line, its 17 aisles with identical horseshoe arches and the total lack of any ornamentation on its white walls achieve a rare elegance. But it is the minaret for which the Koutoubia is most famous. It is similar to but a little earlier than the Giralda in Seville and the unfinished Hassan Tower in Rabat, for which Sultan Yacoub was also responsible. The minaret is perfectly proportioned in relation to the main body of the mosque. The square lantern supports a rounded dome crowned with three golden balls (said to have been presented by the wife of the Sultan as a penance for not observing three hours of Ramadan). The decoration, in the form of tracery carved on to the stone, is simply designed to set off the windows, and is different on all of the four sides. The purity of form is not disturbed by any superimposed ornamentation except for a narrow band of blue tiles at the top which serve to reflect the sky (and purists might prefer them not to be there). Inside, as in the case of the

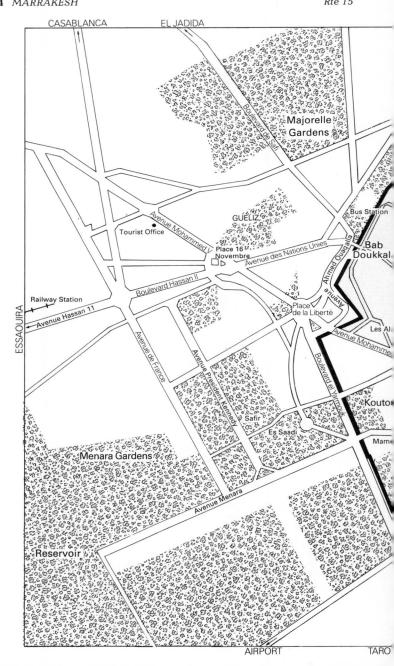

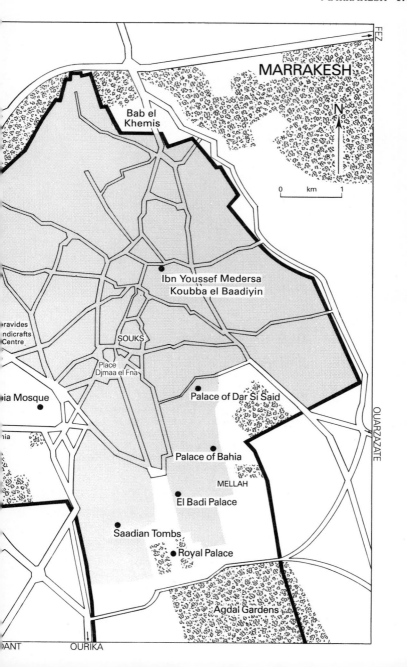

MARRAKESH

FEZ

N

0   km   1

Bab el
Khemis

Ibn Youssef Medersa
Koubba el Baadiyin

ravides
ndicrafts
Centre

SOUKS

Place
Djmaa el Fna

ia Mosque

Palace of Dar Si Said

hia

Palace of Bahia

MELLAH

El Badi Palace

Saadian Tombs

Royal Palace

OUARZAZATE

Agdal Gardens

ANT   OURIKA

Marrakesh scene, with the Koutoubia minaret in the background

Hassan tower in Rabat, there are several chambers and a ramp leading up to the top floor, from which the Muezzin calls the faithful to prayer five times a day.

Very close to the Koutoubia is the most exciting and exotic part of Marrakesh: the square of DJMAA EL FNA. The name, literally translated as 'the Mosque [or Assembly] of the Dead', is taken to refer to the custom of displaying the heads of vanquished rebels or criminals, since the square is known to have been a place of public execution even up to the last century. Since then, and particularly in the heady pre-Independence days, it has been a centre for public meetings and even riots. There have been one or two unsuccessful attempts to close it down and part of it has been covered over and turned into a corn market, but the Djmaa el Fna is still the heart of Marrakesh.

Today it provides constant, ever-changing entertainment, which reaches its climax at sundown and continues late into the night. Here the local tribesmen come to buy and to sell or just to see and to talk. There are story-tellers (for most of the audience cannot read); there are spell-binders and witch doctors: you can have a love potion made or a mixture concocted which will kill your worst enemy, if you can find a language in which to ask for it; if you have a pain to be cured you can overcome the language problem by pointing to the place where it hurts on a sinister tattered chart of the human body, although it might be unwise to rely on their prescriptions; there are dentists displaying rows of teeth that they have pulled out during the day and even some sets of false ones to put in their place; there are religious mystics who often work themselves into a trance and many of their audience too; there are bands playing weird banjo-like instruments and the *Gnaoua* (black musicians who beat huge drums with long curved sticks); there are letter-writers, usually sitting under umbrellas with the tools of their trade scattered around them; there are the sellers of brightly coloured dyes, piles of old bones and little bottles of sickly perfume; there are also the ubiquitous water-sellers and the snake-charmers, who after putting a cobra through its paces will take it out of the basket and wave it under the noses of the bemused spectators.

Between the circles go the acrobats, usually children who manage to bounce on their heads like rubber balls, finishing the right way up with their hands outstretched for coins (a concession to tourism). Many of them drag monkeys along on leads, who will perform for you whether you want it or not. There are hot-dog stalls and numerous charcoal grills on which are sizzling small herring-like fish, unidentifiable pieces of meat and corn-on-the-cob. It all smells quite delicious but should probably not be eaten. This smell, mixed with the inevitable one of mint tea, the hotchpotch sound of the orchestras, the hum of the voices of the story-tellers and the occasional screeches of the holy men are what most characterise the Djmaa el Fna. Would that it were possible to wander from circle to circle unnoticed and unmolested. Children and young boys are particularly pressing with their attentions in this hallowed place. There are several conveniently placed cafés around the square, from the terraces of which you can often have a splendid view of the whole entertainment, without noise or hustle. But the temptation to become part of the pageant usually returns quite quickly, and you slip down and join the throng once more.

The main entrance to the *Souks* is in one corner of the Djmaa el Fna. These cover a vast area and, if you want to see as much as possible in a limited time, it is advisable to take a guide, preferably an official one wearing a badge. Guides can usually be found standing around the entrance. If you engage a guide through your hotel it may cost slightly more but he will have a reputation to keep and may therefore be more reliable. Another reason for taking a guide rather than trying to go it alone is that he will keep away all the others who will want to offer their services or sell you anything from a phial of perfume to a camel.

The *Souks* are a riot of colour, noise and activity, a wealthy storehouse of all the treasures of this vast and varied country. They are grouped into corporations. Thus you will find all the silver merchants in one corner, all the gold merchants in another, and rows of stalls selling exclusively leather-work or copper goods or jewellery. The real fascination is to watch the craftsmen at work, gilding on leather, or inlaying with enamel the sheaths of ornate silver daggers, hammering out copper, embroidering silks or smoothing out the surface of a cedarwood table. You can easily spend a day or two exploring the full extent of the tangle of little streets and absorbing the extraordinary excitement of this industrious and colourful world, with its spicy smells and weird music. All the alleyways are covered by a trellis of latticed reeds so they are relatively cool even in high summer. The best time to visit the souks is fairly early in the morning or late in the afternoon (after 17.00). The siesta is taken very seriously and very little happens in the mid-afternoon. However, business does continue until quite late in the evening.

The historical monuments and splendid palaces built by former sultans are scattered thoughout the old town. One of the most perfect examples of Moorish art is the palace which houses the tombs of the Saadian kings,

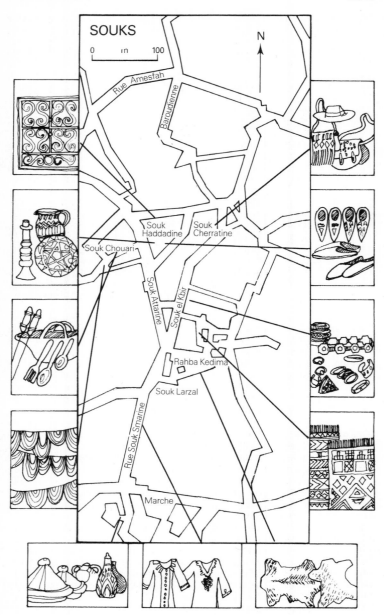

SOUKS

0   in   100

N

Rue Amesfah

Baroudjienne

Souk Haddadine

Souk Cherratine

Souk Chouari

Souk Attarine

Souk el Kbir

Rahba Kedima

Souk Larzal

Rue Souk Smarine

Marche

The Almohade gate, Bab Agnaou, Marrakesh

les tombeaux Saadiens, built by Ahmed Edh Dhahabi (1578–1603), the greatest of the Saadian rulers, at the end of the 16C and paid for with the gold that he had brought back from Timbucktoo. To reach this monument leave the S side of the Djmaa el Fna by the Rue du Bab Agnaou. After a few minutes' walk you reach a small square; go through the *Bab Agnaou* on your left. This is the only surviving Almohade monumental gate in Marrakesh. It is very large and simply decorated, with carving on the stone in the manner of the Koutoubia minaret—unlike the gates of later dynasties which tended to be laden with tiles and decorative columns (as in Meknes). Facing you is the Kasbah mosque, called *El Mansouria* after the Almohade sultan Yacoub el Mansour, who built it at the end of the 12C. Its minaret is exactly contemporary with that of the Koutoubia and was restored in 1965. The narrow path to the Saadian mausoleum goes round to the right of the mosque. The tombs of 66 royal Saadians lie within two buildings, each with three rooms and set in a garden.

On your left as you enter the garden is an *oratory* with a superb mihrab and a lantern supported by four elegant columns. Leading from the oratory and visible from the garden through the next opening is the *Room of the Twelve Columns*, which Ahmed Edh Dhahabi created for his own tomb and those of his sons. Their tombs lie beneath the ceramic mosaic floor marked by finely carved marble slabs, the large central tomb being that of the Sultan himself. Here are stalacticic cupolas and very delicate stucco-work; carved and gilded cedarwood ceilings and walls decorated with soft-coloured mosaic tiles. Light comes from a hidden interior glass dome and creates a special atmosphere. There is a third room which contains the

The Saadian tombs, Marrakesh

tombs of wives and children. The second building, a little older and almost sober in its decoration, contains the tomb of Lalla Messaouda, the mother of Ahmed, and that of Mohammed esh-Sheik, the first Saadian sultan, together with those of more princes.

The gardens are always full of bird-song and have palms and datura standing amidst rosemary, jasmine and roses. In the centre is a square containing simple tombstones belonging to the servants of Saadian royal households. Even the Alouite sultan Moulay Ismael, whose policy it was to destroy all relics of the preceding dynasty, left the Saadian tombs intact. However he did have the area encircled by a wall which no one had succeeded in penetrating until the French discovered it in 1917; it is they who were responsible for the path which today leads around the Kasbah mosque.

Ahmed Edh Dhahabi also built the palace **El Badi**, which means 'the incomparable'. To reach it, return through the Bab Agnaou and turn immediately right towards Place des Ferblantiers: el Badi is on the S side of the place through Bab Berrima. The contemporary historian El Oufrani (1511–1670) relates that 50 tons of marble was imported from Italy and paid for on a pound for pound basis with sugar; he also states that skilled craftsmen came from many different countries and were amply rewarded for their work (unlike the creators of Moulay Ismael's royal palaces who were cruelly exploited Christian slaves). The walls of this incredibly sumptuous palace were 2m thick and the inner courtyard measured 135m by 110m and enclosed gardens watered by 100 pools and fountains (placed above ground level so that irrigation was easier) and with several elegant pavilions faced with marble columns. All this can now only be imagined because the palace lies in ruins: it was systematically destroyed by the jealous Moulay Ismael, but not before all the treasures had been stripped from the walls and dispersed among his own extravagant palaces in Meknes. Today the ruins of El Badi are brought to life by the Folk Festival held every June in what used to be the courtyard. On this occasion the pools are filled and the fountains work. Traces of one or two of the pavilions still remain, the most complete being that of *el Khemsin* (or 'the Fifty'), on the W side, which was once a vast reception hall and named after its 50 marble columns. Another half-ruined pavilion houses a small museum which contains, among other things, an early Almoravide pulpit. It still has its original painted ceiling. Vestiges of royal palaces lie around the perimeter of the courtyard, and on the S side is the enclosure housing today's royal palace or *Dar el Makhzen*, built on Saadian and Almohade foundations and recently superbly restored. It is now again in use by the royal household and therefore not open to visitors.

Next to the Badi Palace is the *Mellah*, reached by returning to the Place des Ferblantiers and going through an archway on the right of Bab Berrima. The Mellah was created by the early Saadian sultan Abd Allah (1574–76), allegedly to protect the sizeable Jewish population from Muslim threats and insults, but also to have them easily accessible for taxation purposes: the Jews in Saadian times represented a considerable source of revenue for the Makhzen. The mellah was once a thriving city within a city. It covered an area of some 18 hectares and included synagogues (a few of which still remain), shops, gardens and houses. Today it differs from the rest of the city only in the unusual height of its houses and the lack of space between them. There are very few Jews left now and the various souks have been taken over by Muslim craftsmen. Having lost its identity it now seems rather sad and neglected in comparison with the colourful souks that lie immediately around Djmaa el Fna.

Two splendid 19C buildings in the vicinity—immediately N of the mellah—are the **Bahia Palace** and the **Palace of Dar Si Said**; the former was the residence of Ba Ahmed, the Chief Vizir to Sultan Moulay el Hassan; the latter was built by his brother Si Said, and has been transformed into a very worthwhile museum. It is probably one of the best museums in Morocco with its wide variety of treasures and everyday objects. (Open every day except Tuesday from 9.00 to 11.45 and from 14.30 to 18.00.) The palace itself is so minutely crafted that it would deserve special attention even if the artefacts were not there. Particularly striking are the painted cedarwood ceilings, seemingly each more beautiful than the last.

The palace is Andalucian in style—built around a patio crowded with fountains and plants. You enter the building along a passageway lined with ancient wooden doors complete with heavy and intricate locking devices. First there is a room containing a variety of children's toys, also made of wood, including what must surely be the forerunner of the Big Wheel, with carriages, each big enough for one child, hanging on four spokes, making a kind of vertical roundabout. The jewellery room is dominated by great Roman-style fibulas as worn by Berber women, together with earrings and elaborate head-dresses. Then there is a room full of weapons, including the long and heavy 'fantasia' rifles which are traditionally held aloft in one hand and shot in the air as the rider gallops along at top speed. Another room contains nothing but copper and brass household utensils; here are the typical kettles with their ornamental stands still used in the hand-washing ceremony before and after a traditional Moroccan meal. Coffee pots, hexagonal sugar boxes typical of Marrakesh, incense burners for driving out evil spirits, and very ornate bowls with conical lids for containing bread. The kaftan room is particularly splendid.

Upstairs is the main reception room, obviously used for family occasions and today arranged as for a wedding. It holds two major pieces of furniture, both made of cedarwood: one is a many-sided two-tiered table used for displaying wedding presents; the other is a traditional marriage chair, intricately painted and with the usual very high seat. The reason for its elevation is two-fold: it was always necessary for the bride to be clearly visible to all the guests; and (perhaps more importantly) it was necessary to discourage her from running away should the first sight of her intended husband be too awful to contemplate (traditionally she would not have met him before the ceremony). The last rooms contain carpets, mainly Berber carpets from the Middle and High Atlas mountains. The colours are predominantly dark red and gold.

The Bahia Palace next door is empty but it certainly merits a visit as a fine example of 19C Andalucian-style domestic architecture. It is built around a large central courtyard with gracious colonnades, fountains and a green and white mosaic floor, which creates an effect of infinite coolness on hot summer days. The palace is approached through an avenue of orange trees, geraniums, datura, jasmine, and a few lofty palms. This is typical of old Marrakesh: one minute the hectic bustle of donkeys and men in the crowded squares; the next the magic of a scented tree-lined path of absolute peace.

On the N side of the Djmaa el Fna (on the far side of the leather souk—Souk Cherratine) is the **Ibn Youssef Medersa**, the largest medersa in Morocco. It is reputed to have housed over 800 students at one time who would have attended lectures in the adjacent mosque of the same name and probably other nearby mosques. It was built by the Merinides in the 14C and then completely rebuilt by the Saadians in 1562 in their exuberant Andalucian style.

You go in through a small entrance hall and a long outer corridor to reach the great rectangular court with its upper storey of students' rooms (approached by a stairway from the entrance hall). The court contains a large pool (unlike the small ablutions fountains of the Fez medersas) which is set in a floor of white marble. The walls are the most remarkable feature, decorated with characteristic Saadian flamboyance. The decoration is comparable with the Courtyard of Lions in the Alhambra of Granada, and it seems likely that Andalucian craftsmen of the same school were responsible for all the most lavish Saadian monuments in Morocco (cf. the tombs described above and the two pavilions added to the central court of the Karaouyine in Fez; Rte 10).

Around the base of the walls is, typically, a layer of softly-coloured mosaic tiles, then delicate stucco arches, with panels of criss-cross patterns carved in stone above, and, at the top of the walls, cedarwood lintels carved with kufic script and a pine cone design. The horseshoe-shaped mihrab in the *oratory* is a particularly fine specimen, with arabesques containing quotations from the Koran, and around it a stucco frieze of swirling designs and the pine cone motif. Another interesting feature is the sculpted marble wash basin which has been placed in the small entrance hall. The figurative nature of its decoration—small heraldic birds—betrays its non-Saadian origin, and it is thought to have been brought over from Cordoba in the 10C. The central pool is said to date back to the 11C and is perhaps the original reason for the medersa being located there. It is possible that it was constructed on the foundations of an earlier religious monument built by the Almoravides.

The *Mosque of Ibn Youssef* across the road was completely rebuilt in the 19C and is of little interest to the non-Muslim visitor. However, if you stand with your back to the S wall of the mosque and look straight ahead towards the souks you will see the *Koubba el Baadiyin*, built by the Almoravides when they founded the city in the 11C as a holy shrine covering an ablutions pool. This is the only Almoravide building that remains intact, and it was only fairly recently discovered, half-buried in rubble from recent destructions and with less interesting structures hard up against it. It is a small and simple square building with a rough dome, but the beginnings of what were to become very familiar designs are apparent in the shapes of the windows and arches. It is worth a closer look.

Marrakesh is justly famous for its gardens, where the visitor is free to wander and where time has little meaning. Most refreshing is the *Menara*, created by the Almohades in the SW corner of the town. It is a vast olive grove containing a large reservoir which is overlooked by a sober 19C pavilion. Today busloads of tourists stop at the steps leading up to the reservoir, gaze a moment into the brackish water, take a quick photo of the pavilion or the ever-present water-sellers, and then drive back into the town. The gardens themselves remain untouched by all this commotion and await the more leisurely visitor. The drive back along the Ave de la Menara affords an unforgettable view of the Koutoubia.

The *Agdal Gardens* to the S of the Royal Palace also date back to the 12C and contain every sort of fruit tree—apricot, fig, orange, plum and pear. The gardens were re-designed in the 19C by Sultan Abd er Rahman (whose son, Mohammed, was later drowned in the reservoir called, somewhat ironically, *Es Sahraj el Hana*, the pool of health). From the roof of the pavilion alongside the water there are distant views of the High Atlas.

Quite different from the other two is the *Majorelle Garden* situated in the N of the new town, just off Ave El Jadida. This small and very contrived botanical garden was created by a Frenchman named Louis Majorelle

The Palmeraie, Marrakesh

during the Protectorate. It has a particularly good collection of cacti and is open only in the mornings.

Marrakesh Gueliz, the new town, is traversed by wide boulevards, lined on both sides by orange and lemon trees or by jacarandas; the scent of the former and the colour of the latter when in flower are unforgettable. The main artery is the Ave Mohammed V, which starts in the district of modern shops, hotels and restaurants, and sweeps through the walls of the old city right up to the Koutoubia itself. A surprising Victorian touch is the preponderance of horse-drawn landaus which will take you to any part of the town (for about 30 dirhams, negotiable in advance). Sitting comfortably in one of these, making slow aristocratic progress through the streets, is one of the most restful and delightful ways of getting to know your way around, and particularly to be recommended at sunset when the whole town and the palmeraie are bathed in a hot rosy hue.

The **Palmeraie**, which covers over 1214 hectares, is one of the great wonders of southern Morocco. A drive along the 8km '*route de palmeraie*', which can be extended to take in the city walls, is highly recommended.

The climate of Marrakesh is considered by many to be one of the most perfect in the world—except of course in the high summer months when it can become very hot, although not unbearable since it is never humid. The temperature for the rest of the year ranges from warm to pleasantly hot. There is very little rain and the air is light and particularly good for anyone suffering from chest, ear, nose or throat complaints. The sun is only occasionally obscured when a sandstorm arrives suddenly and violently from the desert.

There is a wide choice of hotels. You can pay handsomely and stay at the world-famous *Mamounia*—a luxurious palace set in beautiful walled gardens. The atmosphere is dignified and the style of architecture inside is Moorish. Recently a conference centre and banqueting hall have been incorporated which, to a certain extent, have destroyed this world famous hotel's uniqueness, although they have undoubtedly made it more profitable. It is conveniently situated only five minutes' walk from the souks and the Djmaa el Fna. All the rooms are at the back and face the Atlas. Below you is the swimming pool, heated in winter, in its setting of leaning palms, orange, lemon and grapefruit trees and cypresses.

It would be hard to think of a more attractive place than Marrakesh to hold international conferences and many of the big hotels are now equipped with the necessary facilities, the Safir and the Es Saadi in particular. Recommended for sheer pleasure is the four-star *Les Almoravides* with delightful gardens and pool, and the advantage of lying midway between the souks and the modern shops just off Ave Mohammed V. Smaller, cheaper hotels with gardens and pools (and still in the centre of town) include the three-star *Imilchil* and the two-star *Koutoubia*. For a really atmospheric and memorable (though noisy) stay in Marrakesh, go to the one-star CTM hotel which is located on the Place Djmaa el Fna and has a roof terrace from which to observe the fun.

The town is rich in restaurants to suit every mood and many nationalities. There are of course the hotels themselves and the Mamounia is outstanding (at around 300 dirhams a head, at least). There are several modern, French-style establishments in the new town such as *le Petit Poucet* and *les Ambassadeurs*, both on Mohammed V. If you want something really atmospheric and you have a whole evening to spare, there are the Moroccan restaurants, usually housed in former palaces in the old town. These are splendid value although created especially for tourists since Moroccans do not on the whole eat in restaurants. The meal will be plentiful and will certainly include cous-cous and two or three other typical dishes. In summer there will often be dancers to entertain you, maybe a snake charmer and usually a small band. All this, and very often transport from and back to your hotel (which is usually necessary) can be had for around 200 dirhams a head and should be booked in advance through your hotel. Even more exotic are the one or two enterprising places out in the palm grove where you sit in huge tents and, at the end of the lengthy meal, have the chance to see a real 'fantasia' performed in front of the tents. There will usually be troops of Berber musicians and dancers. The music is deafeningly loud but quite intoxicating.

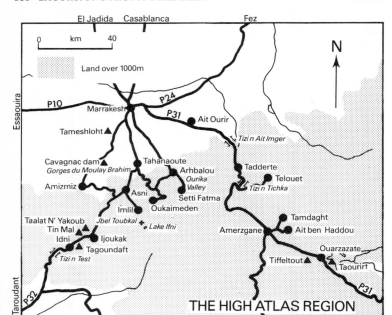

THE HIGH ATLAS REGION

16 Excursions from Marrakesh

A. The Ourika Valley and Oukaimeden

Total distance: c 190km round trip.

Take the main road to Taroudant out of Marrakesh (see Rte 15). The S513 road to Ourika branches left just before leaving the S outskirts of the city. After a flat stretch of about half an hour it begins to climb in gentle spirals alongside a rushing torrent of icy water which is the river Ourika. Villages hang on to the almost vertical sides of the valley. They are difficult to spot from a distance because they are made of the same red earth as the valley itself. Wildly romantic to photograph, they must be less romantic to live in; some of them are indeed deserted and in the process of being slowly eroded away by the wind and rain. No longer under threat of attack by hostile tribes, the inhabitants have moved down into the fertile valley where they cultivate every space. It is particularly lovely in spring when the tiny valley-bottom fields first emerge from the winter snow, their horizontal lines softened later by clouds of almond blossom.

The road continues as far as the hamlet of *Setti Fatma* (63km from

Marrakesh; 1500m alt.) and then gives up as the gorge closes in. This is a good place to start walking and if you call in at the village café you will probably be directed to the 'Walk of the Seven Waterfalls' which starts as a rough path from the grassy sward behind the café and then fairly quickly becomes more of a scramble up the rocks. For the less energetic there are more moderate paths.

There are several modest hotel-restaurants in the Ourika valley, which you will have passed on the way to Setti Fatma, notably *l'Ourika* (with swimming pool) and *chez Ramuntcho* where you can eat copiously while gazing down into the ravine or up at the soaring majestic peaks. You can spend the night there too though accommodation is sometimes fairly basic. There is also the Kasbah Restaurant (in an unmistakably Glaoui building) and, opposite it, the rather stylish Hotel Amnougar with a pool.

The road to **Oukaimeden**, which branches off the Ourika road at *Arhbalou* (24km back towards Marrakesh from Setti Fatma), is only slightly hair-raising and rises gradually to 2650m by means of rather gentle hairpin bends. It is paved all the way. This little settlement should certainly be visited if at all possible for here the mountains rise even more abruptly and splendidly to their great heights and one really is on top of the world. There are two small hotels—*Imlil* and *chez Juju*—which are sporty ski-lodges with cosy accommodation and good food, and there is at least one refuge belonging to the Alpine Club. Oukaimeden offers the best skiing in Morocco. The season runs from December to April (sometimes later). There is one chair-lift and 6 ski-tows and a day pass costs 60 dirhams. There are also facilities for hiring boots and skis. This is not beginner's skiing however; the snow tends to be icy and most of the runs are steep. Nor can one be sure of the snow. It may not come at all or it may come in such superabundance that the only access road is cut off.

For non-winter visitors, walking and climbing are obvious attractions and guides are available to take you up Jbel Oukaimeden or to indicate one of the many tracks going SW towards Imlil. You may also be fortunate enough to spot some of the prehistoric stone carvings. The most accessible ones can be found close to the lake as you enter Oukaimeden. Others could be anywhere and the guides will often know.

Descending from Oukaimeden it is possible to return to Marrakesh by turning left to 23km *Tahanaoute* (instead of right to Ourika). It is not so much the village but the drive to it which is worth the effort for the road is spectacular and the glimpses of the Marrakesh plain through mountain clefts are memorable. After Tahanaoute it is a straight level drive of 30km back to town.

B. Jbel Toubkal via Imlil

64km to **Imlil** and thence on foot or muleback. Return the same way.

For the adventurous, more intensive explorations into the High Atlas can be undertaken either on muleback or on foot. The recommended centre from which to start is Imlil, some 17km along a road going SE from the Berber village of Asni (48km S of Marrakesh on the main Taroudant road; see Route 17). Imlil can provide experienced mountain guides, maps and all the necessary equipment for sale or hire, as well as an array of cafés and shop's and a French Alpine Club hostel.

The most rewarding excursion of all is the ascent of Jbel Toubkal. At 4165m this is the highest mountain in Morocco and climbing it should be well within the capacity of any fit and properly equipped person between the months of April and November. From Imlil the first village—Aremd—is about 1 hour's walk; then walk for 2 hours up the valley to Sidi Chamharouch where there are soft drinks for sale; this is followed by a 3-hour climb up a steep path to the Neltner refuge (3207m). From here there is a fairly stiff scramble to the summit, taking between 2 and 3 hours depending on fitness. The view from the top is truly magnificent and best of all is the clear light of early morning. For this reason many people spend a night at the Neltner refuge, which can be arranged at Imlil and costs 20 dirhams.

Visible from the summit (and a 4-hour walk away) is Lake Ifni, the only lake in the High Atlas. The whole Toubkal area is now a National Park and there are many other tracks, including the 4-hour walk eastwards to Tacheddirt (with refuge) whence you could continue and connect up with either Oukaimeden or the Ouika Valley.

C. Amizmiz

Total distance 110km to **Amizmiz** and back to **Marrakesh**, or c 140km round trip via *Asni*.

A few kilometres out of Marrakesh (see Rte 15) on the Taroudant road a right-hand turn (S507) is signposted **Amizmiz** which lies 53km to the SW. On the way you pass several kasbahs including that of *Tamesloht*, and the *Cavagnac dam* with its great lake behind it.

Amizmiz is a small and charming Berber settlement. Its houses are clustered around a kasbah and a zaouia. It has a small inn and there is a colourful market on Tuesdays, usually attended by a large number of people from neighbouring villages.

After Amizmiz the road becomes a rough track, but none the less scenic as it winds its way through oak and juniper trees before petering out in the middle of nowhere. The quickest way back to Marrakesh is by the way you have come; but a circular trip can be made by taking a turn E at Amizmiz along a wildly beautiful track across the gorges of the Nfiss river, rejoining the main Taroudant road just to the S of *Asni* (see Rte 17).

17 Marrakesh to Agadir

A. Via Chichaoua

Total distance 266km. **Marrakesh**—P10. 77km *Chichaoua*—S511. 189km **Agadir**.

This fast road (P10) across the lower reaches of the Atlas was only completed in 1973. It is straightforward, easy driving and scenically a little dull. First follow the main Marrakesh–Essaouira road as far as 77km

Chichaoua, an ordinary town distinguished only by its carpet industry. The carpets have pink or red backgrounds and are produced in quantity by several co-operatives which will welcome the interested visitor. After Chichaoua the road (S511) turns S and climbs gently to the small town of (45km) *Imi-n-Tanout* and then crosses the TIZI-N-MAACHOU (1300m alt.), which must be one of the lowest and easiest passes in the High Atlas range. The road continues to pick its way through the foothills and finally descends towards the fertile Souss plain with Agadir (see Rte 4) and the ocean beyond.

B. Via the Tizi-n-Test Pass and Taroudant

Total distance 304km. **Marrakesh**—S501. 47km *Asni*—87km *Tizi-n-Test Pass*—90km **Taroudant**—80km **Agadir**.

This picturesque and unforgettable road soars to a precipitous and snowy height of 2100m at the TIZI-N-TEST PASS and then ambles gradually down to the plain of the Souss river to Taroudant and Agadir. For savage beauty of a kind rarely seen, this is a road worth saving your energy for. You should not try to do it in less than six hours, for although the distance is not great, there are many hairpin bends and steep climbs. The road is, however, quite safe and wide enough at all times for passing, though sadly no longer well maintained since most travellers to Taroudant and Agadir seem to prefer the much quicker route via Chichaoua. One cannot but wonder at the ingenuity and courage of the people who built it; it was constructed by the French at the beginning of the 20C as a first step in the pacification of the great 'Lords of the Atlas' (in this area the Goundafi clan), the ruins of whose kasbahs still crown the rocky heights at strategic points along the route. The scenery is ever changing: red-earth villages perched on high escarpments, terraced fields cut into the mountain sides, slopes covered with wild flowers in spring, rushing torrents and, above all else, the mysterious, permanent and untouched snowfields.

The road is flat as far as the small Berber town of Tahanaoute (34km) which overlooks the Gorges of Moulay Brahim and from where a track goes to the ski-resort of c 40km Oukameiden (see Rte 16). It then climbs a further 13km to the very pleasant town of *Asni* (1150m alt.) which appears almost completely surrounded by mountains. Asni can be a delightful spot to spend the night—a fitting half-way house between the hot and exotic attractions of Marrakesh and the cold and rugged Berber country to come. There is a small but very adequate hotel, somewhat pretentiously named *Grand Hotel du Toubkal*. A track starts here for 17km Imlil, the starting point for the trek to the top of *Jbel Toubkal* (see Rte 16).

13km further on is *Ouirgane*, also highly recommended as a stopping place. It has two distinguished hotels, both with swimming pools and good restaurants: *la Roseraie* and *Au sanglier qui fume*. Both also offer facilities for shooting, fishing and camping and *la Roseraie* organises riding expeditions into the mountains in spring and early summer. Next comes the village of *Ijoukak* which spans the Agoundis river. It has a small hotel. A kilometre further on is the village and kasbah of *Taalat N'Yacoub*, and just beyond that a short trail leads to the ruin of the very hallowed **Tin Mal Mosque** (1153). This is all that remains of the 12C stronghold from which the Almohade chief Ibn Toumart (hailed as the Mahdi) and his disciple, Abd el

Mumene, first went out to preach the Unity of God and the need for reform, and then to attack the decadent Almoravides in Marrakesh and Fez. It was also to Tin Mal that the last of the Almohade leaders retreated when the Merinides drove them out of Marrakesh in 1262. The Merinides ruthlessly sacked the town in 1276 but, significantly, left the mosque itself standing, as if even they respected the teachings of Ibn Toumart (who was buried there). Roofless now but noble in its stark setting, Tin Mal affords a unique opportunity for the non-Muslim to see what a mosque is like inside. It still retains its framework of transverse arches and some splendidly tenacious stalactitic vaulting, particularly under the arches leading to the mihrab, which is intact and displays typically Almohade patterns of powerful geometric forms around arabesques and rosettes. The mihrab closely resembles that of the Koutoubia in Marrakesh (which it slightly pre-dates) and it is considered almost certain that the two were designed by the same craftsman. Tin Mal is unique in that the minaret is placed above, and partly behind, the mihrab—minarets are usually positioned at one end of the N wall and no one knows why the architect of Tin Mal decided otherwise.

A little further on the road passes close to another kasbah, perched on a hilltop, called *Tagoundaft*. Both kasbahs were built by the powerful Goundafa tribe who ruled in feudal style over this whole area until the early 20C when they were extinguished by the even more powerful Glaoui clan.

12.5km beyond *Idni*, where there is a modest hotel-restaurant, is the magnificent TIZI-N-TEST PASS, with breathtaking views, especially S over the Souss valley. 37km below the Pass on the other side is the P32 which goes E towards 152km *Tazenakht* and is part of the great W–E transverse route across the south of Morocco, linking the major towns of Agadir, Ouarzazate and Errachidia. 67km along this road is the small town of *Taliouine* with a splendid Glaoui *kasbah* which seems to flow down the hillside. It has good stalactitic carving on the towers and almond trees all around. Next door to it is the 4-star hotel, *Ibn Toumert*, while the more modest *Auberge Souktan* overlooks the kasbah from the opposite side of the valley. It makes a pleasant excursion and there is a rough road going SW to Irherm and 148km Tafraoute.

From the junction with the P32 it is 52km of easy driving to **Taroudant**, an attractive red-earth town completely enclosed in ancient crenellated walls some 6m high. Within this forbidding exterior are olive groves, palm trees and fertile, well-watered fields. This is a town which instantly speaks of past splendours: its origins go back to pre-Saadian times but it was the Saadians, arriving from the Draa valley to the E in the 16C, who made Taroudant their capital. They stayed for 20 years, embellishing and building palaces and ramparts. The town became a prosperous commercial centre, exporting sugar, cotton and indigo to the region of Timbucktoo in exchange for the gold which became a Saadian obsession. Greatly enriched, the Saadians then moved to Marrakesh and Taroudant's importance dwindled fast till it became what it really is today: an unremarkable town but whose magnificent walls lend it great elegance. It is very hot in summer because it is down on the plain and inland, and warm and windy in winter.

Its souks are animated and the artisanat—objects of brass, leather and wrought iron—is attractive if not very original; more collectable is the heavy Berber jewellery. There are also figurines and objects carved out of the soft local stone, which appear more African than Islamic. Just inside the main walls is the old kasbah quarter where the Saadians had their palaces, most of which were destroyed by the Alouite sultan, Moulay Ismael, in the 17C when he put down a rebellion, massacred the entire population and replaced it with Berbers from the Rif. He built a fortress here, of which sections remain. Here too is the *Palais Salam*, once a 19C pasha's palace. It is now probably one of the most enjoyable hotels in Morocco, as much for its friendly service (fresh orange juice appears the moment you arrive) as for the splendour of its air-conditioned split-level rooms opening on to idyllic gardens where the wind rustling through palm fronds sounds just like rain. (A single room here costs the equivalent of £20, breakfast included.)

There is also the *Gazelle d'Or*, an inordinately expensive hotel 2km out of town. It is completely self-contained behind its solid red ramparts and offers every conceivable luxury and amusement including swimming, tennis, riding and falconry in a 10-hectare park. It is closed in the high summer months. More modest hotels offering gardens and pools include the *Saadiens* and the *Taroudant*.

It is 80km from Taroudant to Agadir through the Adminin forest and across the prosperous farmlands of the Souss valley, by way of Ait-Melloul.

18 Marrakesh to Ouarzazate

Total distance 204km. **Marrakesh**—P31. 37km *Ait Ourir*—71km *Tizi-n-Tichka* (—21km **Telouet**)—60km *Amerzgane*—36km **Ouarzazate**.

The TIZI-N-TICHKA PASS, at an altitude of 2260m, is higher but slightly less spectacular than the Tizi-n-Test on the Marrakesh–Agadir road. Nevertheless, this is a driving and visual experience not to be missed; moreover the road is well-maintained and the inclines are properly graded.

Leave Marrakesh (see Rte 15) from the N of the medina, near Bab Khemis, by the P24 (signposted to Kasba Tadla and Fez); then, after 7km, turn right on to the P31 to Ouarzazate. The first town, still on the plain, is 37km *Ait Ourir* which has nothing special to recommend it except its Tuesday market. About 20km further across this fertile stretch, planted with olive groves and fruit trees, the road begins to climb, to cross, first of all, the TIZI-N-AIT-IMGER PASS in the foothills; at 1470m a kind of practice run.

From this point on, standing at every hairpin bend and often perilously close to the edge, are the sellers of amethysts and other semi-precious minerals such as cobalt and topaz. The stones are usually still uncut and sometimes remain within the original rock casing. There are small boys with boxes of goodies who will run up the hill by some hidden short-cut, in order to overtake you and be waiting at the next bend but one. There are also co-operatives with several permanent stalls and a more professional take-it-or-leave-it approach. The range of merchandise is enormous and often includes fossils and local pottery as well as stones. You will need—and be respected for—your best bargaining skills.

The road soars higher, between slopes spotted with oleanders and scrubby oaks, and the last village before the pass is *Tadderte*—a picturesque Berber settlement surrounded by walnut trees and with a modest inn. After 16km you come to the Pass itself, and once over it the atmosphere changes quite markedly. You are now facing the desert, the pre-Sahara, which is cut into by three river valleys—the Draa, the Dades and the Todra—a land of oases and ksour. The ksour (singular: ksar) are small fortified villages of red beaten-earth houses, many with one or two interior courtyards and towers at each corner. The houses are clustered around the chief's house, or kasbah, which will be larger, often painted with whitewash and usually with either two or four square crenellated towers intricately and delicately carved, the degree of decoration depending on the wealth and power of the chief. Since inter-tribal war in the pre-Sahara has ended many of the houses have been abandoned for more comfortable ones lower down in the valley.

The most interesting of the ksour is that of **Telouet**, where the houses are clustered round the now deserted kasbah of the Glaoui family, which looks like a medieval fortress. This can be reached by taking a left-hand turn just after the Tizi-n-Tichka Pass and driving about 21km over good but sometimes steep track through some splendid scenery. The Glaouis dominated a large part of the S in the days before and during the Protectorate, and this palatial kasbah was the very centre of their power guarding, as it did, one of the only two access routes across the mountains to Marrakesh.

The story of the most famous member of the Glaoui family, Thami, also known as the Pasha of Marrakesh or, quite simply, El Glaoui, is a fascinating one. In the aftermath of World War II, which had brought Morocco out of its isolation, the desire for self-determination and independence from France was growing apace. The Istiqlal (Independence) Party regrouped and the sultan, Mohammed V, gave tacit support to the cause of Independence by omitting all reference to the French in his speeches. Later he declared himself openly supportive of Independence and during a formal visit to France asked the Government to institute radical changes forthwith. He achieved very little but the fact that he tried ensured a triumphal return and increasing disobedience and disorder under the French administration.

Meanwhile, Thami el Glaoui, Pasha of Marrakesh and certainly the most powerful man in the S, was showing himself to be a staunch supporter of the French, probably because he (and others like him) feared that any independent Moroccan government would very soon put an end to his almost limitless power and extravagant lifestyle. Aided and abetted by the French government to do all in his power to stem the tide of nationalism, he publicly denounced the Sultan for having sold himself to the Istiqlal party, calling him 'Sultan of Istiqlal but not of Morocco', whereupon Mohammed V bade him leave the palace and never return.

The French continued to support El Glaoui, building up his reputation as 'the uncrowned king of the real Morocco'. In August 1953 he issued a request to the French Government, signed by hundreds of the traditionally rich and powerful who also feared life under an independent administration could be less sweet, calling for the immediate removal of the Sultan whom, they claimed, the people of Morocco no longer recognised. The next day the Sultan and his family were duly exiled to Madagascar. An uncomfortable two years followed during which Morocco was ruled by an elderly puppet sultan, and support grew for the banished ruler, matched by increasing mistrust and dislike of the French. This period of growing disquiet and confusion finally ended in 1955 when el Glaoui once more took the lead; sensing defeat he made a complete volte-face and requested the return of the 'true Sultan' on the grounds that his previous dismissal had been illegal. Tired of the whole affair the French Government acquiesced and brought him back from Madagascar. He went first to Paris where el Glaoui, ever the opportunist, met him and fell to his knees begging forgiveness. He was forgiven with the words: 'we must forget the past and look forward now to the future'.

The *kasbah* of Telouet, former palace of El Glaoui, is now a sad shadow of its former splendour but still—at least from the outside—recognisable as having originally been the home of a person of great wealth and taste. Inside, where there must once have been a superb collection of French and Moroccan furniture and carpets, there is now nothing to see but dilapidated walls, empty rooms and a few staircases. The village below the kasbah is, however, still very much alive.

Telouet merits a visit by reason of its setting and, above all, because of its history: it is a vestigial part of Morocco's really astonishingly recent past—a legacy from the days of the 'Lords of the Atlas', so vividly described by Gavin Maxwell in his book of the same name.

The road to Ouarzazate winds gradually down past the terraced Berber village of *Irherm-n-Ougdal*, with its typical dark-red square kasbah with a tower at each corner. Southern kasbahs are generally smaller and less flamboyant than those of the north.

The road follows the river Imini and at *Amerzgane* (60km from Tizi-n-Tichka) puts out a right-hand branch (P32) which eventually joins up (via Tazenakht) with the other (Tizi-n-Test) road over the High Atlas 220km to the west. Also at Amerzgane is a turning E to the village of *Ait Ben Haddou* (15km)—a spectacular fortified ksar with houses piled up around several decorated kasbahs, all seeming to defy the laws of gravity as they perch on the steep mountain slope. These fortified villages must have been almost totally inviolable but extremely awkward to live in. The importance of this one lay in the fact that (in the days before the French built the present road over the Tizi-n-Tichka) it was connected with Telouet by a track through the mountains, alongside the river Ounila. There are other ruined kasbahs, with attendant ksour, N of Ait Ben Haddou along the remains of this route which is open now as far as Tamdaght; after that it becomes a mule track.

The road continues to Ouarzazate (36km from Amerzgane), flat now and relatively straight. There is a splendid kasbah on your right as you approach the town which is accessible from the Zagora road. This is **Tifeltout**, and its harmonious proportions and soft outlines make it one of the most frequently photographed and filmed kasbahs in Morocco. It is another legacy of the Glaoui family and is now a hotel-restaurant renowned not only for its excellent Moroccan cuisine but also for folklore displays and Berber dancing which take place most evenings in the huge courtyard. There are only eight rooms but space is also available on the flat roof (amongst the storks' nests), either for sleeping or simply for escaping from the somewhat repetitive sound of the Berber troupes. As with the paradores in Spain, little has been altered on the outside and a high standard of comfort has been installed without defacing the essential Moorish dignity and splendour of the building. It is a cool and wonderful place to come to after a long hot journey.

Ouarzazate lies at an important junction between the main routes from the Draa and Dades valleys and Marrakesh. It began as a strategically-placed French outpost, from which to pacify neighbouring Berber tribes. It therefore has no authentic old centre, and the one main street (Blvd Mohammed V) offers little in the way of local colour or lively markets. It does have a Glaoui kasbah—*Taourirt*—which stands at the S end of the town overlooking the river bed. It is in need of repair but parts of it are usually open to the public. Clustered around it is a collection of workshops and stalls and opposite is an official '*centre artisanal*'.

Nevertheless, in the last seven years Ouarzazate has been decreed a

Kasbah near Ouarzazate

major tourist centre and now has two 5-star and five 4-star hotels as well as a variety of small ones, all grouped together in a '*zone hotelière*' behind the town centre.

Standing on the edge of the desert and accessible by three major roads (as well as having its own airport—1km NE of town—with regular flights from Casablanca and Paris), it is an important stopping-off point for the package tours. Perhaps it is in their honour that the pink and crumbling ramparts around Taourirt have been outlined in fairy lights, which give an air of permanent festivity to the town belied by its rather lifeless quality. Discreet floodlighting would have done a lot better.

19   Ouarzazate to Zagora

Total distance 171km.—**Ouarzazate**—73km *Agdz*—98km **Zagora**.

Zagora—22km *Tamgrout*.

Zagora—54km *Tagounite*—34km *Mhamid*.

The first part of this road as far as 73km Agdz is dramatic as it follows the river Draa through the strange surrealistic black shapes of the Jbel Sarhro mountains. *Agdz* is a most attractive market town, with a huge main square busy with cafés and stalls which are hung with colourful Berber carpets and scattered with local pottery and jewellery. This is an excellent place to seek out and bargain for carpets: the selection ranges from quite small prayer rugs, to the sort which is made of silk and needs to be hung on the wall, or large, room-sized carpets in vibrant colours. They do not necessarily have the lasting quality of the more solid Berber rugs from the N, and their price should favourably reflect this fact. Wandering through all the cheerful hubbub of the town are the desert people, tall thin men of aquiline feature and noble gait, looking somewhat aloof from it all.

The Draa valley between Agdz and Zagora must be one of the most intensely populated ribbons of land in the pre-Saharan region. The Draa is one of Morocco's longest rivers, rising in the High Atlas, cutting through the Jbel Sarhro range and then turning W along the S flanks of the Anti Atlas, sometimes disappearing into the desert sand and then reappearing again further on. It eventually pushes its way out to the Atlantic at *Foum-el-oued-Draa* (Mouth-of-the-River-Draa) about 80km SW of Goulimine.

Seen from the road there is nothing but arid, sandy wasteland above, while on the valley floor not an inch of space is left unused. There are cereals of all kinds, and almond, lemon, orange, date and olive trees. Just above the fertile ground live the people in their villages, their simple houses coloured red or ochre, with heavy wooden doors and tiny windows, so that the sun does not enter. These people are industrious. The women who are not working in the fields spin and weave, the old men tan hides or make babouches, the young men tend their crops. The women dress in typical southern Berber style: in black, with their faces unveiled, and adorned with a wealth of silver jewellery. Jewellery holds an important place in the life of Berber women; they wear it every day regardless of how menial their tasks; and it is an integral part of the family capital, to be sold off in times of drought and poor crops, or to be increased and displayed in greater profusion in periods of prosperity.

There are kasbahs all along the route with distinctive tapering corner towers and white outlined windows. *Tamnougalt*, just beyond Agdz, has a particularly good collection of kasbahs.

Just before reaching *Zagora* the road passes through the *Jbel Azlag Gorge* and then emerges on to the great palm-filled oasis, once an important stopping place for camel caravans on the journey between Timbucktoo and Sijilmassa (S of Erfoud). Indeed there is a sign in Zagora which states that it is just 52 days by camel to Timbucktoo. The Saadians set off from this region in the early 16C, going on to conquer the whole of Morocco and also to penetrate deeper than ever before into the region S of the Sahara in search of gold and slaves. Other dynasties had been here before and it was the Almoravides who built the fortress on top of Jbel Zagora, the hill on the opposite bank of the Draa, ideally placed for guarding the caravan route. Behind the hill are traces of earlier occupation in the form of heaps of stones probably marking the burial places of prehistoric chieftains. There is a track which crosses the river and goes up to the fortress which is now, once again, used for military purposes. Casual visitors are therefore discouraged from going all the way. The views are nevertheless spectacular from well below the top.

Zagora does not pretend to be anything other than an oasis—a stopping place for weary travellers—a take-off point for the journey into the unknown, and it has markets on Wednesdays and Sundays which are almost exclusively given over to dates, for centuries the staple food of desert dwellers. There are two delightful hotels with interesting restaurants: the three-star *Tinsouline* in typical kasbah style with pool and all reasonable comfort; and the more modest *Fibule du Draa*, slightly outside town on the edge of the palm grove. There is also the new and rather showy four-star *Hotel*

Club Reda. Electricity as far S as this tends to be on the unreliable side and it is usual to find candles laid out by the bedside ready for the anticipated breakdown. The sudden lack of air-conditioning could be disconcerting on a hot night; fortunately the nights are fairly cool except in the high summer months of June, July and August.

A short EXCURSION 22km from Zagora to the village of *Tamgrout* is recommended. It is reached by a turning off the Jbel Zagora track. Tamgrout was once the seat of the Naciryin—a 17C religious brotherhood—and still possesses a fine library of ancient manuscripts, some of them 700 years old, with ornate and gilded writing on gazelle skin parchment, occasionally dotted with marginal notes made by later scholars. This rare and fascinating library (unlike the Karaouyine in Fez) is open to visitors. Tamgrout has a colourful market on Saturdays where the locally-made distinctive green enamelled pottery is sold, and two reasonable restaurants, the *Draa* and the *Oasis*.

The main road continues S from Zagora—although it deteriorates somewhat—for a further 54km as far as the settlement of *Tagounite*, and then turns W for a further 34km (alongside the Draa) to *Mhamid*.

South of Zagora the landscape is quite changed. The track leaves the river for some 30km and you drive over a bare plateau of black rock. The sun shines relentlessly on the distant, sinister silhouettes of the Jbel Bani range. The view is unreal, but later you rejoin the river and its green ribbon of fertility. At Mhamid even the waters of the great Draa lose themselves in the burning sand and the settlement itself—once a strategic point on the trans-Saharan trade route—seems to be disappearing beneath the desert. Mhamid was attacked by the Polisario in 1980 and is still very much a military post. Visitors are allowed through only with an official guide and a pass from the Caid's office in Zagora. It is probably not worth it unless you intend to travel further into the desert.

After Mhamid there are tracks which may or may not lead you E towards Rissani. They should not be attempted without a guide and, preferably, a four-wheel-drive vehicle. What may look like a straightforward road on the map will turn out to have innumerable side-tracks, forks and bends, and there is absolutely no means of knowing which is the main one, which will fade out after 10km, and which will double back on itself and perhaps take you into Algeria.

20 Ouarzazate to Errachidia including excursions up the Dades Gorge and Todra Gorge

Total distance 309km. **Ouarzazate**—41km *Skoura*—50km *El Klâa des M'Gouna*—24km *Boulemane*—53km *Tinerhir*— 55km *Tinejdad*—24km *Goulmima*—62km **Errachidia**.

The road from Ouarzazate E along the valley of the great Dades river to Boulemane is an easy uneventful 115km, passing first of all the impressive reservoir of El Mansour Eddhabi at the confluence of the Draa and Dades rivers. Not without reason is this road known as '*La Route des Kasbahs*' for as you approach (41km) *Skoura* they become more plentiful and ever more ornate with intricate carving on the towers and delicate wrought iron grilles

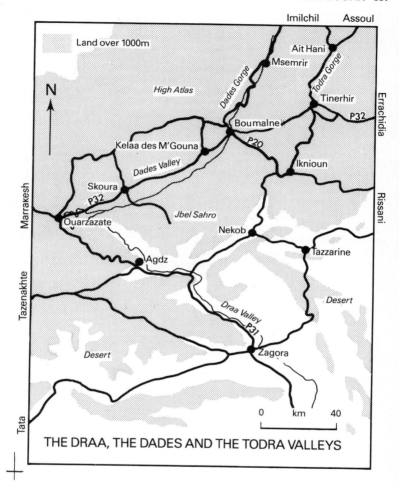

THE DRAA, THE DADES AND THE TODRA VALLEYS

over the windows. Since they are built only of *terre pisé* (earth and straw), the kasbahs are in varying stages of erosion; once they reach a certain point of dilapidation they are simply left to dissolve picturesquely away and new ones are built alongside. Skoura stands in a beautiful palm grove and where there are not palms, there are apricots, almonds, figs and walnuts sharing the fertile ribbon of land next to the river.

El Kelâa des M'Gouna (50km) is famous for its rose water which every other shop in town appears to sell. Rose water (*eau de roses*) is bought in large quantities by Moroccan ladies for rubbing into their faces and hands, and most of it comes from here. There is a rose festival here in May every

Animal market at El Kelâa des M'Gouna

year. Before the season of roses comes that of the almond blossom: clouds
of delicate pink and white flowers rise out of the valley bottom and reach
up towards the weathered kasbah walls, built high on the rocks because
of possible attack from floods or enemies. Kelâa has a delightful hotel, *Les
roses du Dades*, next door to a kasbah ruin.

Drive through 24km *Boulemane*, which has nothing much to offer except
its Wednesday market, and on up the Dades Gorge.

The Dades Gorge

Boulmane—62km Msemrir—32km Ait Hani.

Along this part of the route, before the gorge closes in, the almond trees
are thickly clustered, and the kasbahs, hard to photograph when the sun
is high because they are just the same colour and texture as the surrounding
rock, are especially impressive. The road soars up the sides of the gorge,
turns round and round on itself, plunges down and serpentines up again.
It is narrow and at times precipitous, with a drop of thousands of feet. This
is sporting driving and should not be attempted during or after rain when
the surface becomes slippery. Under dry conditions it is perfectly feasible
in an ordinary car and the views back down the gorge are superb.

After the little village of (62km) *Msemrir*, the country flattens out and becomes less interesting. There is a track which goes E from Msemrir across a range of mountains to 32km *Ait Hani*, at the N end of the Todra Gorge, but do not attempt this without a four-wheel drive vehicle and, even then, only in dry summer conditions. It is quite one of the most spectacular drives in Morocco but with areas so steep and hairpin bends so tight that your nerves, not to mention your car, are strained to the utmost. This is rugged mountain scenery on a leviathan scale and quite untamed. There are no people. The rock is highly mineral and it is tempting to collect specimens of rock crystal, quartz and amethyst.

If, on arrival at Ait Hani, you want more of this excitement continue N to *Imilchil*, but do leave plenty of time. Driving on such unpredictable tracks always takes longer than you think and the many fissures will not show up in failing light. In all, between Msemrir and Imilchil there are 92km of track and this can easily take all of a very long day. There are easier ways of approaching Imilchil (see Rte 13).

From Boulemane there is an easy 53km drive through the Jbel Sarhro mountains to *Tinerhir*, at the S entrance to the Todra Gorge. Tinerhir is one of the great tourist-frequented centres of the pre-Saharan region; and understandably so for it is in a bowl high in the mountains, ringed round with huge sculptured peaks which make a magical silhouette against the setting sun. The colours are hot; the green of the palm grove, tightly wedged in amongst the vertical rock walls, makes a vivid contrast with the dry dusty red. However, Tinerhir has recently developed a metallurgy industry which has caused a mass of concrete dwellings to swamp the old town. Deep within this depressing grey belt some artisanat survives though the ironsmiths who used to fashion window grilles on small forges are understandably fewer in number. Still thriving are the rug weavers—Berber women who work in family groups and go through the whole process of washing, carding, spinning and weaving in houses deep in the Mellah. Needless to say, they are delighted to display their skills and also to sell their rugs which will often seem irresistably cheap. They are immensely proud of their craft and pass it on from generation to generation, many of the rugs using traditional designs and serving as marriage presents. The Mellah itself is worth exploring: the streets are dark and narrow and remarkably cool (if a little dirty). The best way to get there is from the main square behind the Hotel Todra.

The highest building in town is the kasbah-style *Hotel Sargho* which stands right next door to the real original kasbah, now in ruins. Owned now by Kasbah Tours, this hotel concentrates on accommodating large groups. The decor is pretentious, the dining room hot and cramped and the pool area bare and unimaginative.

The Todra Gorge

A road from Tinerhir runs all the way along the bottom of the Todra Gorge. It never takes off and soars up the sides like the Dades road. Todra is a vast fault in the high plateau which separates the High Atlas from the Jbel Sarhro range, comparable with the Grand Canyon at Colorado. The road runs alongside the river and frequently fords it. At the beginning there are one or two glorious glimpses of palm grove between the rocks. As you progress higher 'up the river, the fords become deeper and sometimes impassable. The sky is a slit of light at the top and the rock walls, dark and forbidding, are sometimes brought to life by waterfalls looking like lengths of glinting silver ribbon. Unless you have an all-purpose vehicle you should not attempt to go much further than *Tamattouchte*, for the river begins to fill the gorge and at times the road turns into a row of stones barely discernible under the water. In the dry season you could continue the further 10km or so up to *Ait Hani* and then consider turning W to tackle the exciting mountain road described earlier, descending the Dades Gorge back to Boulemane and Tinerhir, an arduous and time-consuming but utterly memorable round trip of around 175km—not to be undertaken lightly.

The road between Tinerhir and Errachidia is an easy and comparatively dull stretch of 141km across semi-desert country. After 55km it passes through the quaint little town of *Tinejdad* whose women devote themselves to weaving woollen cloth for djellabahs which is greatly prized throughout the country. Here there is a minor road which goes direct to Erfoud (90km). The poor surface of the road is amply compensated for by the attractive villages along it—*Touroug* in particular. The road follows the river Rheris which has created a lush strip of continuous oases, populated and exhaustively cultivated by the Ait Attas—a colourful Berber tribe who once dominated the region and demanded tribute from other less warlike tribes. Ruined hill forts and an extensive graveyard marked with black stones betoken furious battles in the past. Small mounds of sand as far as the eye can see identify underground channels for collecting moisture. Suddenly you are in sandy desert and dunes can creep across the road (which makes it very skiddy). Jorf is a sizeable oasis with a fine triumphal arch and a cool colonnaded centre. From here it is palms all the way to (20km) Erfoud.

Back on the main road and 24km further on is the unremarkable town of *Goulmima* lying within a huge palm grove which hides a number of green-roofed sanctuaries and ancient water mills in its depths. 62km beyond this is *Errachidia*, once *Ksar-es-Souk* but recently renamed after Moulay Rachid, the first ruler of the reigning Alouite dynasty (which originated from this region). This town was created by the French as the administrative and commercial capital of the province of Tafilalet and is today one of the fastest developing areas of the Moroccan interior. Its geographical location gives it an obvious strategic importance: it stands at the crossroads between the great W–E route, which crosses Morocco S of the High Atlas, and the main N–S route connecting Fez with the Tafilalet region and Erfoud by way of the Ziz corridor. For this reason perhaps the town bristles with military and there are barracks to right and left of its magnificent triumphal arch. These exuberant arches are a feature of major southern towns and tend to set high expectations of what is to come. Sometimes they are quite far out of town and look isolated and faintly ridiculous. But this one, standing close to so much manifest progress, is undoubtedly justified.

As you approach Errachidia you will see villages which from a distance look like the usual kind of ksour, so traditional is their appearance. When examined more closely they are found to be newly-built with modern facilities of all kinds, each with its own mosque and market place. The prosperity of this whole region is based on the highly sophisticated and expensive irrigation schemes which were set up in the late 1960s in the wake of disastrous flooding by the then untamed Ziz river. The damage to crops at the time was incalculable and a decision was made to invest in a number of dams to keep the river within bounds and profit from its energy. This done the region is now an agricultural success story and Errachidia is its focal point.

Errachidia has a 4-star hotel (*Rissani*) but since there is little of tourist interest in the town you are strongly recommended to turn S down the valley of the Ziz and to spend as much time as possible in the Erfoud region (see Rte 21).

21 Midelt to Rissani

Total distance 239km. *Midelt*—P21. 72km *Rich*—68km *Errachidia*—11km *Meski*—66km **Erfoud**—22km **Rissani** (1.5km **Sijilmassa**).

From Midelt (see Rte 12) the southbound P21 climbs up into the High Atlas crossing the range via the TIZI-N-TALRHEMT (Pass of the she-camel) (1907m alt.) which marks quite brutally the change between desert and temperate vegetation. The road descends, crossing a bare plateau before reaching the valley of the great river Ziz, just after the turning to 72km *Rich*. (From Rich there is a long but comparatively simple road across the plateau to 110km Imilchil; see Rte 13.) The Ziz has cut a dramatic route across the mountains only to become lost in the desert sands S of Erfoud. The scenery is spectacular as the road enters the gorge, passing first under the *Tunnel du*

The valley of the Ziz

Légionnaire (built by French legionnaires during the Protectorate years and still always guarded) and the river cuts a narrow green strip through stark, precipitous rock walls.

The river may almost completely disappear in the dry season but it can become a violent torrent after rain. It is now disciplined by a complex system of dams and reservoirs of which the Hassan Addakhil Dam, completed in 1971, just N of Errachidia is a good example. Ziz water now irrigates the Tafilalet plain and the area to the south.

Errachidia, 140km from Midelt, is described in Rte 20. The journey between Errachidia and Erfoud, by way of Meski (see Rte 22) is quite simply a joy. After (11km) Meski you begin to catch glimpses of palm trees and fields of crops through gaps in the rock wall. In the middle of the valley are the Ziz waters, in friendlier mood now, glinting in the sun. From now on the ksour become more numerous and the valley throbs with life. These villages, built throughout in beaten earth, are the most characteristic feature of the Ziz valley. They are surrounded by high walls, often minutely decorated with traditional Berber designs and pierced by richly carved archways. Inside are friendly people living a free and tranquil life in the privacy and cool shade afforded by the walls. These are Berber tribes, descended from desert nomads, who have come N in search of fertile plains and rivers. Similar people are to be found in the valley of the Draa, to the W of here, living in similar conditions and working every inch of the land.

The road comes right down into the bed of the Ziz and you drive amongst the palms, oleander and almond trees; children will rush out to wave and to try and sell you baskets of apricots or dates or bunches of flowers. Seen from above, the Ziz valley must look like a green ribbon winding over an infinite stretch of sand and sunburnt rock. It is one endless oasis of date palms.

Erfoud (6000 inhab.) is an attractive town, red and dusty, built in straight lines by the French for controlling the Tafilalet region in the 1930s. It has a market place which is worth exploring if only for its range of desert fossils, but it really wakes up only in September each year, at the time of the date harvest, when the crop is brought in from the desert in baskets made of dried palm leaves, by donkeys. The dates are sorted with meticulous care before being sent to the far corners of the kingdom or for export further afield. There is a Date Festival in October.

The prestigious *Hotel Sijilmassa* which dominates the town from on high and commands one of the loveliest desert views in Morocco has now been turned into a royal palace and is no longer open to the public. The *Hotel Salam*, at the W end of town, with a smaller view and smaller pretentions, has friendly staff, traditional decor and glorious flower-decked swimming pool area.

Erfoud is right in the sandy desert and is therefore a centre from which to make many trips. Tracks branch out in all directions towards the dunes, joining one oasis with the next and disappearing into the desert horizon. A good overall view can be had by driving up Bordj Est, a hillock on the edge of town. The top of it is now occupied by a military outpost and, at time of writing, one is only allowed half-way up. Even this is well worthwhile especially in early evening when the sun slowly sinks behind the hills, creating dazzling contrasts between light and shade.

Rissani lies 22km to the S of Erfoud. The drive is through a continuous oasis of brilliant green squares of flourishing crops, irrigation canals and palms. Just before entering the town, notice the crumbling sections of wall on the left. This is all that remains of *Sijilmassa,* an Arab city dating back

Triumphal Arch, Rissani

to the early 8C. Well placed on the earliest caravan route from the Sahara to Fez, it became notorious for greed, vice and slave trafficking and was several times sacked by both Almoravides and Almohades in their early, most pious years. Barely discernible a few metres up the rough track are the remains of a palace, whilst in the foreground are a marabout and a cemetery. This site seems totally abandoned and will soon disappear altogether beneath the encroaching sands unless something is done.

Rissani's triumphal arch is grand and richly decorated and suggests greater prosperity than is to be found now. The town comprises a cluster of

The kasbah of King Hassan II, Rissani

ksour, small houses grouped within impregnable walls with decorated towers and ornate entrances. Inside are all manner of souks and narrow passageways to be explored, and a charming arcaded market.

This region is proud to have been the cradle of the reigning Alouite dynasty, for it is from here that they emerged in the mid 17C, first conquering the southern oases and then taking Marrakesh and Fez from the Saadians. Many traces of their origins lie here, on the SE side of Rissani and accessible either by walking through the town or by taking the 21km 'Circuit Touristique' (well signposted) around the outside.

Firstly there is the *Mausoleum of Moulay Ali Cherif*, founder of the Alouite dynasty. It was rebuilt in 1955 after the Ziz river overflowed its banks and carried much of the original building away. Not for non-Muslims to enter, its entrance is anyway unremarkable. In front is a huge square where lively markets are held, usually on Sundays. There is a donkey park, but no car park. Men from different desert tribes in flowing robes and turbans bring their wares to sell: strangely shaped pots, leather chests studded with brass, old jewellery, rugs and blankets. It is a fascinating scene.

Behind the Mausoleum—and worth the short walk or bumpy drive—is the beautiful carved entrance to a royal ksar known as *Akbar* which once served to house disgraced members of the Alouite family and the widows and concubines of its leading members.

Oulad-Abd-el-Halim is another royal ksar; its remains include two fine gateways whose design and ornate carving remind one of the great *babs* of Meknes. It is thought to have been lived in by the early governors of the Tafilalet, many of whom were members of the royal family. Today what is left of it houses one or two carefully chosen families who subsist amongst the ruined walls, courtyards and overgrown gardens. Remarkably, some of the painted ceilings survive in apparently excellent condition because, the guides say, they were painted with egg tempera.

Village near Merzouga

A track leaves Rissani S and then E to 29km *Merzouga*, which is well known for its massive sand dunes collectively known as *Erg Chebbi*. People have often been disappointed by the Moroccan desert because so much of it is stony rather than sandy. But here, in the Tafilalet region, the desert comes up to all expectations, with sand dunes in every hot colour. Merzouga is now beginning to capitalise on its undoubted attraction for the more intrepid tourist and several cafés have sprung up, as well as a small hotel (*Hotel des Palmiers*) at the foot of the highest dune.

To the W of Merzouga is a lake, dry for nine months of the year but coming to life from December to March when the water attracts flamingoes and other migrating birds.

The track continues S a further 24km and rejoins the river Ziz at the much smaller oasis of *Taouz*. Beyond lies the Algerian border and the wilderness of the Sahara. There is a track leaving Merzouga which will take you directly back to Erfoud but this is less well-marked than the Rissani one and unless it is early and you have a good sense of direction, it is not wise to attempt it. There are alternative side-tracks and few signposts in these parts; those tribesmen you meet are friendly enough but can usually speak only Berber.

Another worthwhile EXCURSION is along the track signposted 95km *Al Nif*, which branches W from the Erfoud–Rissani road at the Rissani end. There is nothing particular about this part of the road. It takes you through the by now familiar desert scene. But if you are feeling adventurous, you can then turn S to the lovely palm groves of Tazzerine and Mallal as far as Nekob (119km from Al Nif) just before which the track turns N and soars steeply up to cross the Jbel Sarhro range and brings you down to 87km *Boulemane*. This is quite a lot of driving but worth the energy expended because the mountainous part is exceptionally beautiful. It is really very steep in places and takes you up to what seems like the roof of Morocco. The views over seemingly endless ranges are beyond description.

An alternative route from Nekob continues W 44km joining the Draa valley road (see Rte 19).

22 Errachidia to Oujda

Total distance 524km. **Errachidia**—P21. 11km *Meski*—P32. 75km *Boudenib*—124km *Mengoub*—46km *Bouarfa* —115km **Figuig**—185km *Berguent*—83km **Oujda**.

A drive of 11km S from *Errachidia* (see Rte 20) brings you to Meski and the start of the desert road (soon becoming desert track) which takes you 256km to Bouarfa and a further 115km to Figuig, the most easterly town in Morocco. From Bouarfa N to *Oujda* is a further 268km. Obviously this is a very long and tiring journey, but for those who appreciate the vastness of the stony desert, and who want to catch a feeling of the 'empty quarter' it is arguably worth the effort.

The village of *Meski* is famous for its spring which is 2km off the main road. Clearly signposted *La Source Bleue du Meski*, it gushes out from a cleft in the rock into a tank which was erected by French legionnaires for the purpose of swimming. There is an attractive camp site amongst the palms by the water, a modern swimming pool and various cafés and shops, and it costs 2 dirhams just to go and have a look. Small boys (who are not allowed into the campsite area) spring out of the bushes before you get there and invite you for a guided tour of the palmeraie. They are very persistent and highly organised (average age around 9 years) and take you on a delightful 10-minute walk past channels of crystalline water, oleanders and a distant ksar. Two dirhams each for the guide and the '*guardien*' keeps them happy.

The drive from Meski to 245km Bouarfa is remote and featureless with only an occasional point of interest in the form of a mining village or two; and the central section of the road between Boudenib and Mengoub is *piste*. *Bouarfa* was once a garrison town but is now a quiet windswept place living on manganese mining.

Figuig (115km) has great character and it is worth the extra drive to the Algerian border (having come so far) to visit the hottest place in Morocco. Figuig is one of the largest of the southern oases and is said to have over 200,000 palm trees. It consists of seven separate ksour, each with its own individual palmeraie enclosed within crumbling turreted ramparts. It is not hard to believe that until the beginning of this century the seven were constantly in a state of simmering and sometimes quite bloody dispute, usually over the scarce water supplies. Figuig's strategic position on the border with Algeria has involved it frequently in wars with that country, not least during the reign of the expansionist Sultan Moulay Ismael, who in the early 18C first lost it and then won it back again. It was also until recently a departure-point for pilgrims leaving by camel for Mecca.

Today Figuig has undeniable charm and its palms provide welcome coolness wherever you go. Of the seven ksour, some are more worth visiting than others: the largest is *Zenaga* with a modern administrative centre and a welcome café. *El Maiz* is probably the most picturesque with its maze of narrow shady streets and terraced houses. *El Hammam*, as the name implies, boasts a hot spring where people can perform their ablutions before entering the mosque. There are no hotels.

The only way out of Figuig, apart from crossing the border into Algeria, or going back the way you have come, is to take the straight northerly road up to Oujda. The only objects of interest on this long unbending stretch (268km) are the *bordjs* (forts, many in ruins), recalling vividly the story of 'Beau Geste'; some of them make beautiful silhouettes on the desert skyline. The road runs parallel with and at times quite close to the Algerian border and for obvious strategic reasons is maintained in relatively good condition. It cuts a thin swathe of civilisation across this very neglected E flank of Morocco.

After 185km you reach the small town of *Berguent* and the coal-mining area of Jerada lies just to the S of Oujda (see Rte 14).

23 Agadir to Laayoune

Total distance 673km. **Agadir**—10km *Ait-Melloul*— P30. 78km **Tiznit** (— 111km **Tafraoute**—86km **Irherm**)—67km *Bou Izakarn* (—114km *Foum el Hassan*—80km *Akka*—69km *Tata*)—43km **Goulimine**—125km *Tan Tan*— 235km *Tarfaya*—115km **Laayoune**.

Leave Agadir (see Rte 4) by the airport road at the S end of the city and at 10km *Ait Melloul* take the right-hand fork (P30) to 78km Tiznit. The very straight road passes through colourful villages, orange and lemon groves, clumps of cactus and, about 12km N of Tiznit, the first palm trees. The people of this fertile coastal plain of the Souss are lucky: their land is well watered by the Oued Massa which rises in the Anti Atlas mountains and has been dammed up-river to provide irrigation for fruit and early vegetables.

Tiznit is a typical pre-Saharan walled town of considerable charm, with houses that are flat-roofed and red or ochre coloured. It is set in a cluster of palm trees which form a romantic backcloth to the crenellated walls and stocky square towers which are so typical of pre-Saharan architecture. Surprisingly perhaps, this is not an old town at all but was built by Sultan Moulay el Hassan in 1882, albeit enclosing within its walls several existing ksour. The purpose of this town was military. It was built as a base from which to pacify the Chleuh Berbers and later the French were to use it for the same purpose. They kept a large garrison there and used what is today the main square as their parade ground.

Tiznit is often referred to as Morocco's 'silver capital' and its people have long been known for their delicate work in silver—filigree bracelets and necklaces, belts, daggers encrusted with semi-precious stones and much else. The work goes on in small workshops, somewhat grandly called *'fabriques'* which are dotted around the town. You will certainly be pressed to go and see at least one and will notice that the most delicate filigree work is done by young boys, often working in poor light: 'small fingers and good eyes' the explanation goes, but one feels the eyes will not stay 'good' for long in those conditions. A complete range of this work is for sale in the Silver Market—a square of shops with little to choose between them, to be found behind the Mechouar, just inside the Gate of the Three Windows.

But the real glory of Tiznit is its antique jewellery and no-one should miss the *'Ancien Souk'* in rue Si Belid with its rose-coloured walls and its collection of stalls where the old men display their wares. Tiznit is a trading post between N and S: much of the new silver ware is taken by nomads down to the Saharan region (perhaps as far as Mauritania or Mali) where it is exchanged for antiques—filigree jewel boxes lined with camel-skin, caskets in silver with coral or turquoise, ink wells made of camel-bone and silver (for writing koranic texts), heavy necklaces made from silver coins and tiny pieces of coral mounted on fine chains. Much of this stuff is then sold to merchants from the big cities like Fez or Marrakesh who sell it on to the tourists in the souks. The lesson here is obvious. Tiznit (or Goulimine further S), is the place to buy from the widest range and at the lowest prices. But be warned: such treasures often look less impressive (or perhaps too exotic) in a northern European setting.

Apart from the permanent 'Ancien Souk', there are other places to buy. Some of the Berber 'middle-men' rest a while before heading either S to buy, or N to sell and will be delighted to display their wares which they keep in their houses in vast wooden chests. Since their progeny tend to roam the streets as guides (and often very knowledgeable ones they are), it is difficult to avoid the following experience, which will follow a very precise protocol: you are invited in to take tea—first in the outer room and then in the inner sanctum; the treasure chest is then pulled from the wall and the items are lifted out with great pride (the guide acting as interpreter); once everything has been laid before you, 'not for buying, just for looking', a wooden bowl is offered in which to place the objects which particularly please you. (If you *really* do not want to buy anthing at all, it is better to stop at this point, admire the goods and gracefully withdraw.) That done, you are asked to write down on a piece of paper, conveniently to hand, the prices you would be prepared to pay for any of them. The paper will pass backwards and forwards between you in solemn silence as each side changes the figures up or down. Finally a compromise is reached, the articles change hands, the money is counted, the silence is broken and more tea is served. There is an elegant and timeless inevitability about the whole process which is quite delightful.

There is not much in the way of interesting buildings but the *Grand Mosque* has an unusual minaret with small wooden stakes sticking out of it, said to facilitate the dead in their the climb up to Paradise. Next door to the mosque is a sacred spring. Legend claims that there was a town founded here some 1500 years ago in memory of a reformed prostitute who was martyred; it is said that at the moment of her death a miraculous spring gushed forth from the spot where she fell. The spring is called *Source Bleue de Lalla Tiznit* and is still revered as a holy place. And the lady in question is the town's patron saint. Sadly the sacred spring is now no more than a dirty stagnant pool.

For an overnight stay the 3-star hotel *Tiznit* (2 minutes' walk from the walled town) is recommended. Despite its unpromising-looking site next to a petrol station on the main crossroads S of town, it is peaceful inside and the rooms are grouped around a charming courtyard with bougainvillea cascading over the walls, and oleander and rosemary surrounding the small swimming pool. Otherwise, there are one or two simple and atmospheric hotels and a stark but secure campsite inside the walled town.

From Tiznit a road goes W 9km to the attractive beach of *Sidi Moussa d'Aglou*, with its troglodyte fishermen's huts dug into the rock face. There is very little else to see apart from the vast stretches of untouched sand and the magnificent Atlantic rollers. Another road leaves Tiznit westwards and then down the coast to 43km Sidi Ifni. The coastal stretch is lovely and—about 2km after the headland village of Mirhleft—there is a particularly good sandy beach overlooked by a marabout set inside ancient walls.

Sidi Ifni was built in 1934 by the Spaniards (who were finally taking up a right granted to them by the Treaty of Tetouan in 1860 to have a small enclave within reach of the Canaries). They did not leave until 1969. Today Sidi Ifni is a rather depressing has-been sort of place with a large central *Plaza Mayor* (now renamed *Place Hassan II*) which retains its Andalucian garden in the middle with typical pebble mosaic pavement. Ranged around it are the sad and locked up Consulate-General and a collection of decaying pink and white official buildings. Here too the Moroccans have built a new town hall, boldly candy-striped in pink and white as if to revive the jolly mood. There is also a memorial commemorating the date of the Spanish surrender (30.6.69) and a Moroccan fort up on the hill to guard against any future invaders.

From here there is a winding road just managing to retain its narrow central strip of tarmac to 57km Goulimine.

Another road from Tiznit goes E 111km to **Tafraoute**, high in the Anti Atlas: a beautiful but fairly wearing drive of some 2½ hours. The tarmac strip in the middle is just wide enough for one car and the battle to stay on it rather than move on to the rocky hard shoulder is usually won by large and tight-packed Mercedes taxis which claim it as their right. The Anti Atlas range runs parallel with the High Atlas and continues the line of the Jbel Sarhro from the east. Some of the peaks rise to over 2500m; the landscape is rugged and on a huge scale. Kasbahs of red earth, sometimes painted ochre colour, are built high up on the rocks, one above the other, backed by great vertical masses in chaotic shapes. (There is a good example of gravitydefying boulders around the village of Adai, just 3km before reaching Tafraoute.) The area is sparsely cultivated and only the almond trees seem to flourish. Indeed Tafraoute is much visited in early spring when the almond trees are in blossom. The Almond Festival is in mid February but the exact date changes from year to year.

Some of the kasbahs seem remarkably richly decorated and well maintained. This is because many of them are the family homes of the immensely hard-working shopkeepers of the north (*les épiciers*) who work long and hard for many years and eventually convert their fortune into land and houses in the Tafraoute area. The children then stay there with mothers or grandmothers who tend the crops, while fathers continue to make even more money elsewhere.

The town of Tafraoute lies in a kind of amphitheatre—a complete circle of rose-coloured granite rocks perched on top of one another and studded with date palms and almond trees. The best view of the town is from the terrace of the *Hotel des Amandiers*, the most impressive of three hotels, which is built high above the town in traditional kasbah style, and has the usual modern amenities, although the small swimming pool has recently become a casualty of the influx of wealthy bourgeoisie who have used up all the water in the town below.

The town itself is soon explored and merits less time than Tiznit, though it has a fair amount of artisanat and a range of shops and restaurants. The best thing about Tafraoute is its surrounding countryside which offers a wealth of villages to explore and mountain tracks to walk or drive. This is prehistoric rock carving country and local guides are available (from the *Hotel des Amandiers*) to show you where to go. There is also a good large-scale map of the area there to enable you to plan your walks. Particularly recommended is the Ammeln valley (Valley of the Almonds) accessible from 2km up the Agadir road. You will pass village after village, high on ledges on the mountain side, their irrigated fields on narrow terraces beneath them. Also recommended is the village of Agard-Oudad, 3km S of Tafraoute on the 7075 road. Very picturesque, it is sited hard up against a dramatic spur of rock known locally as '*le chapeau de Napoléon*'. One kilometre further on are the rock paintings by a Belgian artist, Jean Veran, which seem to fit quite comfortably into this grandiose setting.

From Tafraoute you can either go all the way to (62km) Irherm (but the road surface definitely deteriorates once you leave the main Agadir road at 24km) and thence N to Taroudant (a further 89km: see Rte 17); or you can stay on the main road all the way to Agadir (127km) passing countless hilltop kasbahs and the small market town of Ait Baha; or you can drive back to Tiznit.

From Tiznit the main road continues S, over the TIZI-MIGHERT PASS (1060m alt.) in the Anti Atlas foothills as far as 67km Bou Izakarn, where you fork right for 43km Goulimine.

Goulimine is frankly a disappointment. This once modest, dignified and eminently Saharan town has now expanded into a noisy commercial centre, depending largely for its prosperity on the groups of tourists who are brought here regularly by coach to see a way of life which no longer exists. The charming colonnaded section (now called Place Hassan II) is still there, right in the middle, but completely engulfed.

The once famous Sunday morning camel market (1.5km out of town on the Tan Tan road) is now almost exclusively given over to goats. The few camels which are there have probably been brought in for butchery only; trading in fine camels goes on the less accessible oases to the south. Berbers of the region are tending to give up their nomadic life style and settle down to raise livestock and grow crops in the plentiful oases, a fact which helps to explain the demise of the camel market. ('Now it is the camels who photograph the tourists' our guide said, somewhat cynically.)

At least the local Berbers retain their romantic image—swathed in sand-repellent indigo blue cotton robes whose dye is so little fixed that the colour comes off on their skins which are permenently tinged with blue—hence their popular name of 'Blue Men'. They wear the ends of their blue, black or white turbans wound round their mouths as a protection against the sand-carrying wind which never ceases to blow, and this undoubtedly adds a touch of mystery to their noble demeanour.

The traditional guedra is also a thing of the past. This erotic dance performed (sometimes for hours on end) by a woman on her knees and moving only the top part of her body, to the accompaniment of clapping and drumming, is now only ever put on for visiting tourist groups. The memorable hot, sticky *guedras* in cafés and tents are gone for ever, it seems, at least from Goulimine.

The 2-star *Hotel Salam* (for those who want to stay over-night) retains vestiges of its former Saharan character and has a flat roof to escape to on a hot airless summer night.

For a night or two in an oasis, take a minor road 19km E from Goulimine to *Tighmert* where a new, traditional style hotel has just opened (*Hotel Taregna*). Whether you actually stay or not, the drive is worth doing, past scores of camels grazing (all the ones you did not see in Goulimine) and a good sprinkling of the typical black Berber tents, made of woven camel hair. These tents are surprisingly cool and spacious inside, last for some 20 years and are usually lined with brightly-coloured rugs.

The oasis of Tighmert is a pleasure to walk around, especially at sundown, and there is a surprising amount of activity going on amongst the palm trees. Thanks to a constant supply of water, these people grow barley, maize, olives, grenadines and quinces, as well as the ubiquitous prickly pear know locally as 'Berber figs'.

From Goulimine the road continues S 125km to *Tan Tan*, an easy drive over a rather bleak stretch of desert. Tan Tan is a modest outpost of a town, and comes to life only in July each year when it has its moussem. This attracts a huge gathering of Saharans and 'blue men' with their camel caravans, some of whom will have come from as far S as Mauritania. West of the town is a fine beach with a few villas and cafés and S of that are the beginnings of a fishing port. From Tan Tan the recently tarmacked road now continues to 235km *Tarfaya*, a rather depressing ex-Spanish town still bearing traces of colonial architecture and fortifications from which to pacify local warlike tribes and, more recently, the Polisario. There is nothing to tempt the visitor to stay here.

The road continues 115km further S to Laayoune which was built by the Spanish to administer the Spanish Sahara after they abandoned Tarfaya in 1956. Since the Spanish withdrawal in 1976 (after the Green March) this town has grown and grown as Moroccans have been given huge incentives to come and settle and work here. No expense has been spared; there is the airport, a huge football stadium, an imposing new mosque and a glass palace commemorating the Green March which overlooks the vast, empty Mechouar Square. To accommodate the growing number of package tours arriving from Paris, Agadir and the Canaries there are two plush hotels—

the Spanish-built *Parador* and the Hollywood-style *Al Massira*—and a host of smaller hotels, bars, discos and cinemas. Amongst all this hectic modern development there nestles the much advertised blue lagoon surrounded by golden dunes. But the sea is 20km away and the beach is next to the new phosphate port.

It is really worthwhile continuing S 540km to the narrow peninsula of Dakhla only if you are really keen to fish for sea bass, sole or red mullet, in which case it would be easier anyway to fly from Laayoune or direct from Agadir. The road is tarmacked all the way but is bleak and featureless; the going is hard and lonely. Serious fishermen will turn to *Sochetur* (72 Blvd Zerktouni, Casablanca; tel. 277513) who organise inclusive fishing trips to Dakhla. Moroccans speak of the intention to develop Dakhla (once Spanish Villa Cesneros) in the same way as Laayoune. So far, however, there is nothing but an airfield, a few pensions, a lot of military paraphernalia and a sad old Spanish cathedral.

The desert E of Goulimine is rewarding to explore. There is a string of small oasis towns at regular intervals and the road is now tarmacked as far as Akka. It starts at Bou Izakarn (43km back from Goulimine) and continues E through the oases of 114km *Foum El Hassan*, 80km *Akka* to 69km *Tata*. There are interesting cacti on the way and plenty of palm trees to provide welcome shade for a picnic. The road is frequently crossed by river beds, which are usually dry and present no problems but can become quite sizeable streams after heavy rain or when the snow in the mountains melts. If this happens the only thing to do is to pitch camp and wait until the waters subside, which they usually do very quickly. Beware of scorpions when sitting down and never put your hand under a stone.

Foum el Hassan lies by the river Tamanart and is therefore well-watered and prosperous. *Akka* is in the middle of a palm grove and *Tata* is a large and beautiful oasis watered by three streams from the Anti Atlas which have made possible a surprisingly lush central square. There are three reasonable hotels and a lively souk on Tuesdays and Sundays.

At Tata you are strongly advised to take the track N 109km to Irherm and thence to Taroudant or Tafraoute. The track does continue E across the desert as far as 152km *Foum Zeguid* (whence it is possible to drive N through Tazenakht to Ouarzazate) but it is poorly maintained; one oasis begins to look very much like another and it is extremely easy to get lost.

INDEX

218

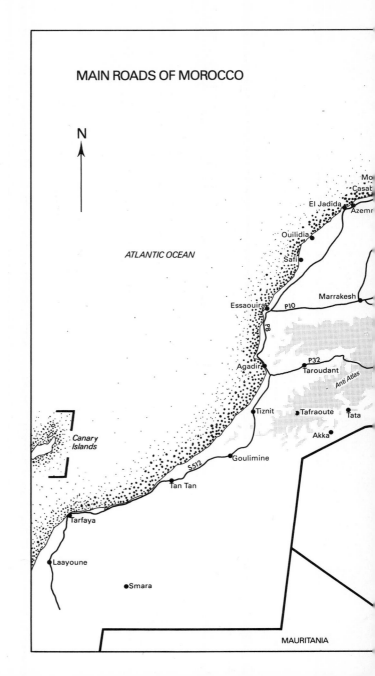

MAIN ROADS OF MOROCCO

N

ATLANTIC OCEAN

Mo
Casal
El Jadida
Azemr
Ouilidia
Safi
Marrakesh
Essaouira
P10
P8
Agadir
P32
Taroudant
Anti Atlas
Tiznit
Tafraoute
Tata
Akka
Canary Islands
Goulimine
S 512
Tan Tan
Tarfaya
Laayoune
Smara

MAURITANIA

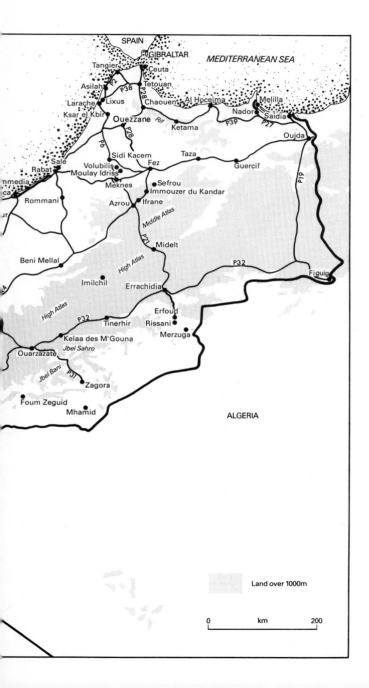

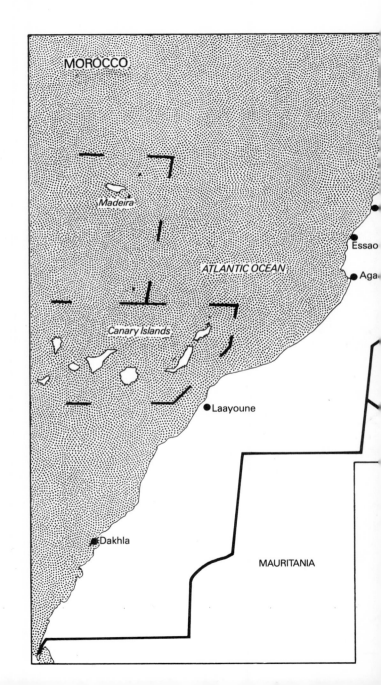

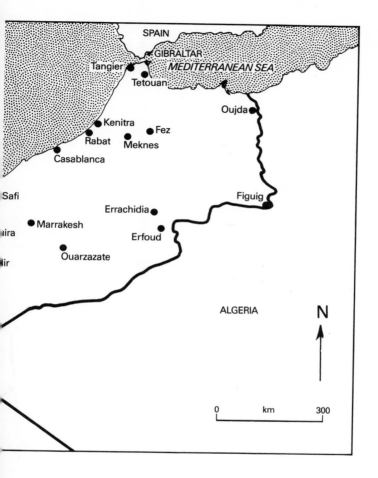